Gender, Interaction, and Inequality

Cecilia L. Ridgeway

Gender, Interaction, and Inequality

Springer-Verlag

New York Berlin Heidelberg London Paris
Tokyo Hong Kong Barcelona Budapest

Cecilia L. Ridgeway
Department of Sociology
Stanford University
Stanford, CA 94305, USA

With four illustrations.

Library of Congress Cataloging-in-Publication Data
Gender, interaction, and equality/Cecilia L. Ridgeway, editor.
   p. cm.
  Includes bibliographical references and index.
  ISBN 0-387-97578-0
  1. Sex role. 2. Social interaction. 3. Sex differences
(Psychology) I. Ridgeway, Cecilia L.
  HQ1075.G464 1991
  305.3—dc20   91-4184

Printed on acid-free paper.

Typeset by Best-set Typesetter Ltd., Hong Kong.
Printed and bound by Edwards Brothers, Inc., Ann Arbor, MI.
Printed in the United States of America.

9 8 7 6 5 4 3 2 1

ISBN 0-387-97578-0 Springer-Verlag New York Berlin Heidelberg
ISBN 3-540-97578-0 Springer-Verlag Berlin Heidelberg New York

Contents

Contributors

CLIFFORD E. BROWN Department of Psychology, Wittenberg University, Springfield, Ohio 45501, USA.

DAVID DIEKEMA Department of Sociology, University of Iowa, Iowa City, Iowa 52242, USA.

JOHN F. DOVIDIO Department of Psychology, Colgate University, Hamilton, New York 13346, USA.

STEVE L. ELLYSON Department of Psychology, Youngstown State University, Youngstown, Ohio 44555, USA.

MARTHA FOSCHI Department of Anthropology and Sociology, University of British Columbia, Vancouver, British Columbia, Canada V6T 1Z1.

JUDITH A. HALL Department of Psychology, Northeastern University, Boston, Massachusetts 02115, USA.

MARK HEDLEY Department of Sociology, University of Arizona, Tucson, Arizona 85721, USA.

CATHRYN JOHNSON Department of Sociology, Emory University, Atlanta, Georgia 30332, USA.

PATRICIA YANCEY MARTIN Department of Sociology, Florida State University, Tallahassee, Florida 32306, USA.

LINDA D. MOLM Department of Sociology, University of Arizona, Tucson, Arizona 85721, USA.

NANCY RHODES Department of Psychology, Texas A & M University, College Station, Texas 77843, USA.

CECILIA L. RIDGEWAY Department of Sociology, Stanford University, Stanford, California 94305, USA.

DAWN T. ROBINSON Department of Sociology, Cornell University, Ithaca, New York 14853, USA.

LYNN SMITH-LOVIN   Department of Sociology, University of Arizona, Tucson, Arizona 85721, USA.

ELLEN M. VECCIA   Department of Psychology, Northeastern University, Boston, Massachusetts 02115, USA.

WENDY WOOD   Department of Psychology, Texas A & M University, College Station, Texas 77843, USA.

Introduction: Gender and the Role of Interaction in Inequality

CECILIA L. RIDGEWAY

Through what mechanisms does gender affect interaction in face-to-face encounters? How does the impact of gender on interaction affect structures of inequality between men and women? To what extent are gendered patterns of interaction, in turn, a product of men's and women's different status and resources in the larger society? These are the questions this book addresses. It does so with the intent of increasing our understanding of the role played by interactional dynamics in explaining gender differences in behavior and gender inequality in society.

Because gender is one of a very few "master roles" that are the foundation for both personal identity and the societal division of labor, it has effects on and is affected by virtually all types of interaction. However, this book focuses primarily on one broad type of interaction: that which is task or goal oriented. This is the sort of interaction that characterizes committees, teams, community groups, juries, classrooms, work groups, and so on. Goal-oriented interaction is the interaction of "work" (paid and unpaid). It is a major social arena in which decisions are made in society about the distribution of material resources and through which individuals gain access to positions of authority and power. Thus, this book focuses on goal-oriented interaction because it is especially relevant for understanding inequalities in men's and women's status and power in society.

Most social scientific efforts to explain gender inequality tend to leap between causal processes at the macrostructural level of socioeconomic organization and causal processes on the individual level of learned behavior and identity. The intermediate level of interaction is often neglected. This is unfortunate not only because interaction and its organization by gender is important in its own right. Interaction is also important because it is itself a key mediating mechanism, or proximal cause, by which many macrostructural as well as individual-level aspects of gender and inequality are accomplished. Consequently, a better understanding of gender processes in interaction is necessary to understand how our society's system of gender stratification operates.

An example might clarify this point. At the macro structural level, two important indicators of men's greater resources, power and prestige, are the persistent wage gap and occupational segregation between men and women. In recent years, a great deal of research has attempoted to pinpoint the causes of these structural indicators with complex and as yet incomplete results (e.g., Baron & Bielby, 1984; Blau & Ferber, 1986; Reskin, 1984; Reskin & Hartmann, 1986). This research has nevertheless shown quite clearly that wage inequality and occupational segregation have persisted over substantial changes in a variety of potentially contributing economic and social structural factors, including rising female labor force participation. How this occurs is a very complex problem, but interaction may provide one piece of the puzzle. I suspect that face-to-face interaction is one important medium through which gender inequality is written into newly developing forms of socioeconomic organization. Consequently, understanding the nature and causes of gender's effects on interaction is crucial to determining if and how interaction contributes to the persistent reproduction of gender stratification in society over changing social structural conditions.

As some psychologists have recently noted (e.g., Eagly, 1987; Maccoby, 1990), a similar case could be made at the individual level about the importance of interaction for the emergence and maintenance of gender differences in individual behavior. For individuals, the ability to learn, enact, and become various socially recognized identities is constrained by the identities or roles they are allowed to play in the organization of interaction. Many aspects of gender roles are taught, evoked and, most importantly, enforced through the structure of opportunities the individual is presented in face-to-face interaction. Because of the relevance of interactional dynamics to individual and social structural processes, this book can be of use to anyone interested in how a social system of gendering operates.

This book seeks to delineate the *mechanisms* or processes by which gender has its effects on interaction. It does not aim for a broad descriptive survey of all possible gender effects in interactional settings. Instead, each chapter scrutinizes theoretical efforts to explain and interpret major empirical findings about gender's effects on crucial aspects of interaction. A variety of theoretical perspectives are represented. Some theories such as those dealing with the status value of gender, structural positions, gender roles, socialization, and gender subcultures are discussed in several chapters. The contributors do not all adopt the same stance toward these theories. Controversies as well as agreements are represented. All contributors, however, are similarly committed to an analytical approach. Each emphasizes the development of causal explanations that can more adequately account for the existing empirical evidence of gender's impact on interaction.

Causal explanations are essential for theory building. In focusing on causal mechanisms rather than descriptive effects, the goal of this volume is to increase our theoretical understanding of the way gender operates in interaction. Theoretical analyses of gender's effects in interaction, in turn, are necessary to understand how such effects might be implicated with individual-level and social structural–level processes in the larger system of gender inequality.

Despite other differences, the contributors to this book all take what might be loosely called a "microstructural" approach to gender and interaction. All agree that individuals come to interaction with certain common, socially created beliefs, cultural meanings, experiences, and social rules. These include stereotypes about gendered activities and skills, beliefs about the status value of gender, rules for interacting in certain settings, and so on. However, as individuals apply these beliefs and rules to the specific contingent events of interaction, they combine and reshape their implications in distinctive ways that are particular to the encounter. As a result, individuals actively *construct* their social relations in the encounter through their interaction. The patterns of relations that develop are not completely determined or scripted in advance by the beliefs and rules of the larger society. Consequently, there is a reciprocal causal relationship between constructed patterns of interaction and larger social structural forms.

The constructed patterns of social relations among a set of interactants can be thought of as micro-level social structures or, more simply, "microstructures." Microstructures include patterned differences that emerge among the interactants in power and prestige, influence, the organization of speaking, nonverbal behavior, situated identities, and social and emotional behavior. As this list indicates, microstructures have both a hierarchical aspect—who has more power and esteem in the encounter?—and a division-of-labor aspect—who does what? The chapters of this book consider how gender affects both the hierarchical nature and the divisions of labor that characterize the microstructures that emerge during goal-oriented interaction.

The concept of interactional microstructures overlaps with the more familiar concepts of small groups, group dynamics, and group structure. Indeed, some contributors to this book explicitly focus on groups in their analyses of gender's effects on interaction. However, the concept of microstructures is broader than that of a small group. By most definitions, groups involve an explicit sense of collective identity in addition to normative patterns of interaction. Microstructures, on the other hand, exist whenever normative patterns of interaction develop among a given set of people, whether or not the people think of themselves as a group. A boss and a secretary, for instance, can develop regular patterns of interaction without an explicit sense that they form a distinct group.

As this suggests, the behavioral arrangements and shared expectations that constitute a microstructure are sometimes quite subtle. Interactants often develop them without being explicitly aware that they are doing so. Yet interactants create microstructures quite quickly, usually after only a few moments of interaction. Furthermore, once created, these patterns themselves become a force that shapes subsequent interaction. This is what makes microstructures of interaction important. They develop as a distinct level of social organization that exerts its own influence both on its individual participants and on larger organizations within which it may be embedded. Thus, microstructures mediate relationships between individuals and larger forms of social organizations. In different ways, each chapter reflects on the importance of gendered interactional micro-structures for understanding either gender differences in individual behavior or gender inequality in larger organizational forms.

A great many task-oriented microstructures are created by the interactions people engage in to fulfill their obligations to a larger or-ganization. Consequently, many, although by no means all, such micro-structures are embedded within larger formal organizations. In some cases, the members of a particular microstructure begin as formal peers in that they all share the same formal position in the organization that brings them together. Juries are formal peers in this sense as are members of the secretarial pool.

In other cases, however, interactants do not begin as peers. They are formally unequal in their position within organizational structure (e.g., boss and secretary). Because of the gendered division of labor in our society, mixed-sex interaction that is goal oriented quite often involves men and women who hold unequal formal positions and, consequently, unequal structural power and authority.

Naturally, such formal differences profoundly affect the patterns of interaction that develop, but interestingly, they do not wholly determine them. In examining gender's effects on microstructures of interaction, it is also important to address how such effects are modified when interactants begin with unequal formal positions. This is especially important for understanding the role interactional dynamics play in maintaining larger organizational aspects of gender inequality. It is just as critical for ex-plaining gender differences in behavior. To what extent are such differ-ences produced by differences in the power and authority of the formal positions men and women occupy? Do men and women act similarly when they are in similar positions of power and authority?

In Chapter 1, Linda Molm and Mark Hedley consider a crucial aspect of this problem. They examine the ways that women and men use power given to them by a formal position to achieve favorable outcomes in interaction. Are men more willing or effective users of power in inter-action or do they just appear so because of their greater access to structural power? Molm and Hedley review the arguments and evidence for structural theories of gender and power use that argue for the latter as well as individual-level theories that locate differences in power use in gendered traits or abilities. They then present their own exchange theory analysis of gender and power use and consider evidence from a series of laboratory experiments to evaluate it. These experiments disentangle gender and structural power by placing women and men in comparably high or low power positions and observing the strategies and effectiveness with which they use power in interaction.

Chapter 2 continues the concern with interaction between formal unequals but, instead of power, Cathryn Johnson focuses on the broader range of leader-follower behavior. She notes that most research in the area asks if women and men in formal leadership positions (i.e., managers) act similarly toward their subordinates. The findings are contradictory, she argues, both because research has been insufficiently linked with theory and because it focuses on leader behavior alone rather than on the interaction between leaders and subordinates. She considers what three available theories would predict about gender's impact on leader-follower interaction. Then she discusses a study that tests these predictions. The results suggest additional dimensions to the ways that gender affects leader-subordinate interaction as well as the way these change over time.

In Chapter 3, Steve Ellyson, John Dovidio, and Clifford Brown return to the question of gender and power, but focus on visual interaction and the role of nonverbal behavior in both establishing and in expressing power differences between men and women. They consider how visual dominance operates both when men and women hold formally unequal structural positions and when they do not. First they examine how the visual dominance ratios of men and women reflect and establish social power in same-sex interactions. Then they move to mixed-sex interaction and examine the effects of the status value of gender, structural inequality, and power striving on the patterns of visual dominance behavior that develop between men and women. Their concern throughout is to evaluate the causal processes that may underlie gender differences in visual interactions. Finally, they consider the relationship of gender differences in visual dominance to those in verbal interaction, as well as the implications of these differences for women's and men's long- and short-term power outcomes.

In Chapter 4, Judith Hall and Ellen Veccia also scrutinize the relationship between men's and women's nonverbal interaction and status and power. However, they focus on touch asymmetry between the sexes. Their particular concern is to evaluate Nancy Henley's (1977) and others' theories that explain touch asymmetry as an expression of men's status advantage over women. Hall and Veccia critically review these theories in light of current evidence on gender and touch and then discuss evidence of their own from two observational studies of touching in mixed-sex dyads, the first in public places like shopping malls and the second at a professional convention. They find that although men do touch women with the hand more than vice versa, the general relationship between touching and sex depends in complex ways on other status differences between the men and women.

Chapters 5 through 7 consider gender's effects on interaction when men and women begin with no formal inequalities in their positions. The gender inequalities that develop in these microstructures are entirely constructed through interaction. In the first of these chapters, Wendy Wood and Nancy Rhodes examine interaction in task groups with an input-process-output analysis that views interaction as the principal mediator between individual attributes such as gender and outputs such as task productivity and patterns of influence. The evidence indicates that in such groups a greater percentage of men's behavior is directed at the task than women's, whereas women have a higher percentage of positive social behavior than men. To explain these differences in interactional style, Wood and Rhodes critically compare socialization theories, theories of gender's status value, and Alice Eagly's (1987) role theory. Then they turn to consequences of men's and women's interaction style and show how these produce sex differences in task performance, leadership emergence, and members' satisfaction with the interaction.

In Chapter 6, Lynn Smith-Lovin and Dawn Robinson also address gender differences in interactional style, but focus more specifically on men's and women's ways of talking and its effects on the conversational dynamics that develop. They review major theoretical orientations to gender and conversational style and the empirical studies each has generated in an attempt to establish the aspects of talk on which men and women systematically differ and the situations in which these differences occur. Concluding that no single theoretical orientation is adequate to the empirical evidence, they offer an integrative alternative based on affect control theory (Smith-Lovin & Heise, 1988). The theory makes formal predictions about the way learned gender identity differences in status, power, and expressivity interact with situations and events to produce gendered conversational styles. They apply their predictions to data on women's and men's interruptions in six-person groups.

In my chapter with David Diekema (Chapter 7), we critically assess theoretical efforts to explain gender differences in interaction in terms of the greater status value attached to being male in society rather than female. For those who are interested in gender inequality, not just gender differences, the status approach is appealing. However, it has been challenged recently by empirical evidence that gender differences in interaction are sometimes greater between same-sex groups than within mixed-sex groups. We assess the expectation states theory of gender's status effects against three possible alternatives: socialized traits, gendered subcultural norms for interactional behavior, and Eagly's (1987) role approach. We make a case for the continuing predictive accuracy and theoretical usefulness of the status approach, but suggest that it be joined with some concepts from other approaches to yield a fully adequate account of the empirical evidence.

Martha Foschi's chapter on double standards (Chapter 8) also takes a status approach to gender and uses expectation states theory. However, Foschi's particular concern is to explain how gender biases the process by which some interactants come to be perceived as more competent than others in task-oriented settings. She reviews evidence that the status value of gender biases evaluations of a person's performances so that men's task contributions are perceived to be better than women's. She expands this account by proposing that status characteristics like gender also activate double standards for the way good or bad performances are used to infer competence. As a result, even when evaluations show that a man and woman have performed equally well, the man's good performance will be taken as a stronger indicator of his ability than will the woman's. Foschi discusses the relationship of this double-standard analysis to attribution arguments and presents some recent data testing her theoretical account.

Chapter 9 returns the book to the formal structural or organizational context with which it began. However, instead of putting primary emphasis on the impact of formal organizational structures on interaction, Patricia Yancey Martin considers how gendered interaction affects organizations. She argues that people in developed nations live much of their lives in and through formal organizations and these organizations are highly gendered. Her concern is to show *how* organizations actively create and sustain gender inequality. They do so through a combination of macrostructural processes such as a gendered labor market and the interactional processes through which the activities of the formal organization actually are carried out and its organizational structure is enacted. The gendered microstructures that emerge from and govern these interactions have critical implications for the maintenance of gender hierarchy within the organization.

The complex empirical determinations and theoretical conclusions of these chapters cannot be simply summarized. However, I would like to conclude this introduction by noting some clear trends or themes that run through all the chapters. First, gender affects patterns of interaction in task-oriented situations in ways that produce inequalities between men and women that perpetuate women's structural disadvantages in larger organizations and society as a whole. Second, these microstructural effects of gender are context specific and depend on the specific power and status attributes of the men and women who interact, whether the interactants are of same or mixed sex, and other such factors. There is little evidence for gender differences in interactional behavior that hold constant across broad differences of context. Third, social structural factors such as the power attached to the positions held by men and women and the lower status value of being female in society account for a great majority of gender differences in interactional behavior. These effects tend to reproduce through interaction men's power and status advantages in society. Finally, however, despite their enormous explanatory importance, structural power and status factors alone do not account for all gender effects in interaction. Multiple analytical approaches are necessary to fully explain gender's impact on interaction.

Acknowledgments. I would like to thank Christina Randall for her hard work on the important task of assembling the index and Martha Foschi for encouraging me to undertake this book.

References

Baron, J.N., & Biebly, W.T. (1984). The organization of work in a segmented economy. *American Sociological Review*, 49, 454–473.

Blau, F.D., & Ferber, M.A. (1986). *The economics of men, women and work.* Englewood Cliffs, NJ: Prentice-Hall.

Eagly, A.H. (1987). *Sex differences in social behavior: A social-role interpretation.* Hillsdale, NJ: Erlbaum.

Henley, N.M. (1977). *Body politics: Power, sex, and nonverbal communication.* Englewood Cliffs, NJ: Prentice-Hall.

Maccoby, E.E. (1990). Gender and relationships. *American Psychologist*, 45, 513–520.

Reskin, B.F. (Ed.). (1984). *Sex segregation in the workplace: Trends, explanations and remedies.* Washington, DC: National Academy Press.

Reskin, B.F., & Hartmann, H.I. (Eds.). (1986). *Women's work, men's work: Sex segregation on the job.* Washington, DC: National Academy Press.

Smith-Lovin, L., & Heise, D.R. (Eds.). (1988). *Analyzing social interaction: Advances in affect control theory.* New York: Gordon and Breach.

1
Gender, Power, and Social Exchange

LINDA D. MOLM AND MARK HEDLEY

One of the most basic indicators of gender inequality is the distribution of power between men and women. Across time, across societies, and across a wide range of settings, men have greater power than women. They have greater access to, and control over, valued resources, and they have greater *formal* power, embedded in positions of authority and codified in law.

At the macro level, this unequal distribution of power is a basic indicator of gender inequality. At the micro level, it raises questions about the relation between interaction and gender inequality. Are men more willing or more effective users of power than women, or do they simply appear so because of their greater access to structural power? Would gender-equal positions of structural power erase any gender differences in power-related interactions—exchange, cooperation, bargaining, and the like? Or do men and women use power differently even when their capacity for power use is equivalent?

In this chapter we examine the relation between gender and power use. We do not address the macro-level question of how men come to occupy positions of greater structural power. Instead, we ask how gender affects the use of structural power in social interaction. Experimental studies that manipulate the structural power positions to which men and women are assigned allow us to disentangle the effects of structural power and gender, and examine how men and women use power when they are placed in equivalent positions of structural power.

We begin by discussing two major kinds of micro theories of gender and power: those that locate gender differences in power use in the individual, and those that locate gender differences in social structure. After reviewing the research conducted in each of these traditions, we report the results of recent analyses of gender effects in a program of research on power and exchange. We evaluate these results in view of previous findings and existing theory, and consider their implications for gender inequality.

The Concept of Power

Power has been conceptualized as a structural potential (Bierstedt, 1950; Emerson, 1962; Wrong, 1968), as a process of behavioral or tactical influence (Michener & Suchner, 1972; Rubin & Brown, 1975; Tedeschi & Bonoma, 1972), and as the successful outcome of influence (Dahl, 1957; Mayhew, Gray, & Richardson, 1969; Simon, 1957). A complete analysis of power must include all three of these facets (see Molm, 1990). In this chapter, we distinguish among these three aspects of power, which we call structural power, power strategies, and power outcomes.

Structural power is the potential power of actors to influence others. It is an attribute of relations, not individuals, and it is determined by the control that actors have over events or resources that others value. Virtually all theories of social exchange, as well as resource theories of power, use some conception of structural power or power capacity in their formulations of power (Bacharach & Lawler, 1981; Blau, 1964; Coleman, 1973; Emerson, 1972; Thibaut & Kelley, 1959). It is structural power that males have greater access to, in organizations, families, and political and economic relations.

Structural power provides actors with the means to exercise influence, but how that power is exercised depends on its strategic use in the process of interaction. Strategic power use is purposive action that takes into account the behavior of other actors. Structural power and strategic action may be conceptualized analytically as "macro" and "micro" levels of power. The "macro" level of power is the structure of control that provides the opportunities and constraints within which the "micro" level of power, the strategic behavior of actors, operates. Even if men and women had equivalent structural power, how they used that power in strategic action might differ.

Together, structure and action produce outcomes of consequence for actors and relationships. Power outcomes represent the relative "success" of power use, i.e., do actors get what they want from the relation? Success may be measured in both absolute and relative terms, by the absolute level of desired benefits that actors acquire, and by how well they do relative to the other actor or actors in the relation. Power outcomes are affected both by actors' relative positions of structural power, and by their strategies of power use (Bacharach & Lawler, 1981; Molm, 1990).

Theories of Gender and Power Use

Theories of gender and power typically try to explain how gender affects either power strategies or power outcomes. Gender differences in power outcomes are explained as a function of gender differences in structural power, or gender differences in strategy. Although the proposed source of these differences varies across specific theories, we distinguish between two major types: individual-level theories, which explain gender differences in power use by individual characteristics of men and women, and structural-level theories, which explain gender differences in power use by differences in the structural positions of men and women. These structural positions provide varying degrees of access to authority and resources in settings such as work organizations, the family, and political and economic institutions.

Individual-Level Theories

Individual-level theories of gender and power propose that gender carries with it certain characteristics, such as personality traits and abilities, that affect power use. Some theories suggest that these differences are biologically based (e.g., Archer, 1976; Wilson, 1975), but most assume they are learned, through the process of socialization for gender roles. Different socialization theories propose somewhat different processes for acquiring gender roles, but all assume that the outcomes of socialization are relatively stable traits that characterize the responses of individuals across situations. It is this assumption of stable gender differences across situations that distinguishes individual-level theories from structural-level theories.

This tradition has its roots in the functionalist work of Parsons (Parsons, 1951; Parsons & Bales, 1955). Parsons proposed that males and females acquire distinctly different roles through socialization, and that these roles are functional for the division of labor in the traditional family unit. Men are socialized to be goal driven, task oriented, and instrumental, whereas women are socialized to be relationally oriented, socioemotional, and expressive in their behavior. Although the functionalism of Parsons's formulation has been rejected (see Meeker & Weitzel-O'Neill, 1977), the concept of distinct male and female roles, shaped through socialization, has continued to be a dominant force in the analysis of gender and social behavior (cf. Spence, Deaux, & Helmreich, 1985).

Most research based on this perspective does not actually study power or power use as we have defined these terms. Instead, researchers study gender differences in motivations and behaviors that are assumed to affect power use. These differences are typically related to the instrumental/expressive dimensions of personality and roles.

An instrumental orientation is expected to include a desire for control and the motivation for individual gain, whereas a relational orientation emphasizes concern for social relations and the rewards of others. Based on this distinction, men are expected to be more motivated to use power for their own gain, and women to be more constrained in power use by considerations of equality in relations. McClelland's (1975) theory of "n power" is based on this distinction. He proposes that power use is motivated by an inner need to affect and control interaction for individual gain. This need, "n power," is predicted to be higher for males than females. Neither hypothesis has been supported by empirical research, however (Smith & Fromm, 1982; Winter, 1988; Winter & Barenbaum, 1988). Nearly half of related research reports no gender differences in n power level, and the relationship between n power and actual power use is tenuous.

Predictions of gender differences in the allocation of rewards have also been based on assumptions of motivational differences. Motivations to maximize individual gain or joint gain are expected to be reflected in preferences for *equitable* or *equal* distributions of outcomes. An equitable distribution allocates rewards or benefits in proportion to individuals' input, whereas an equal one divides rewards equally among all recipients regardless of input. Females are predicted to prefer equal allocations, and males to prefer equitable allocations when it is in their self-interest (i.e., when their own proportion under equity would be greater than an allocation based on equality). This hypothesis has been supported by a number of studies (Dobbins, 1986; Kahn, O'Leary, Krulewitz, & Lamm, 1980; Major & Deaux, 1982). Some researchers have found no gender differences in preferences for equality or equity (e.g., Boldizar, Perry, & Perry, 1988; Parcel & Cook, 1977), however, and others show that allocations based on equality or equity depend on situational variables, such as the specification of performance attributions, rather than on gender (e.g., Wittig, Marks, & Jones, 1980). Carli's (1982) meta-analysis of this literature found the predicted gender difference for equity but not equality. Women tended to take *less* than an equal share for themselves. These gender differences were very small, however, accounting for no more than 1 to 2% of the variance.

Socialization is also expected to produce gender differences in behavioral traits and skills that are assumed to be related to power use, particularly aggression, competitiveness, influenceability, and bargaining skills. Because of socialization, males are assumed to be more likely than females to act aggressively, to compete rather than cooperate, to be resistant to influence, and to display toughness and skill at bargaining and negotiating. To the extent that these behaviors are required for effective power use, males should be more successful power users than females.

Aggression is the most fundamental of these traits because it is often assumed to be the cause of the other behavioral differences as well. Numerous studies, using different methodologies and subjects of different ages, have reported that males are more aggressive than females (see Hyde, 1984, 1986, and Maccoby & Jacklin, 1974, for reviews of this literature). These conclusions have been challenged by other researchers, who find that differences in aggressiveness are situationally dependent (Frodi, Maccauley, & Thome, 1977; Towson & Zanna, 1982). In a recent meta-analysis of aggressive behavior in adult subjects, Eagly and Steffen (1986) found that men both delivered and received more aggression than women. This difference was smaller than many other sex differences, however, and varied with situational attributes of the studies. Their analysis also suggests that gender differences in aggression may result from gender differences in the perception of consequences, such as harm to target and danger of retaliation, rather than from differences in aggressiveness per se.

Evidence for gender differences in cooperation and competition comes primarily from experimental research on mixed-motive games, particularly the Prisoner's Dilemma game. Although the majority of these studies claim support for the instrumental/expressive dichotomy between males and females, findings are highly inconsistent (Rubin & Brown, 1975). Some research reports that females are more cooperative than males (e.g., Aranoff & Tedeschi, 1968; Conrath, 1972; Horai & Tedeschi, 1969; Miller & Pyke, 1973), some find males to be more cooperative than females (e.g., Beddell & Sistrunk, 1973; Gahagan & Tedeschi, 1969; Rapoport & Chammah, 1965), and others report no gender differences (e.g., Tedeschi, Gahagan, Aranoff, & Steele, 1968; Wyer & Malinowski, 1972). A recent meta-analysis of this literature found no support for the predicted gender differences; women were not more cooperative than men in mixed-motive games (Carli, 1982). Studies of coalition formation offer somewhat more support for the stereotypic gender differences. They suggest that women are less likely to play competitively and more likely to form three-way coalitions that do not enhance the probability of winning (Carli, 1982; Uesugi & Vinacke, 1963; Vinacke, 1964).

Another individual-level variable that has been posited to explain the relation between gender and power use is influenceability. Researchers investigating gender differences in social influence have often reported that women are more easily influenced, more conforming, and less influential than men (Eagly, 1978). These studies typically measure changes in opinions in response to persuasive arguments. Meta-analyses of this literature provide some support for the hypothesis that women are more easily influenced than men (Eagly & Carli, 1981). This effect, however, is mediated by the partners' behavior (Carli, 1989). Both men and women use more agreement and positive social behaviors when attempting to influence female partners, a strategy that is more effective than disagreements and task behaviors.

Men and women are stereotypically believed to employ different strategies of influence and different bases of power (Johnson, 1976). They also report using different power strategies in interpersonal relations. Females are more likely to report using indirect, unilateral strategies whereas men say they use more direct, bilateral strategies. Johnson (1976) suggests that these differences arise from gender discrimination in the availability of resources. The findings from experimental studies that examine actual behavior, and control for the availability of resources, are mixed. Some Prisoner's Dilemma studies have found that males are more likely to use tit-for-tat strategies and to vary their choices strategically to optimize individual gain (Kahn, Hottes, & Davis, 1971; Komorita & Mechling, 1967). In coalition-formation games, females tend to present lower initial demands and are more accommodative of others' demands (e.g., Uesugi & Vinacke, 1963; Vinacke, Mogy, Powers, Langan, & Beck 1974). Tedeschi, Schlenker, and Bonoma (1973) and Terhune (1970) conclude that women are less likely than men to use power strategically to maximize individual gain. More recent studies, however, report no consistent gender differences in bargaining skills (Bacharach & Lawler, 1981; Lawler & Bacharach, 1987) or in styles of persuasive influence (Carli, 1989).

Although individual-level conceptualizations of gender differences in power use have dominated the literature, a number of problems weaken the perspective. Much of this literature is characterized by inconsistent findings, unsupported assumptions of gender differences, and ad hoc theoretical discussions. When gender differences are found that support sex-role socialization hypotheses, they generally account for less than 5% of the observed variance (Wallston, 1987; Wallston & Grady, 1985). Often, gender is added as a variable to experiments for control purposes, based on the assumption that males and females are different in most respects of interest to behavioral researchers. Any gender differences found are then "explained" by sex-role socialization theory, whatever form they take (cf. Tedeschi et al., 1973; Terhune, 1970). These studies illustrate the problems with using sex as a proxy for socialized gender roles, without explicitly conceptualizing or measuring the dimensions of those roles or the socialization experiences that are assumed to produce them.

More recent and sophisticated meta-analytic reviews of research on individual sex differences have tried to correct some of these weaknesses. Eagly and Wood (1991) argue that the results of meta-analyses do show significant gender differences in a number of behaviors, and that these differences support Eagly's (1987) gender-role perspective. But these analyses also challenge the notion of transsituational stability that has traditionally characterized individual-level theories. A growing body of evidence shows that specific situational influences are extremely powerful and may determine many of the apparent sex differences that are observed (Spence et al., 1985). We have noted these situational effects on gender differences in aggression, in influenceability, and in reward allocation. Particularly telling are the effects of other people on the behaviors expressed. The gender of the partner, the presence of others, and the public nature of the interaction have all been found to affect the extent of gender differences observed. This pattern suggests that some apparent gender differences may reflect presentational strategies, not stable personality characteristics (Carli, 1982; Spence et al., 1985). Several of these analyses have also found that the sex of the author affects reports of gender differences in influenceability and reward allocation (Carli, 1982; Eagly & Carli, 1981). Male researchers have obtained significantly larger sex differences than female researchers, and most of the research has been done by males. Both patterns—the strong situational effects and the author effects—raise doubts about the extent to which gender differences in power use can be explained by stable, socialized characteristics of males and females.

Structural-Level Theories

Structural theories of power explain gender differences in power use as a function of structural advantages associated with gender in society. The theories argue that males and females do not have equal opportunities to exercise power because of social stratification at the macro level that differentially allocates power resources and status privileges to males and females. Macro-level stratification also produces gender differences in structural power at more micro levels—in the family, among work associates, and so on. Differences in both strategies of power and outcomes of power between men and women can therefore be explained by males' greater structural advantages, rather than socialized characteristics of individuals. Two structural approaches can be distinguished, one based on power and one based on status.

STRUCTURAL THEORIES OF POWER

Structural theories of power propose that gender differences in power use are the result of differential access to structural power. This explanation has been applied primarily to gender differences in nonexperimental studies, in which structural power cannot easily be equalized. Kanter (1977), a leading proponent of this perspective, has argued that many gender differences in power use that are attributed to socialization and individual characteristics are really caused by the relative powerlessness of women in positions of authority. Women who are supposedly in positions of power equivalent to those of men may in fact have less access to resources for influencing others. If the structural power of males and females were equalized, Kanter argues, structural power would "wipe out sex" (1977, p. 200).

Social exchange theories of power (Blau, 1964; Emerson, 1972; Homans, 1974; Thibaut & Kelley, 1959), which also propose that structural power determines or at least influences power outcomes, would be expected to make a similar argument. These theories do not deal explicitly with gender, but they do propose that power use is a function of structural power position. Power is determined not by individual characteristics of actors, but by their structural relations to one another. The critical dimension of relations is how *dependent* actors are on one another for valued resources. The *power* of one actor in a relation derives from the other's *dependence* on him or her. Dependence, in turn, is a function of two variables: how much actors value the resources of exchange, and their alternatives for acquiring those resources. The more actors value the exchange resources that another controls, the greater their dependence. To the extent that actors have alternative sources of valued relations (e.g., more than one friend, more than one work associate who can offer advice), the less dependent they are on any one actor (Emerson, 1972).

When actors have alternative exchange relations, these relations are connected to form larger exchange networks (e.g., dating networks, organizational networks). Within these networks, actors in positions of greater power have greater access to alternative relations and they control resources of greater value for other actors. The theory predicts that actors who are relatively less dependent on others, and thus more powerful, will benefit relatively more from an exchange relation than their more dependent partners.

Most studies that have examined gender differences in power use in social exchange relations report minimal or no effects of gender, suggesting that structural control of resources minimizes gender differences in power use (e.g., Bacharach & Lawler, 1981; Cook & Emerson, 1978; Molm, 1985a). Typically, gender is included only as a control variable in these studies. An exception is Molm's (1985b, 1986) study of gender, power, and legitimation in social exchange relations. This experiment manipulated the gender of subjects assigned to the power-advantaged and -disadvantaged positions of an imbalanced exchange relation (MF, FM, FF, and MM), and manipulated whether that assignment was made randomly or legitimated by the subjects' performances on a preliminary competition (the "winner" of the competition was predetermined). The effects of gender and legitimation on both power strategies and power outcomes (the distribution of reward exchange) were examined.

Molm found only one effect of gender on power outcomes, and that was an effect of the power-disadvantaged actor's sex. Males in the power-disadvantaged position rewarded their partner more frequently than females in the power-disadvantaged position, thus increasing the asymmetry of reward exchange in dyads with a power-disadvantaged male. This finding is directly contrary to the gender stereotype that males are "tougher" and less compliant than females. The gender of the power-advantaged actor made no difference, nor did legitimation of the power positions. Again, this finding opposes the stereotype that males will be better power users than women. The sex of the power-advantaged actor did affect strategies of power use even though it did not affect the outcomes of power use. Actors in exchange relations with power-advantaged males were more likely to take turns giving to each other unilaterally, rather than mutually exchanging rewards at the same time. Females whose power advantage was legitimated tended to adopt a very tough power strategy, rewarding their disadvantaged partners infrequently and only in response to the other's repeated unilateral exchange. These strategies were different, but not more or less effective—they did not produce greater success at obtaining favorable outcomes for either female or male actors.

STRUCTURAL THEORIES OF STATUS

Structural theories of status propose that gender differences in power use result from the status rankings attached to gender by society. These status rankings reflect evaluations of worth and value. Associated with them are normatively shared beliefs that those of higher status (males) have greater competence and more legitimate right to exercise influence, and those of lower status (females) should defer to their influence attempts.

The theory most associated with this perspective is the theory of status characteristics and expectation states (Berger, Conner, & Fisek, 1974; Berger, Fisek, Normon, & Zelditch, 1977). This theory proposes that initial differences in status characteristics such as sex, race, and age affect the distribution of participation, prestige, and influence in groups that are task oriented and collectively oriented. In the absence of information to the contrary, groups that are initially undifferentiated on other characteristics will assume that members with more valued states of the status characteristic are more competent at the group task than those of lower status. These performance expectations, shared by group members who are both high and low on the external status characteristic, will affect the emergent "power and prestige" order of the group. The person for whom higher performance expectations are held will get more opportunities to participate, initiate more actions, receive more positive reactions from other group members, and have more influence on group decisions. This process of status generalization will take place even when the status characteristic has not been previously associated with ability to do the specific task. It can be inhibited by providing information about other, specific status characteristics that contradict the general expectation state attached to the external status (Cohen & Roper, 1972; Freese & Cohen, 1973; Webster & Driskell, 1978).

A number of studies support the hypothesis that gender is a status characteristic that elicits differential performance expectations (Eagly & Wood, 1985; McKee & Sherriffs, 1957; Mischel, 1974; Wiley & Eskilson, 1983). In the absence of information to the contrary, the gender of group members affects the structure of interaction in the predicted ways (Lockheed, 1985; Lockheed & Hall, 1976; Pugh & Wahrman, 1983). As a result of this process, women are disadvantaged. They are less likely to attempt power use and less likely to be successful at influence attempts.

These gender inequalities can be reduced by providing specific information that contradicts performance expectations or by legitimizing high status or high task participation by women (Fennell, Barchas, Cohen, McMahon, & Hildebrand, 1978; Meeker & Weitzel-O'Neill, 1977; Pugh & Wahrman, 1983). Legitimation of a woman's authority can be accomplished in a number of ways, including basing her assignment to the position on her superior competence on the group task or on her motivations to help the group (Ridgeway, 1978, 1982).

The difference between gender socialization and gender status explanations of power use is that gender status explanations predict that gender will affect power use only when gender is activated as a status characteristic. This will occur under one of three conditions: (a) the group members are differentiated on gender, (b) the group task is sex-linked, or (c) a same-sex group is imbedded in a larger organization whose members are predominantly of the opposite sex, thus making gender a salient status characteristic (Ridgeway, 1988). In same-sex groups performing a gender neutral task that is not imbedded in an organization of the opposite sex, no differences in power use should be observed between all-male and all-female groups. Gender socialization theories, in contrast, predict that differences in power use are part of male and female gender roles, learned through socialization, and carried with the individual across situations.

INTEGRATING POWER AND GENDER STATUS

As theories of gender and power use, both social exchange theory and status characteristics theory are incomplete. Exchange theories of power do not address how status characteristics like gender might interact with or alter the effects of structural power, and the theory of status characteristics and expectation states does not address how status characteristics might operate in groups whose members are differentiated on the structural capacity to exercise power and whose interests are partially conflicting. The lack of integration of status and power in a single theory is a puzzling weakness in the structural literature. Here, we consider some of the issues involved in integrating these two theories.

Exchange theory and status characteristics theory propose quite different theoretical mechanisms through which power and status affect behavior. Exchange theory proposes that power affects behavior through the differential control over resources and access to exchange partners provided by structural position. Status characteristics theory proposes that status affects behavior through cognitive processes that link higher status with the expectation of higher performance. What happens when these two mechanisms come together, and gender status is activated in an interactional setting in which (a) actors occupy structural positions of power and dependence in relation to one another, and (b) imbalances in structural power create partially conflicting (rather than collective) interests?

We propose, first, that structural power imposes boundaries on interaction that restrict the impact of external status characteristics. Structural power can override performance expectations in at least two important ways. *First, opportunities to influence are no longer simply a function of interaction.* The structure of power provides some actors with greater opportunity than others, by virtue of their network connections and access to alternatives. *Second, the perception of the benefit of an actor's contributions should not be influenced primarily by his/her status.* Although the value of resources is a subjective determination, and status influences the perception of value (e.g., lower value is attached to work done by women than to that done by men), many resources have value that should be relatively independent of such influence. Therefore, *regardless of status, actors with greater opportunity to engage in exchange relations and actors who control resources of greater value for others should be more likely to benefit from an exchange relation.*

In addition, structural power carries its own performance expectations, that can reinforce or oppose those associated with external status characteristics. Ridgeway (1991) argues that power is the original source of the relation between status and performance expectations. Control over power resources conveys competence, regardless of whether or not power is earned or deserved, and regardless of whether or not power is used. Ridgeway proposes that characteristics like gender acquire status value and come to carry performance expectations when they are associated with power.

Through both resource control and performance expectations, we propose that structural power can determine interaction and the distribution of influence independent of status characteristics. Considerable evidence shows that structural power has direct effects on power outcomes that are not mediated by strategies of power use and that do not depend on intentions or motivations to use power, or even awareness of power (Cook & Emerson, 1978; Molm, 1990). Contrary to Kanter (1977), however, we do not propose that structure "wipes out sex." We believe it can considerably reduce the effects of gender status, but within the boundaries of interaction set by structural power, status characteristics can still influence *how* actors use power, by affecting their strategies and negotiating styles. To the extent that strategies affect power outcomes, gender status can affect outcomes as well.

Gender status is more likely to affect power use when the actors' structural power is unequal. Because positions of power advantage are stereotypically held by men, and positions of power disadvantage by women, gender should be more salient to actors in these structural conditions than to actors in positions of equal power. In other words, we are proposing that positions of power advantage and disadvantage tend to become cognitively associated with gender, so that individuals expect positions of greater power to be held by men, and positions of lesser power to be held by women. Structural power imbalance may even activate gender as a status characteristic in relations that are undifferentiated by gender, in the same way that a sex-typed task can. When power is unequal, cognitive associations between gender and positions of advantage or disadvantage should be activated, even in all-male and all-female groups. In power-balanced relations that are undifferentiated by gender, gender should not be salient as a characteristic that would affect interaction.

In short, the relations between structural power and gender status are likely to be complex. Because structural power determines opportunities and resource control, and because these capacities create their own performance expectations, structural power has the potential to overcome the effects of external status characteristics. But because structural power is historically associated with gender and with expectations that males legitimately deserve greater structural power and are better at using it, it may trigger the very assumptions about gender and power that it should be capable of erasing.

An Exchange Theory Analysis of Gender and Power

To explore some of these ideas, we analyze new data from a recent program of research on exchange and power that systematically manipulates basic dimensions of structural power. As we have seen, one of the weaknesses of the literature on gender and power use is the paucity of empirical research in which power use, and not merely related variables, is actually studied. These data provide an opportunity to analyze the effects of gender on both power strategies and power outcomes under a wide range of differences in structural power. Our analysis includes results previously reported in Hedley (1990) on the effects of gender and structural power on power outcomes. Here, we extend that analysis to include all three aspects of power—structural power, power strategies, and power outcomes.

Three dimensions of structural power were either manipulated or held constant in all of the experiments: power imbalance, average power, and the base of power. The first two, power imbalance and average power, are the traditional dimensions of power in relations proposed by Emerson (1972). *Power imbalance* refers to the difference between the power-dependencies of two actors in an exchange relation, and *average power* refers to the average of their power-dependencies. Power imbalance and average power are attributes of an exchange relation, but they are determined by the position of the relation in a larger exchange network. Each actor's power-dependence on the other is defined by the dependence of that actor on the other relative to the actor's dependence on all actors in the network. The two dimensions can vary independently; i.e., two relations can have the same degree of imbalance but be high or low on the absolute strength of power. Most studies have varied only power imbalance. The independent manipulation of both dimensions of power allows us to examine how males and females respond to variations in total dependency as well as relative dependency.

The third dimension of structural power is the *base* of power: control over rewards or control over punishments. Traditionally, social exchange theories of power-dependence relations have been restricted to power based on control over rewards. In actual power relations, however, most actors control a range of rewards and punishments for each other. As in such relations, our experiments study power use when actors control both rewards and punishments for others in their exchange network. The average power and power imbalance of each base of power in the relation are independently manipulated.

The incorporation of punishment as a base of power is particularly important for studying gender, for some theorists (e.g., Johnson, 1976) have suggested that gender differences in power use may vary for these two bases. Most socialization theories suggest that females will be less likely than males to use punishment-based power because of its association with aggression and its incompatibility with the female role of supporter and facilitator (see Hedley, 1990 for a review of this literature). Structural analyses, however, have suggested that women are more likely than men to use punishment and coercion because they lack reward power in relations (Kanter, 1977; Patterson, 1982). These theorists propose that punishment is not a male or female power tactic, but the tool of actors who are disadvantaged on reward power. By systematically and independently varying dimensions of reward and punishment power, and assigning male and female subjects to equal positions of power, it is possible to examine both the effects of gender per se on the use of punishment power, and the argument that occupants of positions low on reward power are more likely to use coercive techniques, regardless of their gender.

In sum, four dimensions of structural power in the relation between two people (A and B) were varied in these experiments: average reward power, average punishment power, reward-power imbalance, and punishment-power imbalance. When both reward and punishment power were imbalanced, the experiments also manipulated whether the imbalances favored the same actor or different actors.

The effects of these dimensions of structural power on both power strategies and power outcomes are analyzed. *Power strategies* are conceptualized as the contingent use of power resources (rewards and punishments) by one actor in response to another actor's prior behavior. Strategies specify the conditional relations between sequential actions of two different actors, for example, the contingency of A's punishment on B's nonexchange, or the contingency of A's rewarding on B's rewarding. *Reciprocal* strategies are conditional relations between functionally equivalent behaviors of actors, e.g., the contingency of one actor's rewarding behavior on another actor's prior rewarding behavior. *Nonreciprocal* strategies specify the conditional relations between nonequivalent behaviors of actors, e.g., the contingency of rewards on prior punishment (Molm, 1990).

Four power outcomes, corresponding to the dimensions of structural power, measure the amount and distribution of both reward exchange and punishment exchange in the relation: the average frequency of reward exchange in the A-B relation, the asymmetry of reward exchange in the relation, the average punishment exchange, and the asymmetry of punishment exchange. The asymmetry of reward exchange is the traditional measure of power use in power-dependence theory.

The distinction between power strategies and power outcomes allows us to examine the effects of gender on each of these aspects of power. Males and females may differ on one, both, or neither of these aspects. How actors use power, strategically and contingently, is not necessarily related to how successfully they use it. We can examine both differences in style and outcomes.

Method

We analyze the combined data from five experiments that used identical procedures, subject pools, and conceptual and operational definitions of variables. In these experiments, subjects interacted in exchange networks of four actors. The two actors in the exchange relation of interest, A and B, were real subjects; the other two were computer-simulated actors. Each real subject was connected in the network to the other real subject and one of the simulated actors, giving each subject a mutually exclusive choice between two partners on each exchange opportunity. The simulated actors were always in power-balanced relations with their real partners, and they were programmed to behave in a tit-for-tat fashion, but at probabilities less than 1.0 to prevent suspicion.

The exchange networks structured different relations between actors on the dimensions of structural power. Power-dependence relations were manipulated by varying the amount of money subjects could add to each other's earnings (reward power) or subtract from each other's earnings (punishment power) on each of 250 exchange opportunities. Subjects were informed of these values. On each opportunity, subjects chose which of their two interaction partners they wished to act toward, and which action they wished to make, adding a fixed number of points to the other's earnings or subtracting a fixed number of points from the other's earnings. They made these choices simultaneously, without explicit agree-

ments or expressed intentions of whether or when others would reciprocate. In short, these conditions correspond to Blau's (1964) conception of
social exchange as exchange in which the terms and timing of reciprocity
are uncertain. These conditions are similar to those in a wide range of
social exchanges, for example, most exchanges between friends and family
members, as well as many exchanges of help or favors between work
associates or political allies. Because exchanges were nonnegotiated,
however, we cannot examine gender differences in explicit bargaining
techniques. Instead, we examine the contingent use of power resources to
influence the partner's behavior.

Operationally, each actor's reward (or punishment) power over the
other was defined as the number of points that actor could add to (or
subtract from) the other, divided by the total points that the other could
gain (or lose) from both of his/her partners in the network. Average
power and power imbalance were then defined as the average and the
difference, respectively, of these measures of power for each actor. Actual
ratio values of these variables, ranging from 0 to 1, are used for this
analysis. Because the actor favored by punishment-power imbalance was
also manipulated, two separate variables measure that dimension of
power for each actor: punishment-power imbalance favoring actor A, and
punishment-power imbalance favoring actor B. Reward-power imbalance
always favored actor A; i.e., A was the less dependent and more powerful actor.

Quantitative measures of both power strategies and power outcomes
were produced for each network. We used logistic regression analyses to
measure the contingencies between sequential behaviors of A and B in
each relation. The estimated coefficients for the lagged dependence of
one actor's behavior on the other's provide indices of how likely A was to
punish B, or reward B, or not act toward B, based on B's behavior on the
previous opportunity (see Molm, 1990 for a detailed description of this
methodology). These quantitative measures of strategy were then used in
subsequent analyses in combination with structural power, power outcomes, and gender. Power outcomes were measured by the proportion of
exchange opportunities on which A and B rewarded or punished each
other. Average reward/punishment exchange averaged these proportions
for the two actors, and the asymmetry of reward/punishment exchange
took the difference of the two. (The difference of each was calculated so
that higher values of *either* reward exchange asymmetry or punishment
exchange asymmetry favored actor A, indicating that A received relatively
more rewards or fewer punishments.)

Although these experiments were not designed primarily for the analysis
of gender effects, they have a number of advantages for our purposes.
First, no other data set contains the range of systematic variations in
levels of both average power and power imbalance for both reward-based
power and punishment-based power. No comparison of gender effects

under controlled power structures that combine both bases of power has previously been made. Second, this data set contains quantitative measures of power strategies that can be examined in relation to both structural power and power outcomes, making it possible to study the linkages between structure and strategies, and strategies and outcomes, for males and females.

On the other hand, the data set has certain limitations as well. Subjects interacted only in same-sex exchange networks, and they were not told the sex of their partners. We cannot know whether or not subjects assumed their partners were of a particular gender and, if so, which gender. The design thus omits the mixed-sex interactions that most commonly activate gender as a status characteristic. Nevertheless, gender may have been situationally activated, in one of two ways. First, the nature of the task may have activated gender as a status characteristic. Making choices on a computer in a game-like structure to earn money is a task with which males might be more familiar and comfortable than females. If so, males would be expected to exhibit more high-status behaviors, and females more low-status behaviors, just as in a mixed-sex group. Alternatively, positions of power advantage and disadvantage might activate gender as a status characteristic. If so, we would expect to find gender effects when structural power is imbalanced but not when it is balanced.

Results

GENDER AND POWER STRATEGIES

We first analyze how gender affects strategies of power use, either alone or in interaction with structural power. Using hierarchical regression, we regressed measures of the contingent use of rewards and punishment on gender and the structural power variables, and then added multiplicative terms for the interactions between gender and structural power to the equation.

The results, reported in Table 1.1, are for the dyadic averages of the individual strategies of actors A and B. (Recall that actor A was always advantaged, and actor B disadavantaged, in reward power. Depending on the condition, however, either A or B could be advantaged, and the other disadvantaged, in punishment power.) As Table 1.1 shows, we find only one effect of gender that is not conditioned by structure. Males are more likely than females to use punishment in response to the other's non-exchange. All other effects of gender are conditioned by structure. Four structural variables are involved in these interactions: average reward power, average punishment power, reward-power imbalance (which always favors A), and punishment-power imbalance favoring A.

In interpreting these findings, each set of three strategies (the three reward strategies, and the three punishment strategies) is appropriately

TABLE 1.1. Effects of gender and structural power on power strategies (unstandardized regression coefficients, $N = 290$).

Gender and structural power	Power strategies[a]					
	Reward strategies			Punishment strategies		
	R|R	R|N	R|P	P|R	P|N	P|P
Step 1:						
Gender	.08	− .08	.08	− .09	.22*	− .16
Average reward power	1.11	− .88	−1.32*	−1.60**	2.51***	.13
Average punishment power	− .09	− .03	.08	− .41	− .35	1.50**
Reward-power imbalance	−2.10***	1.81***	.79**	.36	− .52*	− .39
Punishment-power imbalance favoring A	.26	− .14	.07	− .54*	.58*	.44
Punishment-power imbalance favoring B	.84	− .51	− .27	− .79**	.87**	.69
F ratio	3.20**	2.70*	3.39**	3.60**	6.06***	2.17*
R²	.06	.05	.07	.07	.11	.04
Step 2—Gender by:						
Average reward power	−2.67	.57	1.50	−.10	1.78	−3.56*
Average punishment power	−1.75	1.10	1.76**	1.25*	− .54	− .81
Reward-power imbalance	−1.80	1.51	1.18*	1.26*	− .76	−1.75
Punishment-power imbalance favoring A	− 11	.06	.00	− .18	1.22*	−1.37
Punishment-power imbalance favoring B	.36	− .44	− .42	.16	.87	− .82
Change in F ratio	1.01	.55	2.59*	2.67*	2.02	2.39*
Change in R²	.02	.01	.04	.04	.03	.04

[a] $i|j$ = the contingency of behavior i on the other actor's prior performance of behavior j, where i and j = R (reward), N (nonexchange), and P (punishment).
*$p < .05$. **$p < .01$. ***$p < .001$.

examined as an interdependent group. The component strategies are not independent. If, for example, the likelihood of A's rewarding increases following B's nonexchange, then its likelihood must decrease after one or both of B's other behavioral categories. Consequently, a significant effect for a single strategy variable in a set suggests that we should examine the entire, interdependent set of variables. We do so in Table 1.2, by gender.

A quick glance at this table shows that structural power has more significant effects on the power strategies of males than of females. A closer examination of the table, and separate analyses (not shown in the table) of these relations for males and females in the "A" and "B" positions reveal different *kinds* of effects by gender, as well. First, structural imbalance affects the power strategies of males in the advantaged power position, but not the strategies of power-disadvantaged males or

TABLE 1.2. Effects of structural power on power strategies by gender (unstandardized regression coefficients, $N = 290$).

Structural power effects	Males	Females
A. Effects of reward-power imbalance on:		
R|R	−3.02***	−1.21
R|N	2.57***	1.06
R|P	1.38***	− .20
P|R	.99**	− .26
P|N	− .90**	− .14
P|P	−1.27*	.48
B. Effects of punishment-power imbalance favoring A on:		
P|R	− .63	− .45
P|N	1.20***	− .03
P|P	− .24	1.13
C. Effects of average reward power on:		
P|R	−1.63*	−1.53*
P|N	3.40***	1.62*
P|P	−1.68	1.88
D. Effects of average punishment power on:		
R|R	− .98	.78
R|N	.52	− .57
R|P	.97*	− .79
P|R	.22	−1.03**
P|N	− .62	− .08
P|P	1.08	1.90**

Note. All effects are estimated after controlling for other structural variables.
*$p < .05$. **$p < .01$. ***$p < .001$.

the strategies of females in either the advantaged or disadvantaged power position. In other words, females in either power position act like power-disadvantaged males. As their reward power advantage increases, powerful males decrease reciprocal reward strategies and increase nonreciprocal reward strategies. Similarly, as their punishment power advantage increases, they decrease reciprocal punishment and increase the contingency of their punishment on the other's nonexchange. These are precisely the kinds of strategies that should make the most effective use of a structural power advantage. Females, like power-disadvantaged males, do not vary the contingency of their rewards or punishments with structural power imbalance.

Second, the average level of reward and punishment power affects the punishment power strategies of females in both power positions, and of males in the power disadvantaged position. (Average punishment power has significant effects on male B's punishment strategies, which do not appear in the averages for A and B shown in the tables.) Females and power-disadvantaged males are more likely to vary their punishment power strategies in response to average power than in response to power imbalance. As the joint capacity for punishment in the relation increases, they are more likely to use punishment in retaliation for the other's punishment and less likely to use it to sanction the other's nonexchange. Increasing reward power, in contrast, increases the use of punishment to sanction nonexchange. Together, these two findings show a tendency to use punishment in response to behaviors on which mutual dependency is greatest. When reward dependency is high, females and power-disadvantaged males sanction the other's failure to reward, and when punishment dependency is high, they sanction the other's use of punishment.

GENDER AND POWER OUTCOMES

Next, we regressed the four measures of exchange outcomes on structural power and gender. Multiplicative interaction terms between structural power and gender were entered in the second step of these regressions, but no significant effects were found. Thus, they are omitted from the results reported here. As Table 1.3 shows, gender significantly affects the frequency and distribution of reward exchange. Relative to the effects of dimensions of structural power, however, these effects are weak. The positive coefficients indicate that both the average frequency of reward exchange and its asymmetry are higher for males than females. Separate analyses for actors in the "A" and "B" power positions show that these effects are produced solely by the effect of gender on the reward exchange of actors in the B position, the position of disadvantage when reward power is imbalanced. Males in this position reward their partner more frequently than do females. As we would expect, this gender effect is evident only when reward power is imbalanced.

TABLE 1.3. Effects of gender and structural power on power outcomes (unstandardized regression coefficients, $N = 290$).

	Power outcomes			
	Reward exchange		Punishment exchange	
Gender and structural power	Average	Asymmetry	Average	Asymmetry
Gender	.08*	.05*	.01	.25
Average reward power	−2.07***	.71***	.23	− .18
Average punishment power	.26**	− .04	− .06	.06
Reward-power imbalance	− .70***	.72***	.01	− .22**
Punishment-power imbalance favoring A	− .22*	.03	.18**	− .04
Punishment-power imbalance favoring B	.03	− .12	.26***	− .11
F ratio	50.30***	22.01***	3.51**	3.20**
R^2	.52	.32	.07	.06

$^*p < .05.$ $^{**}p < .01.$ $^{***}p < .001.$

Surprisingly, gender has no effects on the frequency or distribution of punishment. Instead, the mutual punishment in a relation increases as punishment power imbalance increases, and the actor who punishes more in the relation is the actor who is disadvantaged on reward power. These results support structural theories, which suggest that punishment is the tool of actors who are disadvantaged on reward power, but not socialization theories, which posit greater use of punishment by males. Neither gender nor structural power explains much of the variance in punishment, however.

LINKING STRATEGY WITH OUTCOMES: ARE MALES BETTER POWER USERS?

The results of these analyses raise an intriguing question. If males in power-advantaged positions were more likely to vary their strategies with their structural power, does this pattern explain the higher reward exchange of males in the disadvantaged power position? (In our experiments, remember, males exchanged only with other males, and females with other females.) In short, were males better than females at using a structural power advantage to increase their partners' exchange?

The apparent linkage between these two gender differences is tempting, but statistically we find no support for it. The stronger relation between structure and strategy for power-advantaged males does not explain why their power-disadvantaged male partners rewarded them more frequently. Entering the strategies of male A's or the interaction between their strategies and structural power in the regression equation predicting reward exchange of male B's does not reduce the effect of gender. As far we can tell, these are two distinct kinds of effects.

Implications for Theory

The results of these experiments are notable for their similarities to Molm's (1986) earlier study of power and gender, even though the previous study differed in a number of ways from the experiments in this program. The earlier study examined power in dyadic exchange relations in which the alternative to earning money through exchange was earning it through individual effort. Rewards were the sole base of power, only one condition of structural power was studied, and power strategies were measured by a different technique. Because the experiment was explicitly designed to study gender effects, both same-sex and mixed-sex dyads were studied, subjects knew the sex of their partners, and the legitimation of assignment to the positions of power advantage or disadvantage was manipulated. Despite these very substantial differences, the basic findings of the two studies are very similar: (a) structural power has stronger effects than gender, (b) the effects of gender on exchange outcomes are limited to a higher frequency of rewarding by males in positions disadvantaged in reward power, and (c) males and females differ in power strategies but these differences are unrelated to power outcomes. Whether relations were same-sex or mixed-sex, or whether the partner's sex was known, made little difference. The single effect of gender on exchange outcomes that was observed in both studies is not dependent on the sex of the partner. The first study showed that legitimation of power strengthened this effect, but the absence of legitimation in the second shows that this is not a necessary condition for its appearance. These similarities are significant. They strongly suggest that we are dealing not with minor artifacts of particular experimental settings, but with consistent and meaningful behavioral effects.

What conclusions can we draw from these results, and what are their implications for theory development? First, the results of these studies support our argument that structural power substantially weakens the effects of gender on interaction and influence. When males and females are in positions of equivalent structural power, few effects of gender on exchange outcomes are observed. Gender explains little of the variance in strategy or outcomes.

Second, although the design of these experiments does not allow us to conclusively test between socialization effects and status effects, the results offer stronger support for status characteristics theory than for socialization theory. We find almost no evidence of gender differences in behavior that are transsituational. Only one effect of gender occurred independently of structure: males were more likely than females to use punishment to sanction the other's nonexchange. But males were not more likely to use punishment in general, nor were any other differences in frequency or contingency of behavior observed independently of structure. These results also contradict biological arguments of the relations among gender, aggression, and power use.

The few gender differences that we found also support a status characteristics explanation. If gender status was activated by power imbalance, we would expect gender effects under conditions of structural power imbalance but not balance. And that is the pattern we found: males and females responded differently to structural power imbalance. Males in power-advantaged positions varied their power strategies in relation to their structural power more so than their female counterparts. And males in power-disadvantaged positions rewarded their partners more frequently than females in power-disadvantaged positions. The first finding, the interaction of gender and structure on power strategies, is entirely consistent with a status effect favoring men. Structural power advantage provides an opportunity for influence that high-status actors should be more likely to take advantage of than low-status actors, and that is what the results show.

The second finding is more difficult to interpret. Objectively, females fared better than males in power-disadvantaged positions because they were less likely to engage in unilateral exchange with their less dependent partner. In traditional terms, they were "tougher" and less compliant than their male counterparts. On the surface, this finding appears contrary to both socialization theory and status characteristics theory. But the interpretation of such unilateral exchange as compliance may be wrong. The better exchange outcomes that powerful females obtained may have been the unintended result of higher performance expectations held by males in both power positions. Higher status actors, who have greater performance expectations for themselves, may persist longer in trying to initiate mutual exchange in disadvantaged positions than low-status actors, who have lower expectations that they will be successful in inducing the other's reciprocal exchange. In short, males may have been less likely than females to accept power disadvantage as a constraint on their behavior. Because males expect to be in more powerful positions, they respond to power advantage and power disadvantage in opposite, but parallel, ways. They are more likely than females to use the opportunities of structural power advantage, but less likely than females to recognize the constraints of structural power disadvantage. It is important to remember, however, that our interpretation of these effects as status effects is only valid if power imbalance activated gender as a status characteristic in the same-sex relations. Otherwise, the similarity of findings for same-sex and mixed-sex relations would refute a status explanation.

The responses to average power suggest a somewhat different aspect of gender differences in power strategies. Although relative power provides actors with different *capacities* for influence, their average power is an index of their *incentive* to influence. The greater the absolute dependence of actors on each other, the more they gain from the other's reward exchange and/or lose from the other's punishment. Male actors in power-advantaged positions are not influenced by absolute dependency, but males in power-disadvantaged positions, and females in both power positions, are. The greater their absolute dependency, the more likely they are to use punishment to sanction nonrewarding or punishing behaviors of their partner. As we saw, it is actors who are disadvantaged on reward power who are most likely to use punishment as a power strategy. We believe the greater responsiveness to variations in absolute dependency is also typical, in general, of power-disadvantaged actors. Absolute dependency matters more to these actors. Because they are getting less of what they want from the relation, the subjective value of changes in the absolute magnitude of rewards and punishments is greater for them.

Overall, our analyses of the relation between structural power and strategy suggest that females behave like power-disadvantaged actors, regardless of their power position. Like power-disadvantaged males, they respond strategically to the degree of mutual dependence. Like power-disadvantaged males, they do not respond strategically to power imbalance, even when it is in their favor.

The similarity between females in both power positions, and males in the power-disadvantaged position, is difficult to explain by status characteristics theory. If power imbalance activates gender as a status characteristic, then males should have higher performance expectations for themselves even when they are in a power-disadvantaged position. We would expect them to behave differently than females in the same position. On the other hand, most of our findings, including the tendency for females in both power positions to behave like power-disadvantaged actors, do fit a status characteristics explanation.

Our study does not rule out alternative explanations, however. For example, females may behave more like power-disadvantaged males in their strategic use of power because their dominant structural experience is that of a power-disadvantaged actor. In some respects, this is a socialization explanation, but one that is based not on a notion of internalized, stable traits, but on differential experiences with power that are structurally induced. These effects need not be viewed as stable or unchangeable—clearly, the structure of power currently in effect eliminates most gender differences that might have been created by previous structures—but longer experience under new power structures may be required to eliminate them.

These alternative theories can be tested with experimental designs that manipulate the activation of status characteristics without the ambiguity that has characterized our results. Rigorous test of the effects of status characteristics under conditions of power imbalance should be the highest priority for research in this area. Even with the ambiguity inherent in our findings, however, it seems quite clear that gender differences in power use will not emerge as a compelling explanation of gender inequalities in structural power, or a justification of them. Our results, like those of the individual-level studies, show that gender explains no more than 5% of the variation in any of the measures of power outcomes or power strategies. Structural power explains substantially more. These findings strongly suggest that it is the association of gender with structural power that accounts for apparent gender differences in power use. To the extent that women are structurally disadvantaged, they are seriously impaired in their capacity to use power and to obtain more power resources through exchange. Because these outcomes—which are outcomes of structural power—are associated with gender as well, they reinforce beliefs about women's power use which, in turn, are used to justify and maintain their structural positions.

Acknowledgments. This work was supported by a grant from the National Science Foundation (SES-84 19872) to the senior author. We thank Cecilia Ridgeway for helpful comments on earlier drafts of this chapter.

References

Aranoff, D., & Tedeschi, J.T. (1968). Original stakes and behavior in the Prisoner's Dilemma game. *Psychometric Science, 12*, 79–80.

Archer, J. (1976). Biological explanation of psychological sex differences. In B. Lloyd & J. Archer (Eds.), *Exploring sex differences*. London: Academic Press.

Bacharach, S.B., & Lawler, E.J. (1981). *Bargaining: Power, tactics, and outcomes*. San Francisco: Jossey-Bass.

Beddell, J., & Sistrunk, F. (1973). Power, opportunity costs, and sex in a mixed-motive game. *Journal of Personality and Social Psychology, 25*, 219–226.

Berger, J., Conner, T.L., & Fisek, M.H. (1974). *Expectation states theory: A theoretical research program*. Cambridge, MA: Winthrop.

Berger, J., Fisek, M.H., Norman, R.Z., & Zelditch, M. Jr. (1977). *Status characteristics and social interaction*. New York: Elsevier.

Bierstedt, R. (1950). An analysis of social power. *American Sociological Review, 15*, 730–738.

Blau, P. (1964). *Exchange and power in social life*. New York: Wiley.

Boldizar, J.P., Perry, D.G., & Perry, L.C. (1988). Gender and reward distributions: A test of two hypotheses. *Sex Roles, 19*, 569–579.

Carli, L.L. (1982). *Are women more social and men more task-oriented? A meta-analytic review of sex differences in group interaction, reward allocation, coalition formation, and cooperation in the Prisoner's Dilemma game*. Unpublished manuscript, University of Massachusetts, Amherst.

Carli, L.L. (1989). Gender differences in interaction style and influence. *Journal of Personality and Social Psychology, 56*, 565–576.

Cohen, E.G., & Roper, S.S. (1972). Modification of interracial interaction disability: An application of status characteristics theory. *American Sociological Review, 37*, 643–657.

Coleman, J.S. (1973). *The mathematics of collective action*. Chicago: Aldine.

Conrath, D.W. (1972). Sex role and "Cooperation" in the game of Chicken. *Journal of Conflict Resolution, 16*, 433–443.

Cook, K.S., & Emerson, R.M. (1978). Power, equity and commitment in exchange networks. *American Sociological Review, 43*, 721–739.

Dahl, R.A. (1957). The concept of power. *Behavioral Science, 2*, 201–218.

Dobbins, G.H. (1986). Equity vs. equality: Sex differences in leadership. *Sex Roles, 15*, 513–525.

Eagly, A.H. (1978). Sex differences in influenceability. *Psychological Bulletin, 85*, 86–116.

Eagly, A.H. (1987). *Sex differences in social behavior: A social-role interpretation*. Hillsdale, NJ: Erlbaum.

Eagly, A.H., & Carli, L.L. (1981). Sex of researchers and sex-typed communications as determinants of sex differences in influenceability: A meta-analysis of social influence studies. *Psychological Bulletin, 90*, 1–20.

Eagly, A.H., & Steffen, V.J. (1986). Gender and aggressive behavior: A meta-analytic review of the social psychological literature. *Psychological Bulletin, 100*, 309–330.

Eagly, A.H., & Wood, W. (1985). Inferred sex differences in status as a determinant of gender stereotypes about social influence. *Journal of Personality and Social Psychology, 43*, 915–928.

Eagly, A.H., & Wood, W. (1991). Explaining sex differences in social behavior: A meta-analytic perspective. *Personality and Social Psychology Bulletin, 17.*

Emerson, R.M. (1962). Power-dependence relations. *American Sociological Review, 27,* 31–40.

Emerson, R.M. (1972). Exchange theory, part I: A psychological basis for social exchange. Exchange theory, part II: Exchange relations and networks. In J. Berger, M. Zelditch, Jr., & B. Anderson (Eds.), *Sociological theories in progress* (Vol. 2, pp. 38–87). Boston: Houghton-Mifflin.

Fennell, M.L., Barchas, P.R., Cohen, E.G., McMahon, A.M., & Hildebrand, P. (1978). An alternative perspective on sex differences in organizational settings: The process of legitimation. *Sex Roles, 4,* 589–600.

Freese, L., & Cohen, B.P. (1973). Eliminating status generalization. *Sociometry, 36,* 177–193.

Frodi, A., Maccauley, J., & Thome, P.R. (1977). Are women always less aggressive than men? A review of experimental literature. *Psychological Bulletin, 84,* 634–660.

Gahagan, J.P., & Tedeschi, J.P. (1969). Shifts of power in a mixed-motive game. *Journal of Social Psychology, 77,* 241–252.

Hedley, M. (1990). *Power in social exchange: The question of gender.* Unpublished master's thesis.

Homans, G.C. [1961] (1974). *Social behavior: Its elementary forms.* New York: Harcourt, Brace and Jovanovich.

Horai, J., & Tedeschi, J.T. (1969). Effects of credibility and magnitude of punishment on compliance to threats. *Journal of Personality and Social Psychology, 12,* 164–169.

Hyde, J.S. (1984). How large are gender differences in aggression? A developmental meta-analysis. *Developmental Psychology, 20,* 722–736.

Hyde, J.S. (1986). Gender differences in aggression. In J.S. Hyde & M.C. Linn (Eds.), *The psychology of gender: Advances through meta-analysis.* Baltimore, MD: Johns Hopkins University Press.

Johnson, P. (1976). Women and power: Toward a theory of effectiveness. *Journal of Social Issues, 32,* 99–110.

Kahn, A., Hottes, J., & Davis, W.L. (1971). Cooperation and optimal responding in the Prisoner's Dilemma game. *Journal of Personality and Social Psychology, 17,* 267–279.

Kahn, A., O'Leary, V.E., Krulewitz, J.E., & Lamm, H. (1980). Equity and equality: Male and female means to a just end. *Basic and Applied Social Psychology, 1,* 173–197.

Kanter, R.M. (1977). *Men and women of the corporation.* New York: Basic Books.

Komorita, S.S., & Mechling, J. (1967). Betrayal and reconciliation in a two-person game. *Journal of Personality and Social Psychology, 6,* 349–353.

Lawler, E.J., & Bacharach, S.B. (1987). Comparison of dependence and punitive forms of power. *Social Forces, 66,* 446–462.

Lockheed, M.E. (1985). Sex and social influence: A meta-analysis guided by theory. In J. Berger & M. Zelditch, Jr. (Eds.), *Status, rewards, and influence: How expectations organize behavior* (pp. 406–429). San Francisco: Jossey-Bass.

Lockheed, M.E., & Hall, K. (1976). Conceptualizing sex as a status characteristic: Applications to leadership training strategies. *Journal of Social Issues, 32,* 111–124.

Maccoby, E.E., & Jacklin, C.N. (1975). *The psychology of sex differences.* Stanford, CA: Stanford University Press.

Major, B., & Deaux, K. (1982). Individual differences in justice behavior. In J. Greenberg & R.L. Cohen (Eds.), *Equity and justice in social behavior* (pp. 43–76). New York: Academic Press.

Mayhew, B.H., Gray, L.N., & Richardson, J.T. (1969). Behavioral measurement of operating power structures: Characterizations of asymmetrical interaction. *Sociometry, 32,* 474–489.

McClelland, D.C. (1975). *Power: The inner experience.* New York: Irvington Publishers.

McKee, J.P., & Sherriffs, A.C. (1957). The differential evaluation of males and females. *Journal of Personality, 25,* 356–371.

Meeker, B.F., & Weitzel-O'Neill, P.A. (1977). Sex roles and interpersonal behavior in task-oriented groups. *American Sociological Review, 43,* 91–105.

Michener, H.A., & Suchner, R. (1972). The tactical use of social power. In J.T. Tedeschi (Ed.), *Social influence processes* (pp. 239–286). Hawthorne, NY: Aldine.

Miller, G.H., & Pyke, S.W. (1973). Sex, matrix variations, and perceived personality effects in mixed-motive games. *Journal of Conflict Resolution, 17,* 335–349.

Mischel, H.N. (1974). Sex bias in the evaluation of professional achievements. *Journal of Educational Psychology, 66,* 157–166.

Molm, L.D. (1985a). Relative effects of individual dependencies: Further tests of the relation between power imbalance and power use. *Social Forces, 63,* 810–837.

Molm, L.D. (1985b). Gender and power use: An experimental analysis of behavior and perceptions. *Social Psychology Quarterly, 48,* 285–300.

Molm, L.D. (1986). Gender, power, and legitimation: A test of three theories. *American Journal of Sociology, 91,* 1356–1386.

Molm, L.D. (1990). Structure, action, and outcomes: The dynamics of power in social exchange. *American Sociological Review, 55,* 427–447.

Parcel, T.L., & Cook, K.S. (1977). Status characteristics, reward allocation, and equity. *Sociometry, 40,* 311–324.

Parsons, T. (1951). *The social system.* Glencoe, IL: Free Press.

Parsons, T., & Bales, F.F. (1955). *Family, socialization, and interaction process.* Glencoe, IL: Free Press.

Patterson, G.L. (1982). *Coercive family process.* Eugene, OR: Castalia Publishing Co.

Pugh, M.D., & Wahrman, R. (1983). Neutralizing sexism in mixed-sex groups: Do women have to be better than men? *American Journal of Sociology, 88,* 746–762.

Rapoport, A., & Chammah, A.M. (1965). Sex differences in factors contributing to the level of cooperation in the Prisoner's Dilemma game. *Journal of Personality and Social Psychology, 2,* 831–838.

Ridgeway, C.L. (1978). Conformity, group-oriented motivation, and status attainment in small groups. *Social Psychology Quarterly, 41,* 175–188.

Ridgeway, C.L. (1982). Status in groups: The importance of motivation. *American Sociological Review, 47,* 76–88.

Ridgeway, C.L. (1988). Gender differences in task groups: A status and legitimacy account. In M. Webster, Jr. & M. Foschi (Eds.), *Status generalization: New theory and research* (pp. 188–206). Stanford, CA: Stanford University Press.

Ridgeway, C.L. (1991). The social construction of status value: Gender and other nominal characteristics. *Social Forces, 70.*

Rubin, J.A., & Brown, B.R. (1975). *The social psychology of bargaining and negotiations.* New York: Academic Press.

Simon, H.A. (1957). *Models of man: Social and rational.* New York: Wiley.

Smith, B.L., & Fromm, M.G. (1982). Personality determinants of leadership and participation in a sociotherapy program. *Human Relations, 35,* 433–448.

Spence, J.T., Deaux, K., & Helmreich, R.L. (1985). Sex roles in contemporary American society. In G. Lindzey & E. Aronson (Eds.), *Handbook of social psychology* (Vol. 2, 3rd ed., pp. 149–178). New York: Random its use.

Tedeschi, J.T., & Bonoma, T.V. (1972). Power and influence: An introduction. In J.T. Tedeschi (Ed.), *Social influence processes* (pp. 1–49). Hawthorne, NY: Aldine.

Tedeschi, J.T., Gahagan, J.P., Aranoff, D., & Steele, M.W. (1968). Realism and optimism in the Prisoner's Dilemma game. *Journal of Social Psychology, 75,* 191–197.

Tedeschi, J.T., Schlenker, B.R., & Bonoma, T.V. (1973). *Conflict, power and games.* Chicago: Aldine.

Terhune, K.W. (1970). The effects of personality in cooperation and conflict. In P. Swingle (Ed.), *The structure of conflict* (pp. 193–234). New York: Academic Press.

Thibaut, J.W., & Kelley, H.H. (1959). *The social psychology of groups.* New York: Wiley.

Towson, S.M.J., & Zanna, M.P. (1982). Toward a situational analysis of gender differences in aggression. *Sex Roles, 8,* 903–914.

Uesugi, T.K., & Vinacke, W.E. (1963). Strategy in a feminine game. *Sociometry, 26,* 75–88.

Vinacke, W.E. (1964). Intra-group power relations, strategy, and discussions in inter-triad competition. *Sociometry, 27,* 25–39.

Vinacke, W.E., Mogy, R., Powers, W., Langan, C., & Beck, R. (1974). Accommodative strategy and communication in a three-person matrix game. *Journal of Personality and Social Psychology, 29,* 509–525.

Wallston, B.S. (1987). Social psychology of women and gender. *Journal of Applied Social Psychology, 17,* 1025–1050.

Wallston, B.S., & Grady, K.E. (1985). Integrating the feminist critique and the crisis in social psychology: Another look at research methods. V.E. O'Leary, R.K. Unger, & B.S. Williams (Eds.), *Women, gender, and social psychology* (pp. 7–34). Hillsdale, NJ: Erlbaum.

Webster, M. Jr., & Driskell, J.E. (1978). Status generalization: A review and some new data. *American Sociological Review, 43,* 220–236.

Wiley, M.G., & Eskilson, A. (1983). Scaling the corporate ladder: Sex differences in expectations for performance, power, and mobility. *Social Psychology Quarterly, 46,* 351–359.

Wilson, E.O. (1975). *Sociobiology: The new synthesis.* Cambridge, MA: Belknap Press of Harvard University Press.

Winter, D.G. (1988). The power motive in women—and men. *Journal of Per-*

sonality and Social Psychology, 54, 510–519.

Winter, D.G., & Barenbaum, N.G. (1985). Responsibility and the power motive in women and men. *Journal of Personality, 53,* 335–355.

Wittig, M.A., Marks, G., & Jones, G.A. (1980). The effect of luck versus effort attributions on reward allocations to self and other. *Personality and Social Psychology Bulletin, 7,* 71–78.

Wrong, D.H. (1968). Some problems in defining social power. *American Journal of Sociology, 73,* 673–681.

Wyer, R.S. Jr., & Malinowski, C. (1972). Effects of sex and achievement level upon individualism and competitiveness in social interaction. *Journal of Experimental Social Psychology, 8,* 303–314.

2
Gender, Formal Authority, and Leadership

CATHRYN JOHNSON

Do women and men in official leadership positions act similarly toward their subordinates? The majority of research in the area of gender, leadership, and formal authority addresses this question. One might think it would be easy to answer, but such is not the case. Available empirical evidence provides only contradictory answers. For example, a number of studies show no gender differences in leadership behavior, measured by subordinates' perceptions of their leaders' behavior or by observing actual leader behavior (Adams, 1978; Bartol, 1973; Bartol & Martin, 1986; Birdsall, 1980; Camden & Witt, 1983; Day & Stogdill, 1972; Dobbins & Platz, 1986; Donnell & Hall, 1980; Instone, Major, & Bunker, 1983; Koberg, 1985; Osborn & Vicars, 1976; Rice, Instone, & Adams, 1984; Terborg, 1979).[1] Other studies, however, find evidence for gender stereotypic behavior where women leaders are more person oriented (considerate, appreciative, supportive) than men leaders (Gupta, Jenkins, & Beehr, 1983; Statham, 1988) who are more task oriented (directive,

---

[1] Leadership behavior is measured most often in three ways: (a) subordinate perceptions of the leader are surveyed, (b) actual leader behavior is observed and coded, and (c) interaction between leader and subordinates is observed and coded. Most of the research comparing male and female leadership behavior has relied on subordinate perceptions of leader behavior (Bartol & Martin, 1986, p. 285). Two commonly used measures of leadership behavior are Bales's interaction process analysis (IPA) and Stodgill, Goode, and Day's Leader Behavior Description Questionnaire (LBDQ). Bales's IPA measures four types of behavior: active task behavior (giving opinions, suggestions, and information), passive task behavior (asking for opinions, suggestions, and information), positive socioemotional behavior (agreeing, dramatizing, being friendly), and negative socioemotional behavior (disagreeing, showing tension, being unfriendly) (Bales, 1950, 1972). The LBDQ measures subordinates' perceptions of two dimensions of leadership style: initiating structure (similar to task oriented) and consideration (similar to person oriented) (Stodgill, Goode, & Day, 1963). Initiating structure refers to the extent to which the leader clearly defines her own role and informs followers what is expected of them. Leader consideration refers to the expression of concern for the comfort, well-being, status, and contribution of followers.

instructive, and commanding) (Baird & Bradley, 1979; Eskilson & Wiley, 1976; Fowler & Rosenfeld, 1979). In contrast, yet other studies find men leaders to be more person oriented than women leaders (Winther & Green, 1987), and women leaders to be more task oriented than men leaders (Bartol & Wortman, 1979; Helmich, 1974). Finally, Eagly and Johnson (1990), in a meta-analysis of leadership behavior, conclude that women leaders are slightly more person oriented and less task oriented than men leaders.

Unfortunately this empirical evidence is difficult to interpret because it has rarely been linked to theoretical analyses of gender effects in leader-subordinate relations. A related problem is that previous research has not identified the conditions under which gender differences in leader-subordinate relations will or will not occur.

Three theoretical perspectives are available in the literature that attempt to explain when gender differences will occur. The gender role socialization perspective argues that men and women acquire different personality characteristics, skills, and beliefs that predispose men to be more directive and effective in leadership positions and predispose women to be more concerned for feelings and relationships (Fennell, Barchas, Cohen, McMahon, & Hildebrand, 1978; Martin, 1985; Riger & Galligan, 1980). This approach predicts that leader behaviors will be gender stereotyped in all situations.

In contrast, the structural position approach proposes that women and men who are placed in identical leadership positions with equal access to power resources and status will behave similarly (Kanter, 1977). Positional power in the organization and available power resources are the key to this theory which predicts no gender effects when power is similar for men and women leaders.

The third approach, expectation states theory, argues that gender is a diffuse status characteristic that carries with it general expectations for performance (Berger, Conner, & Fisek, 1974; Berger, Fisek, Norman, & Zelditch, 1977). It also argues that holding a formal position is a reward level that carries with it specific expectations for performance. Both gender and formal position are used as a basis for forming performance expectations that will produce observable inequalities in behavior. However, holding a formal position should have a stronger effect on leader behavior than gender because it is more directly relevant to the work setting. The theory predicts that, in a situation where power is fairly equal for men and women leaders, there will be slight behavioral differences due to the effect of gender.

Given the contradictory empirical evidence and its vague link to theoretical explanations, what do we really know about gender and formal authority? Perhaps the best conclusion is that we have been asking the wrong question, or asking this question in the wrong way. The question is not, do men and women leaders act similarly, but rather, under what conditions do they act similarly.

To address this modified question, I propose five new areas of investigation. The intent of this chapter is to discuss each and its potential to shed light on the relationship between gender and formal authority. I do so by drawing on existing theories and data in the area as well as my own recent study of gender and leader-subordinate behavior (Johnson, 1991).

First, we need to link empirical evidence to theoretical explanations that predict the effects of gender, formal position, and power in interaction. A related and more fundamental question is, what is the proper theoretical specification of the relationship between the effects of power, gender, and formal position in interaction? I will discuss the link between empirical and theoretical perspectives in the first section of the chapter.

Second, most leadership studies focus entirely on the leader's behavior. I argue in the second section that to understand the relationship between gender and formal authority, we must study the *interaction* between leaders and subordinates. At this point, we know very little about the nature of this interaction or about the effect of the gender of subordinate on leader behavior.

Third, leadership studies in laboratory settings traditionally have focused on the behavior of informal leaders (i.e., randomly appointed, achieved, or emergent leaders) in informal task groups, rather than on the behavior of leaders in formal task groups (Anderson & Blanchard, 1982; Brown, 1979; see Wood and Rhodes, Chapter 5 in this volume for a discussion of informal leaders).[2] Because we have in general ignored formal task group interaction, we have also neglected to introduce potentially important organizational variables, such as social composition of an organization and organizational culture, into small group research. In the third section I discuss why the introduction of these variables may enhance our understanding of gender and formal authority.

Fourth, although gender, formal position, and power are undoubtedly important in structuring interaction between leaders and subordinates, they may not be sufficient to explain the nature of formal group interaction. Additional processes may be operating simultaneously that affect

---

[2] Formal task groups differ from informal task groups in that the former are composed of individuals in normatively specified positions usually represented by job titles and determined by the organization. An example of a formal task group is a group comprised of a supervisor and two subordinates. Informal task groups consist of members who are not assigned to any specific positions by an organizational structure or outside authority. Examples of informal task groups include a United Way committee composed of volunteers where no member has been designated chairperson, and problem-solving experimental groups such as Bales's discussion groups (Bales, 1950). Leaders usually do emerge in these groups but they do not have specific job titles.

interaction. I discuss one such process that may be termed the social ease argument in the fourth section. As we shall see, a major difficulty lies in understanding how additional processes interact with gender, formal position, and power processes.

Lastly, despite important reasons for doing so, few studies have examined leader-subordinate interaction over time, either in informal or in formal task groups. It is possible that the nature of the interaction changes once members become familiar with one another. I argue in the final section that if familiarity has an effect, results of leadership studies that are based on data collected from one period of group interaction may give us only a partial picture of the interaction. I then discuss two directions research may take to increase our understanding of time effects.

Theoretical Explanations and Empirical Evidence

In this section I describe three theoretical perspectives that predict the relationship between gender, power, and formal position and their effects on leader-subordinate interaction. I then present and consider the implications of results from a study that tested predictions from each of the three theories against one another.

The first perspective, gender role socialization, posits that gender differences in behavior in organizations are largely due to different socialization processes experienced by boys and girls (Riger & Galligan, 1980). According to this approach, men are taught as little boys to be outgoing and achievement oriented. Women are taught as little girls to be emotionally oriented and reserved in interaction with others (Fennell et al., 1978). The consequences of this socialization are reflected in women and men's behavior in work groups and as leaders in organizations. Results of several previous studies on leaders suggest that the socialization process may affect leader behavior (Baird & Bradley, 1979; Fowler & Rosenfeld, 1979). The validity of this argument has been increasingly questioned, however, for two reasons: the increasing amount of evidence of no gender differences in leadership behavior in organizations (Bartol & Martin, 1986; Dobbins & Platz, 1986; Terborg, 1979), and evidence that leaders' behavior may vary across situations (Eskilson & Wiley, 1976; Perrow, 1986). Structural arguments have been proposed that take into account the context of the interaction.

One such argument, the structural position approach, proposes that gender differences in leadership behavior are a result of unequal access to power and status, not socialized characteristics of the individual. Kanter (1977), a leading proponent of this explanation, argues that apparent gender differences in the behavior of organizational leaders that are attributed to individual characteristics are in fact a result of the relative powerlessness of women in leadership positions. Power, in this case, is defined as, "... the ability to get things done, to mobilize resources, to get and use whatever it is that a person needs for the goals he or she is attempting to meet" (Kanter, 1977, p. 166). Women who are in identical leadership positions with men often have less access to resources to use in supervising and influencing others. As well, these women have less status and clout in the organization and, consequently, behave in ways that reflect their lack of power. Specifically, they are likely to act in a more authoritarian manner (i.e., more critical, bossy, and controlling) toward their subordinates than male leaders. Kanter's explanation suggests that men and women who are placed in identical leadership positions and have equal access to power resources (including equal status symbols) will behave relatively similarly.

Eagly and Johnson (1990) present a slightly different version of Kanter's explanation. They suggest that women and men's behavior should primarily reflect the influence of more specific roles in organizational settings, such as job title, rather than the influence of diffuse gender roles. In addition, criteria that organizations use to select leaders and the process used to socialize them into their roles should minimize tendencies for the sexes to lead or supervise in a stereotypical manner. Eagly's (1987, p. 146) explanation suggests that exposure to relatively clear-cut role requirements would tend to equalize female and male behavior.

The expectation states approach is similar to the structural position approach in that it is a structural argument, though more specific in its explanation, making slightly different predictions. Status characteristics theory, a theory within the expectation states program, argues that gender is a status characteristic that has two states, male and female. These states are differentially evaluated in society in terms of esteem and value, males being more highly valued than females. Gender carries with it general expectations for performance that are incorporated into the small task group whenever gender is activated in the situation. Gender activation occurs in mixed-sex groups because members are differentiated on states of this characteristic. As a result, the theory predicts that, in informal task groups where members are equal on all other status characteristics (e.g., race, age, and education) except gender, both men and women will expect men to perform better at the task, even if gender is irrelevant to the specific task. The theory argues that, because both men and women have higher performance expectations for men, men will be likely to contribute more to the task, have more opportunities to contribute, receive more positive evaluations for their contributions, and be more influential in group decisions than women (Berger et al., 1974; Berger et al., 1977). There is solid empirical evidence to support this formulation of the theory (Lockheed & Hall, 1976; Piliavin & Martin, 1978; Strodtbeck & Mann, 1956; Wood & Karten, 1986).

Expectation states theory offers an analysis of the conditions under which gender will affect behavior in informal task groups, but it has not yet delineated the effects of formal position and gender on behavior in formal task groups. It is possible to expand this theoretical formulation by examining how formal position might be conceptualized in the expectation states program.

In their discussion of the formulation of reward expectations on status situations, Berger and his colleagues (1977, 1985) suggest that in the basic status-reward relationship, there are goal objects defined as the specific privileges, rights, valued positions, and desired objects, such as money and symbols of respect, that are invested with high- or low-status value. These goal objects are associated with reward levels. Individuals who attain high reward levels will expect to receive positively evaluated goal objects. Reward levels are, in turn, associated with similarly evaluated states of task ability. States of task ability are related to states of task success. According to the theory, states of goal objects and reward levels have status significance just like states of characteristics and both relate to perceived task ability, reflected in performance expectations.

It is unclear, however, what the difference between reward level and goal object is in this situation. How would formal position be characterized within this framework—as a goal object or as a reward level?

I argue that expectation states should conceptualize formal position as an abstract reward level that an individual acquires when she or he enters the organization. Associated with this reward level are the more specific rewards called goal objects, such as money, resources used to influence others, status symbols (i.e., office), rights, and privileges. When an individual is hired for a specific position in the organization, s/he expects to receive goal objects (similar to Kanter's power resources) that are commensurate with that position. Both formal position and goal objects combine to form a set of rewards given to the individual by the organization. Formal position is directly linked to perceived task ability and a set of goal objects is indirectly linked through formal position. Therefore, formal position is more relevant to perceived task ability than goal objects. Gender is similar to a set of goal objects in relevancy to task ability since it is also indirectly linked to task ability. However, it is indirectly linked through general expectation states rather than through reward level.

This formulation suggests that, if the reward level for a man and a woman is positive and equal, that is, they both hold identical formal positions, *and* they both receive the same level of positive goal objects, both formal position and set of goal objects will have an equal positive effect on their performance expectations of perceived task ability and task success for self and other. This set of rewards (i.e., formal position and associated goal objects) will be more relevant to task ability than gender, although gender will have a slight effect on performance expectations. As Kanter's argument would suggest, however, it is possible that, in a situation where a man and a woman hold identical positions, the man may receive more positive goal objects than the woman. In this case, the man will have higher performance expectations for self than the woman because he has the advantage of being male and receiving a higher level of specific rewards.

This formulation is similar to Kanter's in that it incorporates the importance of equal access to power resources provided by the organization. Unlike Kanter's argument, however, it suggests that holding an identical formal position has a more direct effect on behavior than goal objects (power resources). In addition, it predicts slight gender effects in mixed-sex groups where formal positions and rewards are equal. Finally, expectation states is more specific than Kanter's explanation in that it links rewards to performance expectations for self and other.

I tested predictions of the three theories against one another in a laboratory experiment consisting of a simulated organization with formal positions (a manager and two employees of a video store) (Johnson, 1991). Males and females were placed in identical leadership positions and had equal access to power resources. Of the three theories, the structural position approach was the most clearly supported by the data. Male and female leaders talked a similar amount of time, had a similar number of speech acts, and were similar in their amounts of agreements and complimenting behavior toward their subordinates. Further, as predicted by the structural position approach, the behavioral data showed that male and female subordinates were similar in active and passive task behaviors and agreements toward the manager, regardless of the manager's gender. As well, they talked a similar amount of time and had a similar number of speech acts. As we shall see below, however, there were several findings that none of the theories could explain.

Obviously, my study cannot be considered a definitive test of the three theories, but it does provide a comparative evaluation of the different predictions derived from them under controlled conditions. We are just beginning to understand the relationship between power, formal position, and gender in formal task groups. Further research is necessary that continues to link empirical evidence with theoretical explanations. Two possible directions are (a) varying the level of power resources for male and female leaders, and (b) creating a more complex organizational hierarchy in the laboratory. To better test the structural position theory we need to compare leader-subordinate interaction in situations where leader power varies across groups. Also, we would benefit from examining leader-subordinate behavior in an organization with more than two levels of positions. One way to accomplish this is to consider the experimenter as the third level of the organizational hierarchy, representing, for example, top management. It would not be difficult to vary the behavior of the experimenter with the leaders to see how this may affect leader-subordinate interaction.

Interaction Between Leaders and Subordinates

Some studies, though few and far between, have examined the nature of the interaction between leaders and their subordinates. A few of these studies have investigated the effect of gender of the subordinates on the behavior of the leader, arguing that the gender of the subordinates has a more significant impact on leader behavior than the gender of the leader. Moore, Shaffer, Goodsell, and Baringoldz (1983, p. 51) reported that leaders, regardless of gender, uttered more statements of disapproval when instructing a male and offered more instruction when directing a female. Winther and Green (1987) concluded that both female and male leaders were more task oriented when working with female subordinates. Instone et al. (1983) found that subjects were more confident of their ability to effectively supervise same-sex rather than opposite-sex workers. Further, Eskilson and Wiley (1976, p. 190) found that both male and female leaders performed in a more leader-like way when leading members of their own gender. In contrast to the above studies, Wexley and Hunt (1974, p. 871) reported that the performance of male and female leaders was not a function of the gender of their subordinates.

Two of the above studies also reported observed behavior of both leaders and subordinates using Bales's (1950, 1972) interaction process analysis. First, Wexley and Hunt (1974, pp. 869–870) found that male and female leaders agreed more with male than female subordinates. Female leaders gave more opinions when working with male rather than female subordinates. In addition, male subordinates showed more release of tension and gave more opinions and orientation when supervised by female rather than male leaders. The authors suggest that male subordinates began to dominate the interaction when interacting with female leaders. On the other hand, female subordinates asked for orientation more often when supervised by male than female leaders. Similarly to Wexley and Hunt, Eskilson and Wiley (1976) concluded that male subordinates had a tendency to ignore the leadership of female leaders. In addition, they also found that male leaders were less leader-like when supervising groups composed of both female and male subordinates than same-sex subordinate groups. They suggest that part of the reason for this may be due to the "rooster effect" where the male subordinate competes with the male leader while in the presence of a female subordinate by performing more leader-like behavior than when in an all-male group.

In addition, West (1984), in her study of the effects of formal position and gender on physician-patient interaction, found that male doctors interrupted their male and female patients far more often than the reverse. In contrast, female doctors were interrupted far more often by male patients than they interrupted them. Female patients interrupted female doctors at about the same rate as female doctors interrupted female patients (pp. 101–102). West tentatively concludes that gender effects can have primacy over status (formal position in this case) when the doctor is a woman. She does not explain under what conditions this may occur.

Results of these studies are interesting, yet difficult to interpret since they have not been clearly linked to theories. The clearest pattern in these results is evidence that male subordinates may not automatically accept the authority of women in higher positions than themselves, suggesting that gender may have a greater effect on interaction than formal position. This also suggests that the legitimacy of women in high formal positions may be questioned by male subordinates. Results from a recent meta-analysis of subordinate evaluations of leaders by Eagly, Makhijani, and Klonsky (in press) provide some support for the importance of legitimacy when looking at subordinate behavior toward leaders. Paralleling the results of the above studies, they found that male followers showed a stronger tendency to devalue women leaders than did women followers, who showed no gender bias in their evaluations. Further, women leaders were devalued more (relative to men leaders) when they adopted "masculine" leadership styles, particularly an autocratic style, than when they adopted other leadership styles, including feminine ones. Unfortunately, none of the studies on leader-subordinate behavior suggests why and under what conditions subordinates question the legitimacy of female leaders by their behavior.

My study also examined the nature of the interaction between formal leaders and their subordinates within four types of groups: a female leader with female subordinates, a female leader with male subordinates, a male leader with male subordinates, and a male leader with female subordinates (Johnson, 1991). Contrary to the several studies mentioned above, I found that male subordinates (as well as female subordinates) acted similarly toward female and male managers.[3] Results also indicated that managers were more directive and talked more than subordinates in all types of groups. Unexpectedly, however, rates of agreements were similar for managers and subordinates, indicating that this behavior did

---

[3] Perhaps male subordinates did not resist female leaders in my study for two reasons. First, leaders were clearly legitimized in their managerial positions. This was accomplished by having the subjects fill out an employment history form that asked them to list the organizations they worked for, their job titles, length of time employed, rate of pay, and duties and responsibilities. Subjects believed that assignment of positions to either manager or employees was based on work experience listed in the employment histories. The employment history form drew upon cultural assumptions that those who have more responsibility in their jobs are more qualified as manager. Second, subordinates clearly recognized that their leader had more available power resources (more information, higher pay, better office, more complex tasks to perform, right to direct subordinates in their tasks). Legitimation of female leaders and clear differential power between positions may have influenced male subordinate behavior toward the leaders.

not differentiate high-positional power members from low-positional power members. Agreements flowed up and down the authority structure.

In addition, several results alert us to the need for reinterpreting some of Bales's (1950, 1972) influential categories for coding interaction when we examine interaction in formal task groups (see Wood and Rhodes, Chapter 5 in this volume for a discussion of Bales's categories). Specifically, managers had higher rates of passive task behaviors (asking questions) and compliments, whereas subordinates had higher rates of active task behaviors (giving opinions and suggestions). Researchers who study face-to-face interaction in informal same-sex and mixed-sex groups interpret asking questions as low-status behavior and offering opinions as high-status behavior. Members with low status provide opportunities for high-status members to offer their opinions by asking questions. Members with high status have more opportunities to contribute to the task and do therefore contribute more to the task. In formal task groups, however, asking questions is not necessarily indicative of low status. In fact, leaders asking their subordinates questions makes intuitive sense. It is not difficult to imagine a situation where an entire meeting may consist of the boss directing questions to his or her subordinates.

Further, for subordinates to give opinions is not necessarily high-status behavior. It might depend on whether the opinion was solicited or unsolicited and, if solicited, by whom. In my study subordinate opinions were more often a result of managers' solicitations, rather than freely given. In this context, a high-status member solicited opinions from low-status members. Giving opinions in this situation was not necessarily high-status behavior. One way to tackle this thorny problem is to suggest that opinions from high-status members, whether solicited or unsolicited, are high-status behaviors. In contrast, solicited opinions by low-status members may be interpreted as low-status behavior, whereas unsolicited opinions by low-status members may be indicative of high-status behavior. Further analysis is needed to examine if this differentiation is useful.

Researchers examining informal task groups also conceptualize positive socioemotional behavior (complimenting, giving encouragement) as low-status behavior. However, in a formal task group setting, complimenting behavior by leaders is not, in and of itself, indicative of low-status behavior. In fact, it may be considered the prerogative of high-status members.

These reinterpretations suggest a rethinking of the meaning of Bales's categories for future research in formal task group behavior, as well as a need for sensitivity to the context in which the interaction takes place. We cannot assume that these behaviors have similar meanings in informal and formal task group settings.

Future research should also include conversational analysis between leaders and subordinates beyond Bales's categories. Kollock, Blumstein, and Schwartz (1985) conducted an in-depth analysis of the conversation patterns of intimate heterosexual and homosexual couples to answer the question, What relationship does power and gender have to the observed differences in men's and women's speech? They used a model of turn-taking derived from the work of Sacks, Schegloff, and Jefferson (1974) and of Zimmerman and West (1975) which assumes that there are implicit rules that govern "polite" and "proper" conversation that participants may or may not follow. Kollock et al. suggest that, "In looking at a conversation we may then ask which persons are violating or ignoring them. The rules of turn taking may not apply equally to all classes of actors" (p. 35). They argue that there are two major elements to the division of labor within verbal interaction: conversational dominance (talking a disproportionate amount of time and interrupting to gain the floor), and conversational support (asking questions, using tag questions, giving minimal responses, agreeing, supporting statements). They contend that power may be more influential in conversational patterns than gender, suggesting that the more powerful partner (whether male or female) in the relationship will engage in more conversational dominance than the less powerful partner, who will engage in more conversational support.

Their results indicated that the more powerful partners were more likely to engage in more conversational dominance (indicated by higher rates of interruptions and lower rates of back channels) than the less powerful partners. However, talking time and question asking seemed linked to power and gender, though not in a simple way (pp. 42–45). It would be interesting to conduct an analysis similar to Kollock et al.'s on the conversational patterns of superordinates and subordinates and compare these results with results of studies that examine conversations in heterosexual and homosexual dyads. This analysis may add to our knowledge of the effects of gender and power in interaction.

Bringing the Organization In

Very few studies have examined leader-subordinate interaction in formal task groups. Most formal task groups are embedded within an organizational structure. Therefore if we are to examine leader-subordinate behavior in formal task groups we need to consider what organizational variables are affecting interaction. The structural position and expectation states approaches do consider the effects of organizational resources and formal position on leader-subordinate interaction. In addition, I argue that at least two other organizational variables are potentially important: social composition of an organization and organizational culture.

There are at least two definitions of social composition of an organization in the literature. First, Kanter's (1977) definition refers to the representation of different types of people in groups in organizations

(p. 208). Kanter suggests four group compositions. Uniform groups are composed of only one social type of person and, therefore, are homogeneous with respect to external status characteristics such as sex, race, and ethnicity. Skewed groups consist of a disproportionate number of one social type over another (ratio of 85:15). Kanter distinguishes "dominants" from "tokens" in this category. In tilted groups dominants are just a "majority" and tokens become a "minority" (ratio of 65:35). Balanced groups consist of a similar number of all social types (pp. 208–209). Kanter argues that relative numbers shape perceptions of organizational members and social interaction. For example, women leaders who have token status may behave differently with their workers than male leader dominants simply because of their token status, and not their gender. Kanter reasons that, because tokens are highly visible, they have additional performance pressure and also carry the burden of acting as a representative of their social category. Several ways to cope with token status are to overachieve or to become socially invisible. According to this explanation, all other things equal, women leaders with token status will act differently from women leaders in uniform, balanced, and tilted groups. No study has directly tested the effects of relative numbers on formal leadership behavior.[4]

---

[4] At least two studies have examined Kanter's theory of proportions in organizations. Both question Kanter's hypothesis that an increase in minority representation will benefit that minority and suggest that there are other variables that intervene between numerical factors and patterns of interaction.

Specifically, Izraeli (1983) examined the effects of proportions of men and women on union officers' perceptions of their own influence and each other's skill levels. She found that changes in group sex proportions had a stronger impact on perceptions of women than of men. Izraeli argues for the need to distinguish Kanter's numeric dominance from institutional dominance. Institutional dominance refers to the dominance of one status group in a particular field, such as banking or child care, whether it happens to be in a majority in a specific interaction or not. She suggests that, "Those who dominate a field of action *over time* come to determine the rules of interaction for strangers who chance to penetrate the boundaries. Neither their culture nor their power is neutralized by numerical reshuffling" (p. 163).

South, Bonjean, Markham, and Corder (1982) tested two theories, Kanter's theory of tokenism and the minority proportion-discrimination hypothesis derived from Blau (1977) and Blalock (1967), on the effects of female employees' proportional representation in work groups on intra- and intergroup relations. In contrast to Kanter's theory and in support of the minority proportion-discrimination hypothesis, they found that, ". . . female representation is negatively associated with the amount of encouragement for promotion females receive from their male supervisors" (p. 598). In addition, they reported that large minority proportions actually had a negative effect on intergroup relations because intergroup contact was reduced by increases in minority group representation. They conclude by suggesting that, "Perhaps the most important finding of this analysis is that purely numerical factors can and do exert fundamental influences on patterns of social interaction" (p. 598).

A fairly different conceptualization of organizational social composition is offered by Ridgeway (1988) who defines it as the representation of different types of members in the organization's positions of authority (p. 196). Ridgeway argues that organizational composition can affect social interaction in organizational task groups. In regard to gender composition, she suggests that gender will be activated for females in organizations where males disproportionately occupy the positions of authority. Disproportionate in this case means that at least 75% of the positions of authority are occupied by the opposite sex. This suggests that in a male-dominated organization, gender will be activated in all-female task groups, as well as mixed-sex groups. According to status characteristics theory, if gender is activated in the small group the general competency assumptions associated with being female rather than male will affect women's expectations for themselves and their male colleagues. In all-female task groups in female-dominated organizations, however, gender will not be activated. This suggests that women in all-female groups in male-dominated organizations will have lower performance expectations for themselves than their counterparts in female-dominated organizations. Ridgeway was not concerned with gender differences in leadership behavior in organizational task groups. If we apply her ideas to formal leadership behavior, however, we can make the prediction that women leaders of all-female task groups in male-dominated organizations may behave in a more gender stereotypic way than women leaders in female-dominated organizations. In other words, maybe leaders in female-dominated organizations interact differently with their subordinates than leaders in male-dominated organizations, depending on their gender. This prediction could be tested by comparing leader-subordinate interaction in male- versus female-dominated organizations.

The introduction of organizational culture into our analyses of formal task groups may also prove useful. In the organization literature, culture is often defined as, ". . . social or normative glue that holds an organization together. It expresses the values or social ideals and the beliefs that the organization members come to share" (Smircich, 1983, p. 344). These values and beliefs are made manifest through symbolic devices such as myths, rituals, stories, legends, and specialized language. Researchers in this area suggest that these symbolic devices can be used to convey, among other things, a philosophy of management. In addition, they suggest that culture conveys a sense of identity for organizational members (Peters & Waterman, 1982), and serves as a device that can guide and shape behavior (Pfeffer, 1981).

It is plausible that institutional cultures vary among organizations, influencing the type of leadership and quality of interaction between leaders and subordinates. In some organizations, for example, employee innovation may be encouraged, whereas in others it may be squelched (Peters & Waterman, 1982). This shared value may influence the type of leadership expected by top management of middle management. The important point here, and one that should be investigated, is that organizational culture may be an intervening variable between gender and leadership behavior.

The Social Ease Argument

Theoretical explanations for gender differences in leader-subordinate interaction focus on the effects of gender, formal position, and power, and their relationships to one another. In addition to gender, formal position, and power, however, other processes may be operating in formal task groups that affect interaction.

In my study of leader-subordinate interaction in formal task groups there were several significant findings that none of the theoretical approaches could explain (Johnson, 1991). I found that both male and female managers offered fewer opinions and suggestions, asked more questions, and were more directive toward opposite-sex subordinates than toward same-sex subordinates. In addition, both male and female subordinates directed more agreements toward each other more often when interacting with an opposite-sex manager than with a same-sex manager. These findings suggest that there is some other process or set of processes operating in the groups in addition to gender, formal position, and power. They indicate that the interaction pattern between leaders and subordinates in mixed-sex groups is qualitatively different than the interaction pattern in same-sex groups.

I argue that the best explanation for these findings is what may be termed a social ease argument. The social ease argument identifies a set of processes that operates in small groups, affecting the level of social ease or tension within the group. For all task groups where members are strangers to one another initially, the social ease argument suggests that there is both uncertainty and unfamiliarity among the group members regarding each others' interaction style and competence at the task. In addition, in many cases, there may be uncertainty about the task itself. This uncertainty and unfamiliarity creates some social tension, an uneasiness, which may be observed in nervous laughter, silences, or body language (e.g., puzzled expressions).

The social ease argument further states that, in groups where members are strangers to one another initially *and* where they also differ on some group category, the level of uncertainty and unfamiliarity may be much greater, creating even higher levels of social tension. A group category may be an external characteristic (e.g., age, gender, race) or any category that distinguishes members from each other (e.g., members of different work groups in an organization or residents of different neighborhoods). Members who are not similar in their group categories may feel somewhat uncomfortable at first, especially if they have had little past experience with dissimilar others in a particular setting or situation. For example, individuals from different work groups in an organization who form a new group may feel uncomfortable at first because each is ignorant of the others' expectations of how groups should be run. Note here that the same group category may cause greater social tension in one situation than in another since categories will vary in their importance to members across situations. For example, members of different neighborhoods may feel more social tension at a zoning meeting than at a United Way allocation committee meeting.

Applying these ideas to task groups where members differentiate on the gender characteristic, members in same-sex groups are likely to be more certain about what the appropriate behaviors and norms are for interaction than members in mixed-sex groups. The standards for mixed-sex interaction may not be as clear, resulting in some tension that is not as pronounced in same-sex interaction (Hall, 1984). This uncertainty may be a result of lack of familiarity with the interaction patterns of opposite-sex members in work settings.

The social ease argument further suggests that, in situations of uncertainty and unfamiliarity, people prefer dealing with others who are similar to themselves (Kanter, 1977). Kanter contends that leaders in a variety of situations are likely to have a preference for socially similar subordinates. As suggested by social comparison theory, people prefer similar to dissimilar others because of their expectations that the former are more likely to hold views similar to their own (Festinger, 1954). In an uncertain situation this may be particularly important. In addition, Kanter argues that interaction (including communication) with socially dissimilar others tends to be perceived as more uncomfortable and unpredictable than interaction with similar others. In support of her explanation, Kanter found that male managers felt uncomfortable when having to communicate with women. For example, they were quoted as saying, "It takes more time," "You never know where you stood," and "I'm always making assumptions that turn out to be wrong" (p. 58). Unfortunately, there were not enough female managers in Kanter's study to examine whether women felt uncomfortable communicating with men in the same way. Cooper and Davidson (1984), in their study of British male and female managers, did find, however, that women managers reported members of the opposite gender as being uncomfortable working with them because of their own gender (p. 41). Men managers did not report a similar experience.

As suggested earlier, both uncertainty and unfamiliarity occur in different degrees depending on whether members are initially strangers to one another and whether they differentiate on group categories. In heterosexual mixed-sex groups, however, an additional process may be operating to create a special type of social tension not found in heterosexual same-sex groups. This process is called the "hidden agenda," which refers to the desire of persons of each sex to be attractive to the opposite sex (Bernard, 1975). Eskilson and Wiley (1976), in their earlier work on leader-subordinate relations in informal task groups, found that, similar to my study, male and female leaders performed more active task behavior when with members of their own gender. They suggest that members in mixed-sex groups may have found it more difficult to concentrate their communications on task behavior than members in mixed-sex groups because of the "hidden agenda." In heterosexual same-sex groups, members are not as concerned with how they are presenting themselves in regard to their attractiveness.

Interpersonal attraction operating in mixed-sex groups may cause social tension, but exactly how and to what degree is not clear. Further research is needed to examine the effects of attraction on social tension in face-to-face formal and informal task groups. To my knowledge, no such studies have yet been undertaken. In addition, the social ease processes that operate in face-to-face informal and formal task groups warrant further investigation. Most important, we need to examine how social tension processes interact with gender, formal position, and power processes within the groups. For example, perhaps social tension processes have their strongest effect only during the initial stages of interaction, whereas the effects of gender, power, and formal position may be more stable over time.

The Effects of Time on Leader-Subordinate Interaction

All three theoretical perspectives on gender differences in leader-subordinate interaction predict that interaction patterns between leaders and subordinates will remain relatively constant over time. They do not consider the possibility that initial interaction may be qualitatively different than later interaction when members are familiar with one another. Bartol and Martin (1986) warn us that the nature of the relationship between females and males in groups may depend on the duration of the interaction. They point out that Schneier and Bartol (1980) found no difference in the proportion of males and females to emerge as leaders toward the end of their 15-week study. The theories' prediction that time will have no effect may be valid, but we have no empirical evidence to support it. Before we assume that interaction patterns will remain constant we had better investigate this assumption.

There are at least two directions that this research could take. First, we can investigate the effects of time on interaction over several group meetings. Second, we can examine the effects of earlier acts on later acts within one period of interaction. Each direction will be discussed in turn.

In a preliminary study, I analyzed the effects of gender, power, and formal position on leader-subordinate behavior over time (Johnson, 1991).

Ten groups consisting of a female manager and two male subordinates were asked to come to the laboratory for 1 hour a week for 3 consecutive weeks. These ten groups were part of my other study mentioned in the first section of the chapter. Behavioral data were analyzed over three time periods: Time 1, Time 2, and Time 3, totaling 30 meetings. Other types of groups were not run due to limited resources. The results indicated that the female managers began to express their opinions more often, asked fewer questions, and became less directive, whereas male subordinates asked more questions over time. It is striking that significant changes in manager behavior occurred between Time 1 and Time 2, indicating that interaction can change noticeably within a short period of time. Interestingly, these changes remained fairly constant in Time 3. Equally striking is the observation that female managers with male subordinates at Time 2 and Time 3 acted similarly to male managers with male subordinates at Time 1 in my other study.

These results, although significant, are not easily interpretable because they could not be compared to results from other conditions. My speculation is that consistent with the social ease argument, changes in manager behavior may have been a result of reduced social tension over time. That is, managers may have become more familiar with their opposite-sex subordinates, resulting in reduced uncertainty and unpredictability. In turn, reduced uncertainty and unpredictability may have decreased feelings of social tension within the group. Although these are only post hoc explanations, it is clear that the results of this exploratory analysis call into question results of studies that examine interaction in task groups at one time period only.

The second direction for research involves the careful analysis of the effects of earlier speech acts on later speech acts within one period of interaction. At this point we have a limited understanding of how initial verbal and nonverbal behaviors may affect later behaviors within a group. For example, imagine the first meeting with the leader and his or her subordinates in the leader's office. In the first case scenario the manager sets the stage of interaction by talking a relatively long time, giving information and his or her opinions before asking the subordinates for their opinions. In the second case scenario, the manager says very little initially, and instead asks for the subordinates' opinions before providing his or her own. In both cases, the first speech act may affect future interaction within that particular encounter. Interaction patterns in both scenarios may look qualitatively different because of the manager's initial speech act.

Further, it is possible that the leader may set the stage for interaction differently across situations, depending on the purpose of the meeting. As Perrow (1986) suggests, we have too often assumed that the leadership style of leaders is constant across situations when, in fact, leaders may vary their style to fit the demands of the situation (p. 95).

Conclusion

The current state of affairs in the area of gender and formal authority looks bleak simply because empirical evidence is very rarely linked to theoretical analyses. In this chapter I have suggested several new directions for research in this area. First, if we are to move this area out of its current static state of confusion, we must clearly link empirical with theoretical work. In doing so we can address the relationship between gender, power, and formal position and how they interact to affect leader-subordinate interaction.

Equally important, I have suggested that our theories should include analyses of leader and subordinate *interaction* rather than leader behavior exclusively. We know very little about the nature of this interaction. I also pointed out that we have neglected in our theories organizational variables that may affect this interaction. I discussed two potentially important variables, social composition of the organization and organizational culture, yet there are probably additional ones as well. I also argued that it is likely that other processes operate simultaneously with gender, formal position, and power, such as social tension. Existing theories focus only on gender, power, and formal position to explain leader-subordinate interaction, excluding other potentially significant processes. Lastly, I noted that our theories assume that leader and subordinate behavior will remain constant over time, but there is little empirical evidence to support this assumption. I argued that we can no longer take this assumption for granted until we have evidence to support it.

In my view, these proposed extensions of current theoretical approaches, along with appropriate empirical tests, will increase our knowledge of the conditions under which gender differences in leader-subordinate interaction will occur.

References

Adams, E.F. (1978). A multivariate study of subordinate perceptions of and attitudes toward minority and majority managers. *Journal of Applied Psychology*, *63*, 227–288.

Anderson, L.R., & Blanchard, P.N. (1982). Sex differences in task and social-emotional behavior. *Basic and Applied Social Psychology*, *3*, 109–139.

Baird, J.E. Jr., & Bradley, P.H. (1979). Styles of management and communication: A comparative study of men and women. *Communication Monographs*, *46*, 101–111.

Bales, R.F. (1950). *Interaction process analysis: A method of small groups*. Cambridge, MA: Addison-Wesley.

Bales, R.F. (1972). *Personality and interpersonal behavior*. New York: Holt, Rinehart, and Winston.

Bartol, K.M. (1973). *Male and female leaders in small groups*. East Lansing: MSU Business Studies.

Bartol, K.M., & Martin, D.C. (1986). Women and men in task groups. In R. Ashmore & F. Del Boca (Eds.), *The social psychology of female-male relations* (pp. 259–310). New York: Academic Press.

Bartol, K.M., & Wortman, M.S. Jr. (1979). Sex of leader and subordinate role stress: A field study. *Sex Roles, 5,* 513–518.

Berger, J., Conner, T.L. & Fisek, M.H. (1974). *Expectation states theory: A theoretical research program*. Cambridge, MA: Winthrop.

Berger, J., Fisek, M.H., Norman, R.Z., & Wagner, D.G. (1985). The formation of reward expectations in status situations. In J. Berger & M. Zelditch (Eds.), *Status, rewards, and influence* (pp. 215–261). San Francisco: Jossey-Bass.

Berger, J., Fisek, M.H., Norman, R.Z., & Zelditch, M. Jr. (1977). *Status characteristics and social interaction*. New York: Elsevier.

Bernard, J. (1975). *The sex game*. New York: Atheneum.

Birdsall, P. (1980). A comparative analysis of male and female managerial communication style in two organizations. *Journal of Vocational Behavior, 16,* 183–196.

Blalock, H.M., Jr. (1967). *Toward a theory of minority-group relations*. New York: Wiley.

Blau, P.M. (1977). *Inequality and heterogeneity*. New York: Free Press.

Brown, S.M. (1979). Male versus female leaders: a comparison of empirical studies. *Sex Roles, 5,* 595–611.

Camden, C., & Witt, J. (1983). Manager communicative style and productivity: a study of female and male managers. *International Journal of Women's Studies, 6,* 258–269.

Cooper, C.L., & Davidson, M.J. (1984). *Women in management*. London: Heinemann.

Day, D.R., & Stogdill, R.M. (1972). Leader behavior of male and female supervisors: a comparative study. *Personnel Psychology* 25: 353–60.

Dobbins, Gregory H. & Stephanie J. Platz. (1986). Sex differences in leadership: how real are they? *Academy of Management Review, 11,* 118–127.

Donnell, S.M., & Hall, J. (1980). Men and women as managers: a significant case of no significant difference. *Organizational Dynamics, 8,* 60–77.

Eagly, A.H. (1987). *Sex differences in social behavior: A social-role interpretation*. Hillsdale, NJ: Erlbaum.

Eagly, A.H., & Johnson, B.T. (1990). Gender and leadership style: a meta-analysis. *Psychological Bulletin, 108,* 233–256.

Eagly, A.H., Makhijani, M.G., & Klonsky, B.G. (in press). Gender and the evaluation of leaders: a meta-analysis. *Psychological Bulletin*.

Eskilson, A., & Wiley, M.G. (1976). Sex composition and leadership in small groups. *Sociometry, 39,* 183–194.

Fennell, M.L., Barchas, P.R., Cohen, E.G., McMahon, A.M., & Hildebrand, P. (1978). An alternative perspective on sex differences in organizational settings: the process of legitimation. *Sex Roles, 4,* 589–604.

Festinger, L.A. (1954). A theory of social comparison processes. *Human Relations, 7,* 117–140.

Fowler, G.D., & Rosenfeld, L.B. (1979). Sex differences and democratic leadership behavior. *The Southern Speech Communication Journal, 45,* 69–78.

Gupta, N., Jenkins, D., Jr., & Beehr, T. (1983). Employee gender, gender similarity, and supervisor-subordinate cross-evaluations. *Psychology of Women Quarterly*, *8*, 174–184.

Hall, J.A. (1984). *Nonverbal sex differences: Communication accuracy and expressive style*. Baltimore: John Hopkins University Press.

Helmich, D.L. (1974). Male and female presidents: some implications of leadership style. *Human Resource Management*, *12*, 25–26.

Instone, D., Major, B. & Bunker, B.B. (1983). Gender, self confidence, and social influence strategies: an organizational simulation. *Journal of Personality and Social Psychology*, *44*, 322–333.

Izraeli, D.N. (1983). Sex effects or structural effects? An empirical test of Kanter's theory of proportions. *Social Forces*, *62*, 153–165.

Johnson, C. (1991). Gender, formal authority and the interaction between leaders and subordinates. *Dissertation Abstracts International*, forthcoming in Vol. 51–12A.

Kanter, R.M. (1977). *Men and women of the corporation*. New York: Basic Books.

Koberg, C.S. (1985). Sex and situational influences on the use of power: a follow-up study. *Sex Roles*, *13*, 625–639.

Kollock, P., Blumstein, P., & Schwartz, P. (1985). Sex and power in interaction: conversational privileges and duties. *American Sociological Review*, *50*, 34–46.

Lockheed, M.E., & Hall, K.P. (1976). Conceptualizing sex as a status characteristic: applications to leadership training strategies. *Journal of Social Issues*, *32*, 111–124.

Martin, P.Y. (1985). Group sex composition in work organizations: a structural-normative model. In S. Bacharach & R. Mitchell, (Eds.), *Research in the sociology of organizations* (Vol. 5, pp. 311–349). Greenwich, CT: JAI Press.

Moore, S.F., Shaffer, L., Goodsell, D.A., & Baringoldz, G. (1983). Gender or situationally determined spoken language differences? The case of the leadership situation. *International Journal of Women's Studies*, *6*, 44–53.

Osborn, R.N., & Vicars, W.M. (1976). Sex stereotypes: an artifact in leader behavior and subordinate satisfaction analysis? *Academy of Management Journal*, *19*, 439–449.

Perrow, C. (1986). *Complex organizations: A critical essay* (3rd ed.). New York: Random House.

Peters, T.J., & Waterman, R.H., Jr. (1982). *In search of excellence*. New York: Harper & Row.

Pfeffer, J. (1981). Management as symbolic interaction: the creation and maintenance of organizational paradigms. In L.L. Cummings & B.M. Staw (Eds.), *Research in organizational behavior* (Vol. 3, pp. 1–52). Greenwich, CT: JAI Press.

Piliavin, J.A., & Martin, R.R. (1978). The effects of the sex composition of groups on style of social interaction. *Sex Roles*, *4*, 281–296.

Rice, R.W., Instone, D., & Adams, J. (1984). Leader sex, leader success, and leadership process: two field studies. *Journal of Applied Psychology*, *69*, 12–31.

Ridgeway, C.L. (1988). Gender differences in task groups: a status and legitimacy account. In M. Webster, Jr. & M. Foschi (Eds.), *Status generalization* (pp. 188–206). Stanford, CA: Stanford University Press.

Riger, S., & Galligan, P. (1980). Women in management: an exploration of competing paradigms. *American Psychologist*, *35*, 902–910.

Sacks, H., Schegloff, E. & Jefferson, G. (1974). A simplest systematics for the organization of turn-taking for conversation. *Language*, *50*, 696–735.

Schneier, C.E., & Bartol, K.M. (1980). Sex effects in emergent leadership. *Journal of Applied Psychology*, *65*, 341–345.

Smircich, L. (1983). Concepts of culture and organizational analysis. *Administrative Science Quarterly*, *28*, 339–358.

South, S.J., Bonjean, C.M., Markham, W.T., & Corder, J. (1982). Social structure and intergroup interaction: men and women of the federal bureacracy. *American Sociological Review*, *47*, 587–599.

Statham, A. (1988). Woman working for women: The manager and her secretary. In A. Statham, E. Miller, & H. Mauksch (Eds.), *The worth of women's work* (pp. 225–243). New York: State University of New York Press.

Stodgill, R.M., Goode, O.S., & Day, D.R. (1963). The leader behavior of United States senators. *Journal of Psychology*, *56*, 3–8.

Strodtbeck, F.L., & Mann, R.D. (1956). Sex role differentiation in jury deliberations. *Sociometry*, *19*, 3–11.

Terborg, J.R. (1979). Women in management: a research review. *Journal of Applied Psychology*, *6*, 647–664.

West, C. (1984). When the doctor is a "lady": power, status and gender in physician-patient encounters. *Symbolic Interaction*, *7*, 87–106.

Wexley, K.N., & Hunt, P.J. (1974). Male and female leaders: comparison of performance and behavior patterns. *Psychological Reports*, *35*, 867–872.

Winther, D.A., & Green, S.B. (1987). Another look at gender-related differences in leadership behavior. *Sex Roles*, *16*, 41–56.

Wood, U., & Karten, S.J. (1986). Sex differences in interaction style as a product of perceived sex differences in competence. *Journal of Personality and Social Psychology*, *50*, 341–347.

Zimmerman, D.H., & West, C. (1975). Sex roles, interruptions and silences in conversation. In B. Thorne & N. Henley (Eds.), *Language and sex: Difference and dominance* (pp. 105–129). Rowley, MA: Newbury House.

3
The Look of Power: Gender Differences and Similarities in Visual Dominance Behavior

STEVE L. ELLYSON, JOHN F. DOVIDIO, AND
CLIFFORD E. BROWN

The concept of social power has, at its core, the ability of one person to influence one or more others or to control the outcomes of others (Ellyson & Dovidio, 1985). Social power may stem from the information a person possesses (informational power), the position that a person occupies (legitimate power), the ability to administer favorable outcomes (reward power) or unfavorable outcomes (coercive power), or from the perception of being knowledgeable in the topic at hand (expert power) (French & Raven, 1959; Raven, 1974). These sources of social power may also be referred to as structural power (see Molm & Hedley, Chapter 1 in this volume). Sex is a characteristic that has traditionally been related to actual and perceived social power. In the United States, men disproportionately occupy positions of social, political, and economic power relative to women (Basow, 1986). In addition, gender stereotypes, in the United States and cross-culturally, characterize men as having greater potency, competence, and strength and associate men with higher status and more instrumental roles (Deaux, 1984; Williams & Best, 1986). This chapter examines the relationships among social power, gender, and human nonverbal power displays, particularly involving visual behavior.

Gender differences in nonverbal behavior are well documented. Hall's (1984, 1985, 1987) meta-analytic reviews of the literature have revealed that women, compared to men, smile more frequently, approach others at closer distances, gaze more during social interaction, orient themselves more directly toward their interaction partner, are more restrained in their body movement, and are more accurate in encoding and decoding skills. In contrast to the clear evidence that gender differences exist, explanations of why these differences occur are less well substantiated. In one explanation, Henley (1977) proposed that gender differences in social power are reflected in patterns of communication. Henley and Harmon (1985) asserted that patterns of communication between men and women provide "a micropolitical structure that underlies and supports the macropolitical structure" (p. 152). This argument implies that either directly or indirectly, consciously or nonconsciously, men and women in our society employ nonverbal behaviors in a manner that both establishes and perpetuates status inequalities between the sexes. In support of this argument, Henley (1977) presented evidence of parallel patterns of communication between high- and low-power interactants and between male and female interactants.

Despite the intuitive appeal of Henley's (1977) framework, the scientific validity of the proposal is still in question (see Hall & Veccia, Chapter 4 in this volume). Most of the behaviors identified by Henley (1977) have not been tested for both gender and power differences. Among the direct tests, some studies (e.g., Henley & Harmon, 1985) have found support for Henley's framework, whereas other studies (e.g., Halberstadt & Saitta, 1987; Stier & Hall, 1985; see also Deaux & Major, 1987) have not. In addition, support for the framework has been stronger for some behaviors than for others. Hall (1987) argued that gender differences can be explained more fully in ways other than Henley's (1977) oppression hypothesis; she suggested several alternative explanations, such as those involving affiliative motives, anxiety, gender-related personality traits, and socialization. Our chapter focuses on how social expectations mediate power-related visual displays between women and men.

Visual behavior has particularly important functions in regulating social interaction and in establishing and conveying social power (see Kleinke, 1986). In nonhuman animal societies, subordinate animals generally direct a large amount of attention toward dominant animals of the group, except when the dominant members gaze at them. Dominant members visually monitor other members of the group more freely, but they give much less attention to any one subordinate animal (Bernstein, 1970; Hinde, 1974). In humans, as in other primates, the stare conveys messages of interpersonal dominance and control (e.g., Edelman, Omark, & Freedman, 1971; Hillabrant, 1974; Thayer, 1969) and is perceived cross-culturally as threatening (Ellsworth, Carlsmith, & Henson, 1972; Watson, 1970). In contrast to other primates, however, humans rely heavily on verbal communication, a factor that mediates how power is communicated by visual interaction.

Exline, Ellyson, and Long (1975) first explored the relationship between social power and visual behavior within the context of the complementary roles of speaker and listener, roles that are quickly and frequently traded in the natural flow of conversation. In particular, they distinguished between the theoretically different visual modes of looking while listening, which increases as a function of interpersonal attentiveness, and looking while speaking, which decreases with cognitive demand or social anxiety. Exline et al. (1975) proposed that persons higher in social power would look less while listening to others because there would be lower need, and therefore lower motivation, to attend to them; persons higher in social power would look more while speaking because they would be more comfortable and have more control, and thus find speaking easier. They defined the ratio of proportion of time spent looking while speaking to the proportion of time looking while listening to another person as the *visual dominance ratio*. Higher visual dominance ratios were hypothesized to be associated with greater social power.[1]

Throughout this chapter, we consider how the visual dominance ratio relates to variations both in structural power and power striving. We begin by examining how the visual dominance ratios of men and women reflect social power in same-sex interactions. The behaviors of men and women are, however, commonly different in interactions with members of the same sex than with members of the other sex (Deaux & Major, 1987). Thus, we next report the results of investigations of visual behavior in mixed-sex interactions characterized by imbalances in structural power and asymmetries in power-striving motivations. Within this section, we examine the impact of well-defined structural power, more uncertain structural power, and power-striving in unstructured situations. In the concluding section, we discuss the similarities and differences between our results concerning nonverbal power behavior and the findings related to gender differences in verbal influence tactics. We also consider the processes that may underlie gender differences and the implications that these differences have for long- and short-term power outcomes for women and men.

Visual Dominance Behavior in Same-Sex Interaction

Investigations of visual dominance behavior in same-sex interaction fall into two general categories: studies of structural power and studies of power striving. The studies of structural power involve situations in which imbalanced power roles are clearly defined or differential resources between participants are salient and relevant. As Molm and Hedley noted in Chapter 1, virtually all social exchange and resource theories of power rely on some conceptualization of structural power. Studies of power striving examine how personal motives for power are reflected in visual interaction.

---

[1] The visual dominance ratio is a function of both proportion of time spent looking while speaking and proportion of time spent looking while listening. Because these factors may reflect different psychological processes, we generally recommend that researchers evaluate the independent contributions of these components of the visual dominance ration as well as the visual dominance ratio itself. In the studies reported in this chapter, analyses of the visual dominance ratio directly and analyses considering the components of looking while speaking and looking while listening yield the same conclusions. To facilitate comprehension of the overall pattern of results, we summarize the data in terms of visual dominance ratios. Separate data for looking while speaking and looking while listening is available in the primary sources that are referenced or through the authors.

Structural Power

Research on same-sex interactions, involving both men and women, provide consistent support for Exline et al.'s (1975) predicted relationship between social power and the visual dominance ratio in situations of structural power imbalance (see Dovidio & Ellyson, 1985). These studies have investigated structural power imbalances relating to particular roles, general status, and task competence. For example, in one study of male problem-solving discussions, Exline et al. (1975, Study 2) recorded the visual behaviors of dyad members distinguished by legitimate power roles, Reserve Officer Training Corps (ROTC) officers and cadets. The visual behavior of the lower power persons, the cadets, was similar to the visual behavior of persons unmarked by power differences (Argyle & Ingham, 1972; Exline, Gray, & Schuette, 1965). Specifically, they looked while speaking to their partners significantly less than they looked while they were listening (producing a visual dominance ratio of 0.61; see Table 3.1). In contrast, the ROTC officers, occupants of the higher power position, exhibited almost equivalent proportions of looking while speaking and while listening (producing a relatively high visual dominance ratio of 1.06).

In subsequent research, Ellyson, Dovidio, and their colleagues demonstrated that visual dominance behavior is a function of other bases of social power in interactions between women. Ellyson, Dovidio, Corson, and Vinicur (1980, Study 1) examined the effects of social status. First-year college women were paired initially with a female confederate

TABLE 3.1. Visual dominance ratios of interactants relatively high or low in established power or power motives in studies of same-sex dyads.

Study	Subject sex	Independent-gvariable	High	(Control) Equal	Low
Established power					
Exline et al. (1975, Study 2)	Male	Legitimate power	1.08	—	0.61
Ellyson et al. (1980, Study 1)	Female	Social status	0.92	0.66	0.59
Ellyson et al. (1981)	Female	Informational power	0.99	0.68	0.58
Power striving					
Exline et al. (1975, Study 3)	Male	Desire for control	1.15	—	0.67
Ellyson et al. (1980, Study 2)	Female	Desire for control	0.96	—	0.67

From Dovidio, J.F., Ellyson, S.L., Keating, C.F., Heltman, K., & Brown, C. (1988). The relationship of social power to visual displays of dominance between men and women. *Journal of Personality and Social Psychology*, 54, 233–242.
Copyright 1988 by the American Psychological Association. Reprinted by permission.

portrayed as having higher status (a college senior who was an honors student already accepted into a prestigious medical school) or lower status (a high school senior who was planning to drop out of school and get a job in a gas station), and then subjects interacted with a peer. As indicated in Table 3.1, subjects who had relatively high ascribed status displayed the highest visual dominance ratios, whereas those in the low ascribed status condition displayed the lowest visual dominance ratios. Intermediate ratios of the percentage of looking while speaking to looking while listening were found during the peer interaction, regardless of the subjects' previous status condition.

In another study, one involving expert power (Ellyson, Dovidio, & Corson, 1981), pairs of female subjects were composed such that the area in which one subject felt expert was an area in which the other subject felt inexpert. Areas of expertise and nonexpertise were thus complementary within each dyad. The visual behavior of each subject was then observed under three conditions: discussion of a topic of expertise, discussion of a topic of nonexpertise; and discussion of a neutral topic, unrelated to either person's expertise. As expected, variations in expert power influenced visual interaction in the same way as did social status with women and legitimate power with men. Three different power-related visual patterns emerged from the same individuals as the relationship between individuals changed within a very short period of time (see Table 3.1): subjects in the expert condition showed the highest visual dominance, whereas those same subjects in the nonexpert condition evidenced the lowest ratio. When discussing the neutral topic, subjects exhibited an intermediate visual dominance ratio. Thus, across three different studies involving diverse manipulations of power imbalance, higher visual dominance ratios were associated with positions of higher structural power. In the next section, we examine how visual dominance behavior may reflect power motives as well.

Power Striving

Two additional studies, Exline et al. (1975, Study 3) and Ellyson et al. (1980, Study 2) extended the work on visual dominance behavior by examining the effects of an individual's desire for control, a personality measure hypothesized to be associated with interpersonal power, on visual behavior. In both studies, men (Exline et al., 1975) or women (Ellyson et al., 1980), who were differentiated by their responses on the control orientation subscale of Schutz's (1958) Fundamental Interpersonal Relations Orientation (FIRO), were paired with same-sex others in a series of discussion tasks. As predicted, consistent with the findings for established social power, high control-oriented men and women in same-sex dyads exhibited nearly equivalent amounts of looking while speaking and while listening (see Table 3.1), whereas low control-oriented men and women evidenced significantly more looking while listening than while speaking (producing relatively low visual dominance ratios). Thus, a personality variable related to *power striving* systematically influenced patterns of visual interaction in dyads in which no power distinctions previously existed in ways similar to the effects of *structural* power imbalances.

To examine across studies the relation between power and visual dominance behavior in same-sex interaction, we performed a meta-analysis (Mullen, 1989; Mullen & Rosenthal, 1985) on the results across the five studies presented in Table 3.1. On the average, persons high in structural power displayed higher visual dominance ratios than did persons low in structural power (Ms = 1.02 vs. 0.62). This effect was statistically significant, $Z = 8.75$, $p < .001$, and of substantial magnitude, mean $r = .726$ (fail-safe number = 144). In addition, focused comparisons indicated that the effects were not significantly different between studies of male or female dyads ($p > .63$) or between studies of structural or desired power ($p > .24$). These results suggest that, at least in same-sex interaction, the visual dominance ratio has a generalizable and strong relationship to interpersonal power.

Given the robustness of the relationship between the visual dominance ratio and power, it is possible that a relatively high ratio may be an effective strategy for gaining power and influence. The instrumental value of high visual dominance ratios for communicating power is supported by studies investigating the attributions made by observers as a function of visual behavior in interactions between members of the same sex. Dovidio and Ellyson (1982, Study 1) found that observers' assessments of male and female actors' interpersonal power increased as the actors' ratios of looking while speaking to looking while listening increased through three different ratios (25–75%, 40–60%, 55–45%). Another study (Dovidio & Ellyson, 1982, Study 2) further demonstrated that power ratings increased directly with the percentage of looking while speaking whereas attributed power decreased with the percentage of looking while listening. Also, consistent with the notion that visual dominance behavior may be used, perhaps unconsciously, as part of a strategy for influence and power, Exline et al. (1975) reported that ROTC officers who displayed higher visual dominance ratios in their laboratory study had received higher leadership ratings during a summer military training camp four months earlier. In a laboratory study, Linkey and Firestone (1986) demonstrated that higher visual dominance ratios were associated with more successful outcomes between men.

Summary

In summary, research on visual interaction in same-sex interaction yields a consistent pattern of results. First, persons occupying positions of higher structural power in situations in which power roles are established and persons striving for power in unstructured interactions display higher visual dominance ratios. Second, observers reliably decode these messages and make attributions of greater power as a direct function of these ratios. Third, in actual interactions, higher visual dominance ratios are associated with greater success in obtaining resources.

People, however, commonly behave in different ways in same-sex than in mixed-sex interactions. Deaux and Major (1987) propose that "gender-related behaviors are influenced by the expectations of perceivers, . . . the target, and situational cues" (p. 369). Maccoby (1990) argues that gender differences in behavior patterns emerge primarily through socialization and in social situations. Boys and girls, who display minimal differences when observed individually, develop distinctive interactional styles. Boys develop a style that is marked by dominance, self-display, influence, assertion, and competition; girls develop a style characterized by agreement, suggestiveness, interest in mutuality, and social binding. Maccoby proposes that as boys and girls grow older, these styles, which tend to be successful in same-sex interactions, are maintained in cross-sex encounters. Thus, on joint tasks men are more likely to initiate and direct activities and to interrupt women, and they are less likely to respond to their partners' attempts to influence them. In contrast, "women may wait for a turn to speak that does not come, and thus may end up talking less than they would in a women's group. They may smile more than men do, agree more often with what others have said, and give nonverbal signals of attentiveness" (p. 518). According to Maccoby, women find themselves at a disadvantage in cross-sex interaction and, perhaps in part because of their lack of success, women's behavior may be more complex than men's. On the basis of conclusions such as Maccoby's and Deaux and Major's that suggest the need to consider a broader range of interactional contexts, our more recent research has focused on the nonverbal behavior of women and men in mixed-sex interaction. In the next section, we consider the ways that the visual dominance ratio reflects structural power imbalance and power-striving motives in interactions between men and women.

Visual Dominance Behavior in Mixed-Sex Interaction

Berger and his colleagues (Berger, Rosenholtz, & Zelditch, 1980; Berger, Wagner, & Zelditch, 1985), in their expectation states theory, presented a framework that may be useful in understanding how sex and behavioral expressions of power are related in task-oriented situations. Specifically, Berger and his colleagues proposed that social interactions are accompanied by differential expectations about the status of men and women, because sex is systematically associated with prestige and status in everyday life. Berger et al. (1985) referred to characteristics of individuals (such as sex or race) that give rise to differential status expectations as diffuse status characteristics. These expectations, in turn, can generalize to a broad range of situations and, through a process of behavioral confirmation of expectancies similar to the self-fulfilling prophecy (Darley & Fazio, 1980; Harris & Rosenthal, 1986), affect power-related behavior and perceptions across a variety of social contexts (Berger et al., 1985; Eagly, 1983; Meeker & Weitzel-O'Neill, 1985). Thus, as expectation states theory suggests, sex, as a diffuse status characteristic, is linked to greater social power and influence for men than for women in mixed-sex interactions because men in our society are assumed to be more generally competent than women.

Because sex, like all other status characteristics, operates through competence expectations, its impact is moderated by the presence of information directly relevant to each interactant's ability to perform the assigned task (Berger et al., 1985) or by structural power (Ridgeway, 1990; see also Molm & Hedley, Chapter 1). More direct information about competence or status has a greater impact on expectations and behaviors than do inferences based on diffuse status characteristics. In particular, when unambiguous cues about status or competence on a particular task are available, these cues take precedence over diffuse status characteristics and primarily determine power-related behaviors and impressions of ability and influence. When cues are ambiguous or indicate equivalent status or competence among interactants, diffuse status characteristics affect expectations, behaviors, and interaction outcomes. Thus, sex- and task-relevant information may combine to produce outcomes according to a weighted averaging model (Berger et al., 1985; Hembroff & Myers, 1984). For example, Wood and Karten (1986) found that when no information about task-relevant ability was made available to interactants, men engaged in more task-oriented behaviors than did women, and that, perhaps because of these behavioral differences, men were perceived as being more competent than women. When information (actually false feedback) about task-relevant ability was provided to mixed-sex groups, however, sex differences did not occur, but individuals presumed to be high in ability made more task-oriented contributions than did interactants presumed to be low in ability.

Our research used this framework to examine how structural power and power striving relate to visual interaction between women and men. In particular, in the next three subsections, we examine the visual behaviors of men and women when the situation (a) involves asymmetry in well-defined structural power roles; (b) reflects less secure, and perhaps less legitimate, imbalanced power roles; and (c) is characterized by differences in motivations and incentives for power.

Well-Defined Structural Power

In a series of studies, we investigated how situation-specific power factors and the diffuse status characteristic of sex influence nonverbal power-related displays in mixed-sex interactions. With respect to expectation states theory, Ridgeway (1990) proposes that power is the fundamental basis of the relation between status and performance expectations. Although most of the work on expectation states theory has focused on actual and perceived competence, and therefore mainly informational and expert power, other sources of power seem to operate in similar ways. With respect to legitimate power, military rank (Berger, Cohen, & Zelditch, 1972) and professional status on a hospital ward (Caudill, 1958) systematically affect expectations and behavior on relevant tasks. In addition, there is some evidence that reward power and coercive power are related to expectation states. Webster (1969) and Webster and Sobieszek (1974) reported that an evaluator has relatively high status in an interaction by virtue of his or her structural position and may become the source of status expectations among interactants through differentiated appraisals of others' performances. In this section, we examine the effects of expert power, reward power, gender-based task familiarity, and actual knowledge on visual interaction in mixed-sex dyads.

One of our studies (Dovidio, Ellyson, Keating, Heltman, & Brown, 1988) used a procedure involving expert power that followed the method of Ellyson et al. (1981), discussed earlier. Mixed-sex dyads were formed with members of complementary areas of expertise in non–gender-linked areas, and visual behavior was then observed under three conditions: discussion of a topic of high male expertise, discussion of a topic of high female expertise, and a control discussion that involved a topic that was unrelated to either person's expertise. On the basis of expectation states theory (Berger et al., 1985), we predicted that in the conditions in which

TABLE 3.2. Visual dominance ratios of men and women relatively high or low in established power or in unstructured interactions in mixed-sex dyads.

Study	Independent variable	Subject sex	High	Unstructured (Control)	Low
Dovidio, Ellyson, et al.	Informational	Men	0.98	0.89	0.60
(1988, Study 1)	power	Women	1.03	0.53	0.54
Dovidio, Ellyson, et al.	Reward	Men	1.08	1.23	0.84
(1988, Study 2)	power	Women	1.20	0.70	0.61
Dovidio, Brown, et al.	Task	Men	1.78	1.02	0.27
(1988)	familiarity	Women	1.24	0.46	0.26
Brown, et al.	Task	Men	0.86	0.73	0.39
(1990a)	familiarity	Women	0.82	0.61	0.43
	Informational	Men	0.60	—	—
	power	Women	0.50	—	—

expertise was varied, expertise would primarily determine patterns of visual behavior. That is, when men were expert, they were expected to show high visual dominance ratios, whereas women were predicted to display low visual dominance ratios. When women were expert, they were predicted to exhibit high visual dominance patterns, whereas men were expected to display lower visual dominance ratios. In the condition in which the topic was unrelated to either person's expertise, it was hypothesized that sex, operating as a diffuse status characteristic, would relate to visual patterns: men were expected to show higher visual dominance ratios than were women.

The results, which are presented in Table 3.2, showed the expected interaction between expertise and sex ($p < .01$). As predicted, both men and women high in expertise displayed higher visual dominance ratios than their partners who were low in expertise; expert women were as likely to display their power nonverbally with male partners as were expert men with female partners. In addition, men in the control condition exhibited higher visual dominance ratios than did women. In the control condition, men's patterns of looking while speaking and while listening resembled their behaviors in the high-expertise condition, whereas women's patterns resembled their behaviors in the low-expertise condition. These findings are consistent with the hypothesis that in the absence of situation-specific status differences, sex is a status cue.

Whereas the expertise variable in this study was an individual-differences variable (and thus could have various correlates), reward power was experimentally manipulated in another study (Dovidio, Ellyson et al., 1988, Study 2). During this experiment, mixed-sex dyads discussed three topics that were not gender related. Their first discussion was a control condition: there was no imposed distinction between the dyad members. For the second discussion, one member was assigned to evaluate the other member's contribution and was given the power to reward the other person with extra laboratory credit. The roles were reversed for the third discussion topic. Based on the assumption that reward power is conceptually comparable to expert power, we hypothesized that a pattern analogous to the results of the previous study would occur.

This hypothesis was confirmed. The overall patterns of visual interaction displayed as a function of sex and reward power closely resembled the patterns obtained as a function of sex and expertise (see Table 3.2). The Condition × Sex analysis of visual dominance ratios revealed an interaction ($p < .07$). When they were high in reward power, both sexes exhibited relatively high visual dominance ratios. When they were relatively low in reward power, men and women displayed lower ratios. When reward power was not manipulated, men and women again showed different visual patterns: men had a high visual dominance ratio that was similar to their ratio when they were high in power; women had a relatively low ratio that was comparable to their ratio when they were low in power.

A subsequent study (Dovidio, Brown, Heltman, Ellyson, & Keating, 1988) extended this line of research by investigating the effect of a task-relevant cue—degree of gender-based familiarity with a discussion topic—on expressions of power between women and men. Mixed-sex dyads discussed a masculine task, a feminine task, and a non–gender-linked task. To the extent that gender-based familiarity relates to bases of social power such as expertise and information, it may affect informational social pressures (Deutsch & Gerard, 1955). To the extent that gender linkage of the task has impact upon perceptions of socially appropriate behavior, it may affect normative social influence (Deutsch & Gerard, 1955). According to Berger et al. (1985), status in task-oriented groups may be based on actual task competence (informational variables) or on social roles (normative variables). Thus, for both of these reasons, task familiarity may function as a basis of status in expectation states theory.

This study also extended our previous work by examining a range of nonverbal and verbal behaviors, besides visual behavior, hypothesized to be related to power. The nonverbal power-related variables studied were percent of time spent looking while speaking, percent of time spent looking while listening, rate of gesturing with one's hands, number of chin thrusts, and frequency of smiling. Previous research has reported that higher power is communicated by, in addition to higher visual dominance ratios, higher rates of hand gesturing during speech (Dittman, 1972; Henley, 1977); greater frequencies of chin thrusts (Camras, 1980; Henley, 1977), nonsmiling poses (Henley, 1977; Keating, 1985) and relatively infrequent smiling behavior (Frieze & Ramsey, 1976). The verbal behaviors we examined were the frequency of speech initiations and the total amount of speech. Higher power interactants initiate speech more often (Rosa & Mazur, 1979) and speak more overall (Capella, 1985); interactants who speak most are also chosen as leaders most often (Mullen, Salas, & Driskell, 1989).

As expected, systematic differences in the behaviors of men and women emerged on the gender-linked tasks (Table 3.3). Significant multivariate interactions between task gender and participant sex were obtained for both nonverbal and verbal power-related behaviors ($ps <$ .001). On the masculine task, men displayed more nonverbal and verbal power-related behaviors than did women: men looked significantly more while speaking and less while listening, gestured more, and spoke more often for longer periods than did women. On the feminine task, women exhibited more power than men on most of the nonverbal and verbal measures: they looked more while speaking and less while listening, gestured more, and spoke more often and held the floor longer than did men. Also as predicted, on the non–gender-linked task, men displayed

TABLE 3.3. Verbal and nonverbal behaviors of men and women in mixed-sex discussions of gender-linked tasks.

Measure	Masculine topic		Feminine topic		Non-gender-linked topic	
	Male	Female	Male	Female	Male	Female
Verbal[a]						
Time speaking	50%	18%	24%	42%	45%	24%
Speech initiations	14.6	10.7	11.5	14.1	15.8	13.8
Nonverbal[b]						
Looking while speaking	47%	22%	19%	40%	36%	29%
Looking while listening	26%	81%	71%	32%	36%	63%
Rate of gesturing	.14	.03	.04	.09	.09	.03
Frequency of chin thrusts	1.88	0.20	1.45	0.21	1.54	0.38
Frequency of smiling	10.1	14.4	12.5	14.4	9.1	12.0
Frequency of self-touching	6.3	6.5	5.9	6.8	6.2	6.3
Frequency of laughing	3.9	6.0	4.4	6.6	3.9	5.4

Note. For tests of the univariate effects, *dfs* = 1, 23.
[a]For the multivariate effects for verbal behavior, *dfs* for F_m = 2, 22.
[b]For the multivariate effects for nonverbal behavior, *dfs* for F_m = 5, 19.
From "Power displays between women and men in discussions of gender-linked tasks: A multichannel study" by J.F. Dovidio, C.E. Brown, K. Heltman, S.L. Ellyson, and C.F. Keating, 1988, *Journal of Personality and Social Psychology*, 55, pp. 580–587.
Copy right 1988 by the American Psychological Association. Reprinted by permission.

greater power both nonverbally and verbally than did women. In this condition, men looked more while speaking (but not reliably) and significantly less while listening, gestured more, and spoke more and more often than did women. Only two measures originally assumed to be power-related failed to show the predicted interaction pattern. Across all conditions, and independent of power, women smiled more often than did men, and men had a higher frequency of chin thrusts than did women.

Consistent with our previous research (see Table 3.2), men and women displayed their highest visual dominance ratios on tasks traditionally associated with their sex and the lowest visual dominance ratios on tasks linked to the other sex. On the non–gender-linked task, men had higher visual dominance ratios than did women. The comparability across studies of the findings for the visual dominance ratio and the similarity of results for other measures hypothesized to be related to power within this study provide convergent support for how visual dominance contributes to the communication of expectation states within Berger et al.'s (1985) model.

Supportive of expectation states theory, on the gender-linked tasks in this study, task gender had a stronger impact on visual dominance behavior than did the sex of the participants. The process by which task gender moderated visual dominance patterns was, however, elusive.

Expectations of competence on gender-linked tasks may involve *actual* task-specific knowledge, *presumptions* of task-specific knowledge, or both. Consequently, we (Brown, Dovidio, & Ellyson, 1990a) further examined the hypothesis that people are more visually dominant when they feel relatively more competent on a task and investigated whether these feelings come from actual greater knowledge or from presumed knowledge based on task gender. In this study, mixed-sex dyads discussed two masculine, two feminine, and two non–gender-linked tasks. To manipulate actual knowledge, for one set of masculine, feminine, and non–gender-linked tasks both subjects received prior information concerning the problems and the solutions. Participants received no special training on the other set of three tasks, providing a direct replication of our previous study. We expected that men would show higher visual dominance ratios than would women on the masculine and the non–gender-linked tasks, whereas women would display higher visual dominance ratios on the feminine task. Furthermore with the hypothesis that actual knowledge (informational power) can be a critical moderating factor, we predicted that, because of the importance of actual competence in task-relevant situations, training would reduce the sex differences in visual dominance patterns.

In general, the results supported the hypothesis that actual and presumed knowledge are important moderators of power-related behaviors between men and women for gender-linked tasks. Replicating our previous research, when subjects did not receive special training, there were consistent task-gender differences in visual dominance behavior (see Table 3.2): a Task × Sex interaction was obtained ($p < .01$). Men had a significantly higher visual dominance ratio than did women on the masculine task (0.86 vs. 0.43) and a somewhat higher ratio for the non–gender-linked task (0.73 vs. 0.60); women had a higher visual dominance ratio than did men on the feminine task (0.80 vs. 0.39). When sex differences in task-specific knowledge were substantially reduced by training, however, sex differences in visual dominance patterns were eliminated. Men and women who had received training exhibited similar visual dominance ratios on the masculine task (0.68 vs. 0.58), the non–gender-linked task (0.64 vs. 0.56), and the feminine task (0.47 vs. 0.36).

The finding that visual dominance ratios were generally low in the training conditions suggests that power imbalance (relative power), rather than average power (absolute power), is a critical determinant of the visual ratio. Emerson (1972) proposed that two fundamental dimensions of power relations are power imbalance and average power. Power imbalance refers to the relative power of interactants; average power reflects the overall level of absolute power possessed by the interactants. If absolute power were the critical factor, men and women who were trained would be expected to show consistently high visual dominance ratios, comparable to the patterns exhibited by men on the masculine task and women on the feminine task when no training was involved. Although we did not anticipate this result, the conception of social power and dominance as relative is consistent with various theorists of human and nonhuman power relations (see Ellyson & Dovidio, 1985; Mitchell & Maple, 1985). Most of our previous research on visual dominance behavior has investigated situations that involve interactions between relatively high-power and low-power persons. The results of this study suggest the importance of future research disentangling the effects of power imbalance and average power. In Chapter 1, for example, Molm and Hedley proposed that whereas "relative power provides actors with different capacities for influence their average power is an index of their incentive to influence" (p. 22). Not only are the dimensions of power imbalance and average power potentially important for their independent effects, but also for their interactions with gender.

Up to this point, then, our findings indicate that in unstructured interactions men display higher visual dominance ratios than do women. Women without structural power use visual patterns in mixed-sex interaction that are uncorrelated, at least as indicated by same-sex research, with obtaining resources and having influence. A meta-analysis of the results across the four comparisons between the visual dominance ratios between women and men in unstructured interactions, summarized in Table 3.2, revealed that men had systematically higher visual dominance ratios than did women ($Ms = 0.99$ vs. 0.57). This effect was statistically significant, $Z = 5.71$, $p < .001$, and of substantial magnitude, mean $r = .604$ (fail-safe number $= 44$). In mixed-sex interactions, in which roles were well defined and resources were salient, higher power men and women both exhibited higher visual dominance ratios than their lower power partners (see Table 3.3), $Ms = 1.08$ versus 0.50, $Z = 8.95$, $p < .001$. The effect size was large, mean $r = .819$ (fail-safe number $= 120$), and comparable to the effect size obtained for same-sex interactions. No sex differences were obtained within the high-power conditions ($p > .62$). Across the low-power conditions presented in Table 3.3, however, women displayed somewhat lower visual dominance ratios than did men, $Ms = 0.48$ versus 0.53, $Z = 1.78$, $p < .075$, mean $r = .201$. Overall, the results for structural power are clear and consistent and support Berger et al.'s (1985) expectations states theory. Sex differences in visual dominance behavior in situations in which power is relevant but not fully established are discussed in the next section.

If we conceptualize a continuum of interaction types from unstructured, at one end, to well-articulated roles, at the other end, our mixed-sex studies discussed thus far define the endpoints of this dimension. Questions remain, however, about gender differences within interactions at intermediate levels of this unstructured-to-established power dimension. The two questions we pursue in the remainder of this chapter are: (a) Are less well-defined power roles of men and women responded to in ways similar to clearly established structural roles?; and (b) Are the visual patterns associated with power striving in mixed-sex interaction the same as those adopted by women and men in same-sex interaction?

Less Well-Defined Power Roles

With respect to the first question, research demonstrates that the achievements of women have traditionally been devalued relative to men's, unless the accomplishments are formally recognized and validated (Pheterson, Kiesler, & Goldberg, 1971). In simulated hiring decisions, for example, women are generally evaluated less positively than men for high-status positions (Fidell, 1976; Firth, 1982) unless information directly relevant to job performance is available (Gerdes & Garber, 1983; Heilman, 1984; see Dipboye, 1985, for a review). Meeker and Weitzel-O'Neill (1985), drawing on theories of social exchange, distributive justice, and status, proposed that social status moderates the legitimacy of task contributions, and thus status within specific groups. They hypothesized that persons with high status outside the group are allowed to earn status within the group by making task contributions that are accepted by other members. In contrast, the task contributions of persons with low status outside the group are perceived by others as selfishly and competitively motivated, not directed toward the benefit of others in the group. Thus, for persons of low social status, task contributions, by themselves, are not generally perceived as a legitimate way to earn higher status within the group. Concerning gender, Meeker and Weitzel-O'Neill report, "Since men have higher status than women, raising one's own status relative to status of others is legitimate for men but not for women" (p. 389). Consequently, unless they have legitimately been assigned higher status than others, women may be reluctant to seek or exert power in overt ways, and group members may not readily expect or accept their task and leadership contributions.

Consistent with this framework, leadership and power have traditionally been perceived as masculine (Broverman, Vogel, Broverman, Clarkson, & Rosenkrantz, 1972; Schein, 1973), and biases have been found against women who aspire to power or status equal to that of men (Etaugh & Kasley, 1981; Etaugh & Riley, 1983). These biases may also stem from the fact that males are culturally considered (by both men and women) as more legitimate candidates for positions of power and status (Meeker & Weitzel-O'Neill, 1985). Perhaps because of anticipated negative evaluations within mixed-sex interactions, women may be justifiably hesitant to display power or they assume that they are less dominant than their male partner—even when others may perceive them as a leader (Snodgrass & Rosenthal, 1984). Armitage and Snodgrass (1989), for example, found that women are less likely than men to assume leadership in mixed-sex interaction, particularly when their partner is dominant or the task is masculine. Thus, it appears likely that sex differences in power-related behaviors will generally occur within mixed-sex interactions, except when structural power imbalance is well established and validated.

To evaluate this hypothesis, we examined the visual dominance behavior of women in mixed-sexed interaction across three different leadership conditions with varying degrees of situational legitimacy. Two conditions approximated the endpoint conditions of the unstructured-to-established power continuum, and thus provide a conceptual replication of our previous work. The third condition was designed to reflect an intermediate, less secure power position.

In this study (Ellyson, Dovidio, Halberstadt, & Brown, 1990), subjects initially interacted on a discussion task in groups composed of two men and two women. After this discussion, subjects voted for a group leader for the next task. They were informed that the person voted the leader at the end of the study would receive an extra reward, three times the normal credit for participating in the study. In the established power (mandate) condition, female subjects were informed that everyone else had voted for them. In the unstructured (control) condition, subjects were given no information about the outcome of the vote. In the intermediate power (ahead) condition, subjects were informed that they were leading in the voting, but that it was a split vote. Mixed-sex dyads were then formed for the second discussion task.

Women with established structural power roles (the mandate condition), as expected, displayed higher visual dominance ratios ($p < .057$) than did women leaders who were simply ahead in the voting ($Ms = 1.00$ vs. 0.80). In fact, women who were ahead in the voting exhibited visual dominance ratios that were somewhat lower than those of women in the control condition (0.85). To evaluate further the behavior of women in the ahead condition, an additional control condition was run in which male subjects were similarly informed that they were leading the voting. Comparing the two ahead conditions, women leaders showed a lower visual dominance ratio ($p < .05$) than did men (0.80 vs. 1.04). Thus, in positions anything short of firmly established roles, women displayed relatively low levels of social power nonverbally. In contrast, men in insecure power positions displayed high visual dominance ratios, equivalent to the ratios of women with firmly established power positions. Thus, with respect to our original question, these results suggest that the power roles of men and women may be recognized differently by women themselves. That is, women in intermediate power roles (e.g., in the ahead condition) may underestimate their power or question their legitimacy given the equivocal support from their coparticipants. Perhaps as a consequence, they behave in a nondominant manner. Furthermore, the nondominant behavior of women, such as in our ahead condition, could lead to a self-fulfilling prophecy (Harris & Rosenthal, 1985). Both male and female observers who viewed these interactions on videotape and were unaware of the leadership conditions attributed somewhat less power to women in the ahead condition compared to women in the mandate condition and significantly ($p < .05$) less power compared to men in the ahead condition. Women in the mandate condition, who displayed high visual dominance ratios, were perceived to be as powerful and competent as the men.

Meeker and Weizel-O'Neill (1985) proposed that the legitimacy of women's leadership in mixed-sex groups is undermined by women's lower social status than men's. The results of our experiment are consistent with that hypothesis. When women's status was legitimatized by unanimous support (in the mandate condition), women displayed their power directly with a high visual dominance ratio and were perceived by observers as powerful. In circumstances of uncertain support (in the ahead condition and the unstructured condition), men appeared to be more legitimate candidates for leadership than women: men expressed higher power non-verbally and were perceived as more powerful than were women. Concerns about legitimacy may similarly hamper women's efforts to strive for power in mixed-sex interaction. We examine the relationship between power striving in mixed-sex groups and visual dominance behavior in the next section.

Power Striving

With respect to the second question, we have recently investigated whether the visual patterns associated with power striving in mixed-sex interaction are the same as those adopted by women and men in same-sex interaction. We previously found that in same-sex interactions women and men high in control orientation displayed higher visual dominance ratios than those low in control orientation (Ellyson et al., 1980, Study 2; Exline et al., 1975, Study 3). In two studies, we examined the relationship between control orientation and visual dominance behavior in mixed-sex interaction.

In one study of women's visual behavior (Brown, Dovidio, & Ellyson, 1990b), female subjects, either high or low in FIRO control orientation, interacted sequentially on discussion tasks with male and female partners (in counterbalanced orders across groups) who were both either high or low control-oriented themselves. In general, the pattern of visual behavior exhibited by high and low control-oriented women corresponded to the pattern we found in unstructured mixed-sex interactions in our previous research. Overall, women displayed significantly lower ($p < .005$) visual dominance ratios when interacting with men than with women, $Ms = 0.48$ versus 0.73. Although the interaction involving the subject's control orientation was not statistically reliable ($p < .15$), the pattern of means suggested that the power striving strategies of women may be different in interactions with men than with women. Specifically, whereas high control-oriented women exhibited somewhat higher visual dominance ratios than did low control-oriented women when interacting with other women, $Ms = 0.80$ versus 0.66, high control-oriented women displayed *lower* visual dominance ratios than did low control-oriented women when interacting with men, $Ms = 0.43$ versus 0.54. Kimble and Musgrove (1988) examined the visual dominance behavior of high- and low-assertive women in confrontations with men. They similarly found no significant difference in the visual dominance behavior of high- and low-assertive women.

One interpretation of these findings, which contrast with our results for same-sex interaction (see Table 3.1), is that even women motivated for power and control may experience insecurity and feelings of low power with men (Snodgrass & Rosenthal, 1984), perhaps as a consequence of unsuccessful influence attempts or lower perceived legitimacy of their power compared to men (Meeker & Weitzel-O'Neill, 1985). Alternatively, the low visual dominance ratios of women high in control orientation may reflect the use of different and perhaps more indirect methods of influence with men than with women. That is, women may exert power as much as men but may use different power strategies than men (see Johnson, 1976; see also Molm & Hedley, Chapter 1), but may be equally successful. To evaluate the replicability of the differences in visual behavior between high and low control-oriented women and to explore these possible explanations for differences, we conducted another experiment that examined not only visual patterns but also interaction outcomes.

In this study (Mehta, Dovidio, Gibbs, Miller, Huray, Ellyson, & Brown, 1989, Study 1), mixed-sex dyads were composed of one member high and the other member low in FIRO control orientation. Each dyad was presented with problem-solving tasks that involved ranking solutions (e.g., rank the priority of five people to be saved from a sinking ship) and, based on pretesting, were not gender linked. Subjects first formulated individual solutions, and then in a discussion session they generated a group solution. A finding that high control-oriented women are as influential as are high control-oriented men but display lower visual dominance ratios would support the explanation of different influence strategies; a finding that high control-oriented women are less influential would support an ineffectiveness explanation.

Overall, the results were consistent with the hypothesis that the visual correlates of cross-sex influence attempts are different for men and women. A Control Orientation × Sex interaction was obtained ($p < .05$). In particular, high control-oriented men had higher visual dominance ratios ($p < .05$) than did their low control-oriented female partners, $Ms = 0.85$ versus 0.65. High control-oriented women, however, had somewhat *lower* visual dominance ratios than did their low control-oriented male partners, $Ms = 0.48$ versus 0.59. Both high control-oriented men and women, though, were more influential ($p < .05$), based on the correspondence of the group solution to each individual's initial ranking, in determining task outcomes than were their low control-oriented partners. Thus, whereas a high visual dominance ratio was associated with greater influence for men, this was not the case for women.

Nonverbal behaviors have multiple meanings, and it is possible that low visual dominance ratios can be used to communicate messages other than low power. Signs of low power and submissiveness may alleviate concerns about an aggressive reception and thus may be perceived as affiliative cues (Givens, 1978; Moore, 1985). It is also possible that, whereas men employ strategies that are direct and overt, women use indirect strategies, such as appearing attractive and affiliative, to gain control and influence in mixed-sex interactions. According to Meeker and Weitzel-O'Neill (1985), because of their lower social status, "before task contributions from a woman are expected or accepted, there must be evidence that she is cooperatively motivated" (p. 389). The different patterns of visual behavior displayed by high control-oriented men and women in our research may thus be reflective of different objectives and perhaps different influence strategies in mixed-sex interactions.

To examine how visual dominance behavior may relate to different objectives in mixed-sex interaction, we (Mehta et al., 1989, Study 2) investigated the behavior of men and women under three different goal conditions: to be influential, to be likable, and no explicit goal. One person in each dyad was randomly assigned to receive a different goal instruction in writing before each of three tasks. In a condition designed to motivate subjects to control the outcomes of the interaction, the goal for one subject was "to convince the other person of your views." In a condition designed to elicit an affiliative motivation, the goal was "to make yourself likable to the other person." In a control condition, the person was instructed simply to discuss solutions to the problem with the other person. Throughout the study, the other subject was unaware that the partner was assigned goals.

Male and female subjects displayed different patterns of visual behavior as a function of the goal conditions: a Sex × Goal interaction ($p < .05$) was revealed for visual dominance behavior. As expected (see Figure 3.1), men displayed relatively high visual dominance ratio, assumed to directly reflect power, when they were being convincing and, consistent with our previous research, in the control condition. When they were trying to appear likable, they displayed lower ratios ($p < .062$ compared to the discuss condition, and $p < .01$ compared to the convince condition). As illustrated in Figure 3.1, women displayed equivalently low ratios across all three conditions. Yet, when women were motivated to be convincing, they could be as influential as men who received the same instructions. That is, when they were instructed to control

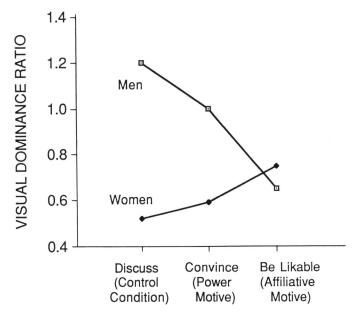

FIGURE 3.1. The effects of assigned goal on the visual dominance behavior of men and women in mixed-sex interaction. From "Sex Differences in the Expression of Power Motives Through Visual Dominance Behavior" by P. Mehta, J.F. Dovidio, R. Gibbs, K. Miller, K. Huray, S.L. Ellyson, and C.E. Brown, 1989. Paper presented at the Annual Meeting of the Eastern Psychological Association, Boston, MA. Copyright 1989 by Mehta et al. Reprinted by permission.

the outcomes, women displaying low visual dominance ratios were as effective in their influence attempts as were men with high visual dominance ratios. Thus, what may be high power nonverbal behavior for women appears to differ as a function of the sex of their partners.

Summary

The findings from the research on visual behavior in mixed-sex interactions are more complex than those obtained from the studies of same-sex interactions. Consistent with Berger et al.'s (1985) expectation states theory, both men and women possessing established power (based on expertise, reward power, and task familiarity) exhibited higher visual dominance ratios than did their lower power partners. Explicit training that helped to equate for knowledge about the assigned task eliminated sex differences in visual dominance behavior. In addition, what is perceived as legitimate structural power may differ for men and women. In one study, female leaders showed high visual dominance ratios when they received unanimous support from their group but not when they received only majority support; men displayed high visual dominance ratios when they just had majority support. Also consistent with expectation states theory, in unstructured interactions sex is a status cue: across four studies, men displayed high visual dominance ratios whereas women showed low visual dominance ratios (see also Ridgeway & Berger, 1986).

The research examining power striving in mixed-sex interactions also produced a complex, but intriguing, pattern of results. The findings for power-striving men in mixed-sex interactions replicated the results for same-sex interactions: men high in control orientation and men instructed to control outcomes displayed high visual dominance ratios. In contrast to the findings for men and for women in same-sex interactions, women striving for control displayed low visual dominance ratios. Thus, the visual behavior of women appears to be more variable and context-related than the visual behavior of men, perhaps reflective of differences in perceived legitimacy of their power or of different influence strategies.

Implications and Conclusion

In general, our research indicates that sex differences in power-related nonverbal behaviors exist and that these differences are systematically related to the interaction context. Supportive of Berger et al.'s (1985) expectation states theory, our studies consistently demonstrated that women who were in secure and well-defined structural power positions exhibited their power nonverbally as directly as did men, in both same- and mixed-sex interactions. In mixed-sex situations in which power was less well defined or secure, however, women displayed relatively low visual dominance ratios, whereas men exhibited relatively high visual dominance ratios. As Berger et al. (1985) and Ridgeway and Berger (1986) proposed, sex operates as a status cue when explicit competence or status information is unavailable.

In addition, we found that what is perceived as a status cue may differ for women and men in mixed-sex interactions. These differences may result from the internalization of traditional gender stereotypes that characterize men as more competent, more powerful, and better suited for leadership than women (Basow, 1986; Broverman et al., 1972). Consequently, men may tend to assume leadership in mixed-sex interactions whereas women may feel insecure in leadership positions and tend to relinquish these roles. Consistent with this explanation, Eskilson and Wiley (1976) found that in mixed-sex groups, women were less likely to perceive themselves as leaders or to seek a leadership role. Other research finds that female leaders perceive themselves to be less dominant than do male leaders (Snodgrass & Rosenthal, 1984), and female managers evaluate their job-related performance less favorably and rate their ability lower than do male managers (Deaux, 1979). In terms of process, women are less likely than men to take command of an interaction, are more likely to adapt themselves to the man's lead, and are less likely to engage in debate or initiate confrontation (Davis, 1978; Hogg & Turner, 1987). Also, women in simulated organizational settings make fewer influence attempts and display lower levels of self-confidence than do men (Instone, Major, & Bunker, 1983). Eagly (1987) concluded from a meta-analytic review of the group interaction literature that men exhibit more task-oriented behaviors (such as giving information and offering opinions) than do women; women engage in more socioemotional behaviors (such as expressing support for others) than do men. Thus, gender and gender stereotypes shape the perceptions and power-related behaviors of both male and female interactants.

Our research further suggests that women may systematically modify their power strategies as a function of social context. In same-sex interactions, power-striving women and men both demonstrated high visual dominance ratios. In mixed-sex interactions, power-striving women displayed low visual dominance ratios, whereas power-striving men exhibited high ratios. Nevertheless, these women were as successful in influencing their partners as were men. These findings move beyond the domain of expectation states theory and suggest the subtlety of interpersonal, perhaps unconscious, influence tactics. The issue therefore moves from whether men and women show different visual patterns to what the function of these different patterns are.

It is noteworthy that our findings for nonverbal behavior in some ways parallel the results of studies of verbal interaction. Research on verbal behavior indicates that men and women in mixed-sex interaction adopt different communicative strategies for gaining power. Johnson (1976) argued that men and women differ in their base of power: men express power in ways that are direct and concrete, and women express power in ways that are indirect and personal. Specifically, in influencing others, men confront and overtly demonstrate abilities to reward and punish. Women, in contrast, manipulate, draw on their relationship with the person being influenced, and may feign helplessness to achieve their objectives. Consistent with Johnson's (1976) reasoning, Falbo and Peplau (1980), in a study of people in intimate relations, found that men were more overt in their expressions of power motivations than were women. Participants' questionnaire responses indicated two dimensions of manipulation: directness and bilaterality. Direct tactics of manipulation involve asking, telling, and talking; indirect tactics include hinting, negative affect (e.g., "I pout or threaten to cry if I don't get my way"), positive affect (e.g., "I smile a lot"), and withdrawing. Examples of bilateral, or interactive, strategies are persuasion, bargaining, and reasoning; unilateral strategies include withdrawing and laissez-faire (e.g., "We do our own thing. I just do it by myself."). Falbo and Peplau found that women report using indirect and unilateral strategies such as hinting, withdrawing, and positive and negative affect to influence partners. Men, in contrast, report using direct and bilateral strategies such as asking, telling, and talking. Supportive of Falbo and Peplau's conclusions, Howard, Blumstein, and Schwartz (1986) found that women commonly used tactics of influence with men that tended to be indirect and unilateral, such as dropping hints, using flattery, pleading, and crying. Our results for nonverbal behavior are consistent with the findings for verbal behavior, but *only* for mixed-sex interaction. In same-sex interactions, men and women exhibited similar nonverbal power strategies.

Why do women in mixed-sex interactions use more indirect power strategies than men? One reason may be that women anticipate possible noncompliance from men, whereas men expect compliance from women (Falbo & Peplau, 1980). Similarly, Maccoby (1990) suggested that women feel at a disadvantage in mixed-sex interactions. These assumptions are not unfounded. Butler and Geis (1990) in a study of emergent leadership in mixed-sex groups found that female leaders received more negative affective responses (furrowed brow, tightening of the mouth, nods of disagreement) and fewer positive affective responses (smiles, nods of agreement) than did male leaders. In addition, Eagly and Wood (1982) demonstrated that women were presumed to be less influential in mixed-sex interactions than were men, except when established status differences were explicit. Apparently, greater status value may accrue to a person simply by being male. Meeker and Weitzel-O'Neill (1985), in their framework concerning gender roles and group interaction, hypothesized that persons with low social status can enhance the perceived legitimacy of their contributions and raise their status within the group by demonstrating that they are cooperatively, not competitively, motivated. Perhaps the indirect and apparently affiliative displays of women in our research reflect this strategy.

Research on verbal behavior also supports the hypothesis that strategy differences may not simply be related to gender, but instead may be based on presumed power inequality. Cowan, Drinkard, and McGavin (1984) examined Falbo and Peplau's (1980) model using children and adolescents (6th, 9th, and 12th graders) and their parents. It was assumed that children were of equal status with same-sex peers but were of lower power relative to their parents. Cowan et al. (1984) found that "feminine" manipulation strategies (unilateral and indirect) were employed more with parents, whereas "masculine" strategies (direct and bilateral) were used more with peers. When relative power was controlled, no sex difference in influence strategies emerged. Kipnis, Schmidt, and Wilkerson (1980) obtained analogous results in a study of the relations among supervisors, coworkers, and subordinates in industrial organizations. Across both sexes, higher status and greater power were associated with more direct and overtly assertive tactics. A high visual dominance ratio may be one relatively direct manifestation of power (Dovidio & Ellyson, 1982, 1985; Linkey & Firestone, 1986).

The findings that women directly express their power nonverbally in interactions with other women but use indirect verbal and nonverbal power tactics in mixed-sex interactions may reflect adaptations to their traditional double bind. Women who violate stereotypic expectancies and express their power directly and overtly may produce reactance and resistance from men; women who conform to the traditional feminine stereotype are likely to be perceived as weak and incompetent (Denmark, 1980; O'Leary, 1974). One positive consequence of this adaptation is that women may have a broader repertoire of influence strategies, drawing on both nonverbal and verbal resources, than do men. In our studies, high power was consistently associated with high visual dominance ratios for men; for women, the relationship between visual behavior and power and influence was more complex, depending on the sex of the other interactant and the nature of the context. Another positive aspect of women's indirect influence strategies in mixed-sex interactions is that, to the extent to which the behaviors also convey approachability and likability, women may achieve influence and control in subtle ways that do not generate the negative consequences that overt power behavior frequently engenders for men as well as for women.

The patterns of nonverbal behaviors, particularly visual dominance ratios, displayed by women in the research presented in this chapter may have some negative consequences as well. Although low visual dominance ratios can be personally and interpersonally effective in terms of the immediate interactions, the fact that observers attribute low power to persons who display low visual dominance ratios, regardless of the sex of the interactants (Dovidio & Ellyson, 1985), may undermine the advancement of women to positions of significant power and prestige. Competence, confidence, and control—attributes associated with a high visual dominance ratio—are perceived to be central aspects of a successful (and masculine) leadership style (Schein, 1973). Thus, nonverbal tactics that may be effective for obtaining resources in the short term may be ineffective for achieving high levels of status and influence over the long term.

The fact that women still have not achieved proportionate social, economic, and political power in the United States is well documented. Women, for example, continue to be substantially underrepresented relative to men in positions of corporate, government, and educational leadership (Morrison & Von Glinow, 1990). Only 3.6% of board directorships in Fortune 500 companies and 4.4% in the health industry are held by women (Von Glinow & Krzyczkowska-Mercer, 1988). Women in management and executive positions earn significantly less than men (Drazin & Auster, 1987; Nelton & Berney, 1987), even when controlling for education and work experience (Frieze, Olson, & Good,

1990). In the United States government, women occupy 8.6% of the senior executive service positions (U.S. Office of Personnel Management, 1989). In higher education, Sandler (1986) reported that colleges and universities, on the average, have only 1.1 women holding the senior positions of dean or above. These disparities persist despite considerable evidence that women and men in management roles have similar aspirations, values, personalities, and motivations (Dipboye, 1987; Howard & Bray, 1988; Powell, 1988). Although there are many factors that could account for the disparities in leadership achievement (see Morrison & Von Glinow, 1990), it is possible that gender differences in nonverbal behavior may be a contributing, but largely overlooked, factor. How the characteristics, motivations, and aspirations shared by women and men differentially translate into behavior may play an important role in determining success. Nonverbal behavior that *appears* to reflect low power, whether due to social expectations, insecurity, or indirect influence tactics, could produce lower evaluations of women leaders by both men and women and impede their advancement to positions of major responsibility and influence.

In conclusion, the data we have gathered on gender-related nonverbal behavior and on nonverbal correlates of power lead us to appreciate more fully the complexity and subtlety of social interactions between men and women. Our research on gender and power has examined three general sources of influence that contribute to the variations in nonverbal displays. We have focused on (a) the individual (man or woman, motivated by personality or incentive), (b) the person with whom the individual interacts, and (c) the interaction context into which both interactants are drawn. This context exists at multiple levels, from broad cultural norms and expectations to the more narrow demands and microstructure of a given situation and interaction. Our results provide evidence of the complex processes of interaction that may develop and evolve in more naturalistic settings. We believe that these findings suggest promising directions for the future research, involving both field and longitudinal studies, that is needed to illuminate the system of short- and long-term relationships among gender, power, and nonverbal behavior, and to understand the process, and not simply the outcome, of social power.

Acknowledgments. The authors would like to thank the following students whose considerable efforts were instrumental in one or more of the studies described in this chapter: Jannice Bailey, Brad Bowman, Christine M. Carson, Randi L. Corson, Tom Cross, Cynthia L. DeBlasio, Tessa L. Edeburn, Lori Fridell, Beverly J. Gibb, Robyn Gibbs, Tamara Helmich, Mindey Hershey, Robert Hoppe, Kimberly Huray, Kimberly Jaeger, Christina Kelley, Renee M. Kisak, Kristen Kling, Liz Koenreich, Parastu Mehta, Thomas A. Melfo, Claudia Meyer, Diane Mikolay,

Kimberly Miller, Frank Mondeaux, Kathyrn A. Moran, Nancy A. Morrison, Sharon K. Morrison, Clifford Pollack, Francisco Ramos, Maureen E. Riley, Kathy Riester, Sheila Rioux, Michelle Riske, Adelle Schultz, Vanessa Shami, Ty Shaikh, Jill Siegfried, Kenneth Silverman, Mark Soine, Angia Staccia, Marnie Tobriner, Sharon Wagner, Warren Wright, Narissa E. Velasquez, Deborah Vinicur, and Bonnie J. Yurcho.

The authors are grateful to Cecilia Ridgeway for her valuable comments and suggestions on an earlier version of this chapter.

Research in this chapter was supported in part by the Department of Graduate Studies at Youngstown State University, the Colgate University Research Council, the Pew Foundation, the Wittenberg University Faculty Research Fund Board, and the Wittenberg Faculty Development Organization.

References

Argyle, M., & Ingham, R. (1972). Gaze, mutual glance, and proximity. *Semiotica*, *6*, 32–49.

Armitage, M. & Snodgrass, S.E. (1989). Women's assumption of leadership with men on masculine and feminine tasks. *Proceedings and Abstracts of the 1989 Annual Meeting of the Eastern Psychological Association, Vol. 60*. Glassboro, NJ.

Basow, S. (1986). *Gender stereotypes: Traditions and alternatives* (2nd ed.). Monterey, CA: Brooks/Cole.

Berger, J., Cohen, B.P., & Zelditch, M., Jr. (1972). Status characteristics and social interaction. *American Sociological Review*, *37*, 241–255.

Berger, J., Rosenholtz, S.J., & Zelditch, M., Jr. (1980). Status organizing processes. *Annual Review of Sociology*, *6*, 479–508.

Berger, J., Wagner, D.G., & Zelditch, M., Jr. (1985). Introduction: Expectation states theory. In J. Berger & M. Zelditch, Jr. (Eds.), *Status, rewards, and influence* (pp. 1–72). San Francisco: Jossey-Bass.

Bernstein, I.S. (1970). Primate status hierarchies. In L.A. Rosenblum (Ed.), *Primate behavior: Developments in field and laboratory research* (Vol. 1, pp. 71–109). New York: Academic Press.

Broverman, I.K., Vogel, S.R., Broverman, D.M., Clarkson, F.E., & Rosenkrantz, P.S. (1972). Sex-role stereotypes: A current appraisal. *Journal of Social Issues*, *28*, 59–78.

Brown, C.E., Dovidio, J.F., & Ellyson, S.L. (1990a). Reducing sex differences in visual displays of dominance: Knowledge is power. *Personality and Social Psychology Bulletin*, *16*, 358–368.

Brown, C.E., Dovidio, J.F., & Ellyson, S.L. (1990b). *Visual dominance behavior of women in same- and mixed-sex interactions*. Unpublished manuscript, Department of Psychology, Wittenberg University, Springfield, OH.

Butler, D., & Geis, F.L. (1990). Nonverbal affect responses to male and female leaders: Implications for leadership evaluations. *Journal of Personality and Social Psychology*, *58*, 48–59.

Camras, L. (1980). Animal threat displays and children's facial expressions: A comparison. In D.R. Omark, F.F. Strayer, & D.G. Freedman (Eds.),

Dominance relations: An ethological view of human conflict and social interaction (pp. 121–136). New York: Garland STPM Press.

Capella, J.N. (1985). Controlling the floor in conversation. In A.W. Siegman & S. Feldstein (Eds.), *Multichannel integrations of nonverbal behavior* (pp. 69–103). Hillsdale, NJ: Erlbaum.

Caudill, W. (1958). *The psychiatric hospital as a small society.* Cambridge, MA: Harvard University Press.

Cowan, G., Drinkard, J., & McGavin, L. (1984). The effects of target, age, and gender on use of power strategies. *Journal of Personality and Social Psychology, 47,* 1391–1398.

Darley, J.M., & Fazio, R.H. (1980). Expectancy confirmation processes arising in the social interaction sequence. *American Psychologist, 35,* 867–881.

Davis, J.D. (1978). When boy meets girl: Sex roles and the negotiation of intimacy in an acquaintance exercise. *Journal of Personality and Social Psychology, 36,* 684–692.

Deaux, K. (1979). Self-evaluations of male and female managers. *Sex Roles, 5,* 571–580.

Deaux, K. (1984). From individual differences to social categories. *American Psychologist, 39,* 105–116.

Deaux, K., & Major, B. (1987). Putting gender into context: An interactive model of gender behavior. *Psychological Review, 94,* 369–389.

Denmark, F. (1980). Psyche: From rocking the cradle to rocking the boat. *American Psychologist, 35,* 1057–1065.

Deutsch, M., & Gerard, H. (1955). A study of normative and informational influence upon individual behavior. *Journal of Abnormal and Social Psychology, 51,* 629–636.

Dipboye, R.L. (1985). Some neglected variables in research on discrimination in appraisals. *Academy of Management Review, 10,* 116–127.

Dipboye, R.L. (1987). Problems and progress of women in management. In K.S. Koziara, M.H. Moskow, & L.D. Tanner (Eds.), *Working women: Past, present, and future* (pp. 118–153). Washington, DC: BNA Books.

Dittman, A.T. (1972). *Interpersonal messages of emotion.* New York: Springer Publishing.

Dovidio, J.F., Brown, C.E., Heltman, K., Ellyson, S.L., & Keating, C.F. (1988). Power displays between women and men in discussions of gender-linked topics: A multichannel study. *Journal of Personality and Social Psychology, 55,* 580–587.

Dovidio, J.F., & Ellyson, S.L. (1982). Decoding visual dominance: Attributions of power based on relative percentages of looking while speaking and looking while listening. *Social Psychology Quarterly, 45*(2), 106–113.

Dovidio, J.F., & Ellyson, S.L. (1985). Patterns of visual dominance behavior in humans. In S.L. Ellyson & J.F. Dovidio (Eds.) *Power, dominance, and nonverbal behavior* (pp. 129–150). New York: Springer-Verlag.

Dovidio, J.F., Ellyson, S.L., Keating, C.F., Heltman, K., & Brown, C. (1988). The relationship of social power to visual displays of dominance between men and women. *Journal of Personality and Social Psychology, 54,* 233–242.

Drazin, R., & Auster, E.R. (1987, Summer). Wage differences between men and women: Performance appraisal ratings versus salary allocation as the locus of bias. *Human Resource Management, 26,* 157–168.

Eagly, A.H. (1983). Gender and social influence: A social psychological analysis. *American Psychologist*, *38*, 971–981.

Eagly, A.H. (1987). *Sex differences in social behavior: A social role interpretation*. Hillsdale, NJ: Erlbaum.

Eagly, A.H., & Wood, W. (1982). Inferred sex differences in status as a determinant of gender stereotypes about social influence. *Journal of Personality and Social Psychology*, *43*, 915–928.

Edelman, M.S., Omark, D.R., & Freedman, D.G. (1971). *Dominance hierarchies in children*. Unpublished manuscript, Committee on Human Development, University of Chicago.

Ellsworth, P.C., Carlsmith, J.M., & Henson, A. (1972). The stare as a stimulus to flight in human subjects: A series of field experiments. *Journal of Personality and Social Psychology*, *19*, 302–311.

Ellyson, S.L., & Dovidio, J.F. (1985). Power, dominance, and nonverbal behavior: Basic concepts and issues. In S.L. Ellyson & J.F. Dovidio (Eds.) *Power, dominance, and nonverbal behavior* (pp. 1–28). New York: Springer-Verlag.

Ellyson, S.L., Dovidio, J.F., & Corson, R. (1981). Visual behavior differences as a function of self-perceived expertise. *Journal of Nonverbal Behavior*, *5*, 162–168.

Ellyson, S.L., Dovidio, J.F., Corson, R.C., & Vinicur, D. (1980). Visual dominance behavior in female dyads: Situational and personality factors. *Social Psychology Quarterly*, *43*(3), 328–336.

Ellyson, S.L., Dovidio, J.F., Halberstadt, A.G., & Brown, C.E. (1990). *Nonverbal and verbal power displays between men and women*. Unpublished manuscript, Department of Psychology, Youngstown State University, Youngstown, Ohio.

Emerson, R.M. (1972). Exchange theory, part I: A psychological basis for social exchange. In J. Berger, M. Zelditch, Jr, & B. Anderson (Eds.), *Sociological theories in progress*. (Vol. 2, pp. 38–87). Boston: Houghton-Mifflin.

Eskilson, A., & Wiley, M.G. (1976). Sex composition and leadership in small groups. *Sociometry*, *39*, 183–194.

Etaugh, C., & Kasley, H.C. (1981). Evaluating competence: Effects of sex, marital status, and parental status. *Psychology of Women Quarterly*, *6*, 196–203.

Etaugh, C., & Riley, S. (1983). Evaluating competence of women and men: Effects of marital and parental status and occupational sex-typing. *Sex Roles*, *9*, 943–952.

Exline, R.V., Ellyson, S.L., & Long, B. (1975). Visual behavior as an aspect of power-role relationships. In P. Pliner, L. Krames, & T. Alloway (Eds.) *Nonverbal communication of aggression* (pp. 21–53). New York: Plenum Press.

Exline, R.V., Gray, D., & Schuette, D. (1965). Visual behavior in a dyad as affected by interview content and sex of respondent. *Journal of Personality and Social Psychology*, *1*, 201–209.

Falbo, T., & Peplau, L.A. (1980). Power strategies in intimate relationships. *Journal of Personality and Social Psychology*, *38*, 618–628.

Fidell, L.S. (1976). Empirical verification of sex discrimination in hiring practices in psychology. In R. Unger & F. Denmark (Eds.), *Women: Dependent or independent variable?* (pp. 779–782). New York: Psychological Dimensions.

Firth, M. (1982). Sex discrimination in job opportunities for women. *Sex Roles, 8,* 891–901.

French, J.R., & Raven, B. (1959). The bases of social power. In D. Cartwright (Ed.), *Studies in social power* (pp. 150–167). Ann Arbor, MI: University of Michigan Press.

Frieze, I.H., Olson, J.E., & Good, D.C. (1990). Perceived and actural discrimination in the salaries of male and female managers. *Journal of Applied Social Psychology, 20,* 46–67.

Frieze, I.H., & Ramsey, S.J. (1976). Nonverbal maintenance of traditional sex roles. *Journal of Social Issues, 32,* 133–141.

Gerdes, E.P., & Garber, D.M. (1983). Sex bias in hiring: Effects of job demands an applicant competence. *Sex Roles, 9,* 307–319.

Givens, D.B. (1978). The nonverbal basis of attraction: Flirtation, courtship, and seduction. *Psychiatry, 41,* 346–349.

Halberstadt, A.G., & Saitta, M.B. (1987). Gender, nonverbal behavior, and perceived dominance: A test of the theory. *Journal of Personality and Social Psychology, 53,* 257–272.

Hall, J.A. (1984). *Nonverbal sex differences: Communication accuracy and expressive style.* Baltimore, MD: Johns Hopkins University Press.

Hall, J.A. (1985). Male and female nonverbal behavior. In A.W. Siegman & S. Feldstein (Eds.), *Multichannel integrations of nonverbal behavior* (pp. 195–225). Hillsdale, NJ: Erlbaum.

Hall, J.A. (1987). On explaining gender differences: The case of nonverbal communication. In P. Shaver & C. Hendrick (Eds.), *Sex and gender: Review of personality and social psychology,* Vol. 7. Beverly Hills: Sage.

Harris, M.J., & Rosenthal, R. (1985). Mediation of interpersonal expectancy effects: 31 meta-analyses. *Psychological Bulletin, 97,* 363–386.

Harris, M.J., & Rosenthal, R. (1986). Four factors in the mediation of teacher expectancy effects. In R.S. Feldman (Ed.), *The social psychology of education: Current research and theory* (pp. 91–114). New York: Cambridge University Press.

Heilman, M.E. (1984). Information as a deterrent against sex discrimination: The effects of applicant sex and information type on preliminary decisions. *Organizational Psychology and Human Performance, 26,* 386–395.

Hembroff, L.A., & Myers, D.E. (1984). Status characteristics: Degrees of task relevance and the decision process. *Social Psychology Quarterly, 47,* 337–346.

Henley, N.M. (1977). *Body politics: Power, sex, and nonverbal communication.* Englewood Cliffs, NJ: Prenctice-Hall.

Henley, N.M., & Harmon, S. (1985). The nonverbal semantics of power and gender: A perceptual study. In. S.L. Ellyson & J.F. Dovidio (Eds.) *Power, dominance, and nonverbal behavior* (pp. 151–164). New York: Springer-Verlag.

Hillabrant, W. (1974). The influence of locomotion and gaze direction on perceptions of interacting persons. *Personality and Social Psychology Bulletin, 1,* 237–239.

Hinde, R.A. (1974). *Biological basis of human social behavior.* New York: McGraw-Hill.

Hogg, M.A., & Turner, J.C. (1987). Intergroup behavior, self stereotyping, and the salience of social categories. *British Journal of Social Psychology, 26,* 325–340.

Howard, A., & Bray, D.W. (1988). *Managerial lives in transition.* New York: Guilford.

Howard, J.A., Blumstein, P., & Schwartz, P. (1986). Sex, power, and influence tactics in intimate relations. *Journal of Personality and Social Psychology, 51,* 102–109.

Instone, D., Major, B., & Bunker, B.B. (1983). Gender, self confidence, and social influence strategies: An organizational simulation. *Journal of Personality and Social Psychology, 44,* 322–333.

Johnson, P. (1976). Women and power: Toward a theory of effectiveness. *Journal of Social Issues, 32,* 99–110.

Keating, C.F. (1985). Human dominance signals: The primate in us. In S.L. Ellyson & J.F. Dovidio (Eds.), *Power, dominance, and nonverbal behavior* (pp. 89–108). New York: Springer-Verlag.

Kimble, C.E., & Musgrove, J.I. (1988). Dominance in arguing mixed-sex dyads: Visual dominance patterns, talking time, and speech loudness. *Journal of Research in Personality, 22,* 1–16.

Kipnis, D., Schmidt, S.M., & Wilkerson, I. (1980). Intraorganizational influence tactics: Explorations in getting one's way. *Journal of Applied Psychology, 65,* 440–452.

Kleinke, C.L. (1986). Gaze and eye contact: A research review. *Psychological Bulletin, 100,* 78–100.

Linkey, H.E., & Firestone, I.J. (1986, August). *Dominance: Nonverbal behaviors, personality trait, and interaction outcome.* Paper presented at the 94th Annual Convention of the American Psychological Association, Washington, DC.

Maccoby, E.E. (1990). Gender and relationships: A developmental account. *American Psychologist, 45,* 513–520.

Meeker, B.F., & Weitzel-O'Neill, P.A. (1985). Sex roles and interpersonal behavior in task-oriented groups. In J. Berger & M. Zelditch, Jr. (Eds.), *Status, rewards, and influence* (pp. 379–405). San Francisco: Jossey-Bass.

Mehta, P., Dovidio, J.F., Gibbs, R., Miller, K., Huray, K., Ellyson, S.L., & Brown, C.E. (1989, April). *Sex differences in the expression of power motives through visual dominance behavior.* Paper presented at the Annual Meeting of the Eastern Psychological Association, Boston, MA.

Mitchell, G., & Maple, T.L. (1985). Dominance in nonhuman primates. In S.L. Ellyson & J.F. Dovidio (Eds.) *Power, dominance, and nonverbal behavior* (pp. 49–66). New York: Springer-Verlag.

Moore, M.M. (1985). Nonverbal courtship patterns in women: Context and consequences. *Ethology and Sociobiology, 6,* 237–247.

Morrison, A.M., & Von Glinow, M.A. (1990). Women and minorities in management. *American Psychologist, 45,* 200–208.

Mullen, B. (1989). *Advanced BASIC meta-analysis.* Hillsdale, NJ: Erlbaum.

Mullen, B., & Rosenthal, R. (1985). *BASIC meta-analysis: Procedures and programs.* Hillsdale, NJ: Erlbaum.

Mullen, B., Salas, E., & Driskell, J.E. (1989). Salience, motivation, and artifact as contributions to the relation between participation rate and leadership. *Journal of Experimental Social Psychology, 25,* 545–559.

Nelton, S., & Berney, K. (1987, May). Women: The second wave. *Nation's Business,* 18–27.

O'Leary, V.E. (1974). Some attitudinal barriers to occupational aspirations in women. *Psychological Bulletin, 81*, 809–826.

Pheterson, G.S., Kiesler, S.B., & Goldberg, P. (1971). Evaluation of the performance of women as a function of their sex, personal history, and achievement. *Journal of Personality and Social Psychology, 19*, 114–118.

Powell, G.N. (1988). *Women and men in management*. Newbury Park, CA: Sage.

Raven, B.H. (1974). The comparative analysis of power and preference. In J. Tedeschi (Ed.), *Perspectives on social power* (pp. 150–167). Chicago: Aldine.

Ridgeway, C.L. (1990). The social construction of status value: Gender and other nominal characteristics. *Sociology Working Paper Series*, University of Iowa, Iowa City.

Ridgeway, C.L., & Berger, J. (1986). Expectations, legitimation, and dominance behavior in task groups. *American Sociological Review, 51*, 603–617.

Rosa, E., & Mazur, A. (1979). Incipient status in small groups. *Social Forces, 58*, 18–37.

Sandler, B.R. (1986, October). *The campus climate revisited: Chilly for women faculty, administrators, and graduate students*. Washington, DC: Project on the Status and Education of Women, Association of American Colleges.

Schein, V.E. (1973). The relationship between sex role stereotyping and requisite management characteristics. *Journal of Applied Psychology, 57*, 95–100.

Schutz, W.C. (1958). *FIRO: A three-dimensional theory of interpersonal behavior*. New York: Holt, Rinehart, & Winston.

Snodgrass, S.E., & Rosenthal, R. (1984). Females in charge: Effects of sex of subordinate and romantic attachment status upon self-ratings of dominance. *Journal of Personality, 52*, 355–371.

Stier, D.S., & Hall, J.A. (1984). Gender differences in touch: An empirical and theoretical review: *Journal of Personality and Social Psychology, 47*, 440–459.

Thayer, S. (1969). The effect of interpersonal looking duration on dominance judgments. *Journal of Social Psychology, 79*, 285–286.

U.S. Office of Personnel Management (1989). *Report on minority group and sex by pay plan and appointing authority* (EPMD Report No. 40, March 31, 1989). Washington, DC: U.S. Office of Personnel Management.

Von Glinow, M.A., & Krzyczkowska-Mercer, A. (1988, Summer). Women in corporate America: A caste of thousands. *New Management, 6*, 36–42.

Watson, O. (1970). *Proxemic behavior: A cross-cultural study*. The Hague: Mouton.

Webster, M.A., Jr. (1969). Sources of evaluations and expectations for performances. *Sociometry, 32*, 243–258.

Webster, M.A., Jr., & Sobieszek, B.I. (1974). *Sources of self-evaluation: A formal theory of significant others and social influence*. New York: Wiley.

Williams, J.E., & Best, D.L. (1986). Sex stereotypes and intergroup relations. In S. Worchel & W.G. Austin (Eds.), *Psychology of intergroup relations* (pp. 244–259). Chicago: Nelson-Hall.

Wood, W., & Karten, S.J. (1986). Sex differences in interaction style as a product of perceived sex differences in competence. *Journal of Personality and Social Psychology, 50*, 341–347.

4
Touch Asymmetry Between the Sexes

JUDITH A. HALL AND ELLEN M. VECCIA

Ever since the appearance of Henley's ground-breaking study on sex differences in touch, textbook writers and many others have spread the word that men touch women more than vice versa, a difference said to be caused by the disparity in men's and women's social status (Henley, 1973). Henley (1973, 1977) provided a syllogistic analysis of the relations of status, touch, and sex that has seemed compelling to many: Higher status individuals have a touching privilege that they exercise in order to express and maintain their status advantage; men have higher status than women; therefore, touching between the sexes is asymmetrical in quantity, with men touching women more than vice versa.

More recently, Henley and LaFrance (1984) predicted a specific connection between status and this touching asymmetry: "[M]en touch women much more than women touch men and . . . this pattern becomes even more clear cut when women lack status advantages such as age or social class" (p. 359).

It is our goal in this chapter to review what is known on touch asymmetry between the sexes and to present two new studies that address the crucial question of the role of status in mixed-sex touching. In studying the role of status it is important to measure status independent of sex rather than to treat sex itself as the operational definition of status, since the hypothesis that status explains touch asymmetry becomes unfalsifiable when dealt with in this way. As part of our treatment.of the status issue, we also review evidence for the overall relation of status to touching.

Touch Asymmetry Between the Sexes: Previous Literature

Since Stier and Hall's (1984) review of sex differences in touch, we have learned of no additional observational studies on sex differences in touch. There has been one participant-observation study, which we shall mention later. Stier and Hall found the literature to be completely inconclusive on the question of asymmetry—that is, which sex is more likely to touch in opposite-sex interaction. Most of the studies were small and they used different operationalizations of touch, for example rates of touch, duration of touch, and the number male-to-female and female-to-male touches seen in a sample of cross-sex touches.

Disregarding studies of children, which tended to find higher levels of female-to-male touch, there was no significant overall asymmetry. This was true across all 14 studies of adults as well as for the subset of 10 studies that used the commonest way of reporting the data—the number of opposite-sex dyads showing male-to-female (MF) versus female-to-male (FM) touch. In such studies, the proportion of dyads showing MF (or FM) touch can be tested against a proportion of .50, which is what one would expect if neither sex produces the preponderance of touches.

However, among the studies of adults were two that bear particular scrutiny. Henley's original study (Henley, 1973), though extremely small, showed significant MF asymmetry, with 77% of the opposite-sex touches being initiated by males (23 MF to 7 FM). Major's replication (Major, Schmidlin, & Williams, 1990; first reported in Major, 1981), using a much larger sample, also found significant MF asymmetry, though by a smaller margin (60%, or 274 MF to 186 FM). Both of these studies limited their observation to intentional touches with the hand—the hand being selected, presumably, as most likely to express dominance by one sex over the other. Compelling though these two studies in concert seem, they are offset in the total analysis by the bulk of nonsignificant studies and by one, of college students standing in cafeteria lines, which found significantly more FM touching (66%, or 38 FM to 20 MF) (Willis, Rinck, & Dean, 1978). The participant-observer study mentioned earlier (Jones, 1986) was based on subjects' logs of all the touches they were involved in over a period of time. This study found more FM than MF touch for a subset of touches called "controlling."

Thus, the evidence regarding asymmetry is extremely mixed, though the Henley and Major studies stand out as a pair consistent in both methodology and results. It is also noteworthy that studies based on introspection and self-report have also tended to find more MF than FM touch (Stier & Hall, 1984). Of course, results of such studies must be taken with a grain of salt because of the obvious possibility of sex-stereotype bias (the Jones article is borderline in this regard because it was based on subjects' reports of actual incidents rather than general recollections).

In light of the mixed results to date, it is important to consider factors that might account for different results across studies (Major, Schmidlin, & Williams, 1990). Based on the available studies, the following factors bear examination:

Setting. All studies have been in public places such as malls, streets, and
airports. Within this constraint, Henley's MF advantage was found only

outdoors (but Major found no difference between indoors and outdoors). Different kinds of public locations might make a difference,
too—work versus social, for example.

Relationship. Most studies have observed people in naturally occurring
dyads—that is, people who presumably already knew each other well
enough to be together in public. It is easy to imagine that the norms
governing the sexes' touching of each other might vary with how
intimate a couple is, or with the particular kind of relationship the
members have with each other.

Age. Henley's MF advantage was found only in couples under 30. Other
studies did not analyze touch asymmetries by age.

Intentionality. Henley's and Major's studies excluded unintentional
touches; most other studies did not make this distinction.

Nature of touch. Henley's and Major's studies only included touches with
the hand, whereas other studies included all initiating parts. No study
has looked at touch asymmetries for morphologically or functionally
different kinds of touches.

Status. Clearly, if status is to be implicated as an explanation for sex
asymmetries in touch, then it must be analyzed in conjunction with sex.
This has not been done so far in the literature.

In the two studies to be reported below, some of these factors were
explored. The first study was done in public settings, like much of the
literature; the second was at a large professional convention. The first
study used observation of naturally occurring dyads; the second included
dyads of this sort but also people newly introduced. Both studies coded
age, by decade; in the first, ages went from teens on up and in the
second, from twenties on up. In both studies, unintentional touches were
either excluded from analysis or not recorded. In both, efforts were made
to analyze asymmetries for different kinds of touch. And, finally, in the
second study great effort was put into measuring the relative status of the
two participants in each touch, so that status could be controlled for while
looking for asymmetries in touch.

Status and Touch: Previous Literature

So far, like most authors, we have dealt with status as an "obvious"
factor to look at in trying to understand any touch asymmetry that might
be found. But what, in fact, does the literature show regarding the
relation of status to touch? In their 1983 review, Edinger and Patterson
cited no observational studies of status and touch other than Henley
(1973). Stier and Hall (1984) located only a few more and, to our knowledge, no new ones have appeared since then.

In a nutshell, though people clearly *believe* that touch initiation is a
privilege of having higher status, the observational literature can neither

support nor refute this. The introspective, self-report evidence comes from studies by Brown and Ford (1961), Henley (1977), and Radecki and Jennings (Walstedt) (1980). Observational studies have taken several forms, which are summarized below.

Henley (1973) inferred the "SES" (socioeconomic status) of people touching in public places. Major, in an earlier report of her 1990 replication study (Major, 1981), presented results for presumably the same operational definition of status. However, as pointed out in the Stier and Hall (1984) review, the operational definition of "SES" was vague and seemed to blur the distinction between SES as an attribute of a person and the relative status of two people as a function of situational or role requirements. Henley gave the example of "waitress-customer" but these two role categories do not necessarily differ in SES (i.e., the customer could have equal, higher, or lower income, education, or occupational status than the waitress). Moreover, it is not clear in this example which party would have the higher situationally or role-defined status: the waitress serves the customer and so may be considered subordinate, but the customer is dependent on the waitress, which suggests the opposite. Furthermore, it is not clear whether the SES measure was confounded by the participants' sex. In any case, both of these studies found tendencies for the "higher SES" person to touch the lower more often than vice versa (significant only in Henley). Together, the two studies were significant (Stier & Hall, 1984).

Goldstein and Jeffords (1981) chose a different approach. Rather than viewing strangers and guessing about their relative statuses, these investigators ascertained status using objective data for a sample of male legislators in a state house of representatives, during legislative sessions. Sources of status data included committee membership and standing and past government service. In this study, the *lower* status individual was somewhat more likely to touch the higher status than vice versa ($p = .07$).

Yet a third approach was taken by Juni and Brannon (1981), who varied dress or title as an experimental manipulation of status. In one experiment, subjects touched a low status "blind" person (actually a confederate) somewhat more than a high status "blind" person ($p = .07$). In a second experiment, the manipulation of status had no overall effect but there was a tendency for the high-status male to be touched *more* than the low-status male.

Age is the one remaining conceptualization of status that we know of in the observational literature. As Stier and Hall (1984) indicated, a variety of studies have found that older individuals are more likely to touch younger ones than vice versa, though the literature is not completely consistent on this and not all authors make an assumption that age functions as a status variable in the context of touch (Heslin & Boss, 1980).

A final group of experimental studies takes yet another approach. Instead of treating status (conceptually) as an independent variable and touch as a dependent variable, these studies treat touch as the independent variable and dominance as the dependent variable by presenting a variety of touch scenarios to judges in photos or videotape and asking for ratings of dominance (Forden, 1981; Henley & Harmon, 1985; Major & Heslin, 1982; Summerhayes & Suchner, 1978). The clear finding of these studies is that touch increases the relative dominance of the initiator.

This last result adds an interesting complexity to the status-touch issue. Let us assume that higher status individuals do indeed have a prerogative to touch—a privilege—such that they feel relatively free to touch lower status individuals. Perhaps the higher status individual is also motivated to *express* his or her status (social dominance, social power) by touching lower-downs—to remind them of their lower status and thus to "keep them in their place." As argued by Henley (1977), such touch may perpetuate the status imbalance, which is certainly consistent with the photo and videotape experiments mentioned above.

However, these same experiments provide a motivational basis for *lower* status individuals to want to touch higher status ones, precisely because it may be a subtle but effective way of elevating their own status. Thus, touching higher-ups may be a smart strategy, though one that may entail risk since the higher-up may regard the touch as "uppity" or as suggesting more of a personal relationship than the higher-up desires. Because to initiate touch also increases the perception of one's warmth (Major & Heslin, 1982), such "upward" touching may also build affective bonds that help neutralize a status difference, now or at a later date. Touching higher status others may also serve emotional needs with no evident instrumental purpose. For example, we are all familiar with scenes showing an adoring crowd straining to touch its idol, perhaps to absorb some of his or her glory vicariously. Consistent with this image, in Goldstein and Jeffords's study (1981), the governor was touched by many but did not himself touch other legislators.

Translating high-low status into the male-female distinction, this analysis suggests *countervailing* touching motives on the part of males and females. It is perhaps not surprising that the literature on touch asymmetry between the sexes has mixed results.

In sum, the observational literature is mixed in results as well as decidedly ambiguous as to what "status" means. In our second study to be described below, we attempted to address these gaps. We modeled our study after that of Goldstein and Jeffords (1981) in that we observed touches in a closed social group (the annual convention of the American Psychological Association). Because individuals' names and institutions were visible on their name tags, the names could later be associated with personal and institutional status indicators gleaned from independent sources.

Study One: Touch Asymmetry in Public Places

In this study (Hall & Veccia, 1990) observers sampled pairs of people who were together in public places and observed them for 10 seconds. Observers used a timing device (equipped with an earplug) that emitted a tone every 10 seconds, which was used for selecting subjects randomly and to mark the beginning and end of observation periods. During the observation interval, the observers dictated information about the dyad members (age, for example) and their activities into a hand-held micro-cassette tape recorder. If a touch was seen, its character, duration, and intentionality were noted. If the selected dyad was already touching when the observation period began, the character of the in-progress touch and other relevant details were noted. For all dyads, the sex composition of the dyad was noted, and if a touch occurred the sex of the initiator was recorded if this could be confidently judged. Observation took place in 20 different public locations including shopping malls, movie lines, subway stations, an airport, and busy streets.

Out of 4,500 dyads, 681 or 15% engaged in touch. Roughly half of these touches were already in progress when observation started. Fourteen percent of the 681 were coded as unintentional and were omitted from analysis. This plus the elimination of touches for which the initiator's sex could not be judged (which was almost always when the touch was already in progress) reduced the sample to 317 touches. Finally, since our present concern is with the question of asymmetry between the sexes, only the 240 touches occurring in mixed-sex dyads are discussed further.

Shown in Table 4.1 are these 240 touches, broken down by the sex of the initiator and target (MF versus FM) and whether the touches were new (occurring during the 10-second observation period) or in progress (already happening when observation began). The asymmetries are clearly opposite for these two kinds of touch. For new touches, MF touch prevailed ($\chi^2(1) = 4.76$, $p < .05$). For in-progress touches, FM touch prevailed ($\chi^2(1) = 4.10$, $p < .05$). The bottom row of the table shows that when the two kinds of touch are combined, there is no touch asymmetry whatever.

TABLE 4.1. Touch asymmetry in mixed-sex dyads, by new and in-progress touches (Study 1).

Temporal occurrence	MF	FM
New	67 (60%)	44 (40%)
In progress	53 (41%)	76 (59%)
Total	120	120

Note. MF means male-to-female touch; FM means female-to-male touch. Figures in parentheses are row percentages.

As mentioned earlier, two important earlier studies looked only at touches with the hand. To replicate this methodology, we divided our touches into those initiated with the hand and those initiated with other body parts (mainly the arm). We then looked again for asymmetries as a function of new and in-progress touches. For hand touches, MF touch exceeded FM touch; the p value associated with this difference was only .15, however. Thus, in terms of statistical significance our study did not definitely confirm the findings of Henley (1973) and Major, Schmidlin, and Williams (1990); however, in terms of magnitude our result was similar to that found in the latter study. For nonhand touches, FM touch prevailed but not significantly ($p < .20$).

Finer breakdowns produced one significant difference: FM touch significantly exceeded MF touch for in-progress, nonhand touches ($p < .05$). Also, a marginally significant difference was found showing more MF touch for new touches with the hand ($p < .10$). Analysis using even finer breakdowns revealed that two kinds of touch showed striking (and opposite) sex differences: males engaged significantly more in the "arm around" gesture with females than vice versa ($p < .001$), whereas females engaged much more in the "arms linked" gesture (i.e., arm in or through the other's arm) with males than vice versa ($p < .001$). The arms linked gesture was particularly prevalent in touches that were already in progress, accounting for the predominance of FM touches in progress.

Another way of replicating earlier research was to stratify by age. When the sample was divided into dyads in which both members were under 30 versus 30 and over (paralleling Henley, 1973), it was strongly apparent that for the younger group, MF touch prevailed whereas in the older group, FM touch prevailed. Both of these differences were significant at the $p < .05$ level. A finer breakdown by age revealed the dramatic pattern shown in Table 4.2. The linear trend for age for the MF percentage (or its opposite, the FM percentage) was highly significant (Rosenthal & Rosnow, 1991). A final analysis revealed that this decrease in MF touch

TABLE 4.2. Touch asymmetry in mixed-sex dyads, by age of dyad (Study 1).

Age of dyad	MF	FM
Teens	16 (73%)	6 (27%)
20s	58 (56%)	46 (44%)
30s	28 (49%)	29 (51%)
40+	7 (21%)	26 (79%)

Note. MF means male-to-female touch; FM means female-to-male touch. Figures in parentheses are row percentages. Age groups 40 and up were collapsed because of low frequencies. Table excludes mixed-age touches and touches for which age was unrecorded.

as age increased (and the opposite for FM touch) was evident but not quite significant for hand touches and was highly significant for nonhand touches.

To summarize the important findings of this study, there was no overall asymmetry between the sexes, consistent with Stier and Hall's (1984) conclusion for the literature as a whole. However, differences did occur as a function of age and body part—both factors implicated in earlier research. The age difference was such that increasingly in dyads of more advanced age, females were likely to be the initiators. No previous research on these questions has looked at older dyads in sufficient numbers to detect this effect. Therefore, the much-cited MF asymmetry found by Henley (1973) appears to be a phenomenon limited to *younger couples*, at least in the kinds of settings and relationships observed in this study. Further, though there was a tendency for MF asymmetry to show up for touches with the hand, the significant asymmetries showed up for nonhand touches—"arm around" (for which MF touch prevailed) and "arms linked" (for which FM touch prevailed).

Interpretation of observational data is, of course, extremely difficult. It would be nice to be able to cast these results directly into a theoretical framework relating status or dominance to the sex differences. But we do not think this is possible. First, we are not prepared to claim that any of the kinds of touch observed are inherently more dominating or status-reflecting than the others. Males and females may each control or dominate the other in their preferred ways. Second, the age effects cannot be interpreted with confidence because age is undoubtedly correlated with life-stage events—for example, the older couples were probably more likely to be married or in long-term relationships. Therefore, role differences may be responsible for the sex differences across different ages. However, one thing is clear: these age effects challenge any simplistic view of touch as expressing status or dominance, unless one is prepared to say that the status difference between the sexes reverses itself completely from adolescence through middle age. Since it probably does not, one must acknowledge that forces other than, or in addition to, the expression of relative status are at work when the sexes touch each other.

If status is a factor in mixed-sex touching, then obviously it has to be measured independent of sex in order for our understanding to advance. Our next study was conducted with this aim in mind.

Study Two: Touch Asymmetry at a Professional Convention

The data for this study were obtained by two observers who attended the 1989 convention of the American Psychological Association for the sole purpose of collecting data on touch (Veccia & Hall, 1991). Observations were conducted in a variety of settings at the convention such as poster sessions and social hours, with emphasis on the nonclinical divisions of the organization. Because of the time constraint imposed by the length of the convention, touches rather than dyads were observed in this study. That is, observers looked for the occurrence of a touch rather than observing dyads for a fixed period of time. There are drawbacks to this sampling methodology for some research purposes (Stier & Hall, 1984). However, it is an acceptable methodology when one's purpose is to compare MF to FM touch. Only those touches that were actually observed to occur were included; touches in progress were not recorded. In this chapter we will be concerned only with cross-sex touches.

It was not practical to record data by dictation in this study. Thus, to remain as unobtrusive as possible, the observers recorded data on data sheets that were kept concealed in either a notebook or a convention program. For each touch, information was recorded on dyad composition (sex and age judged by decade), the form of touch (e.g., hold, rub), body parts involved (e.g., hand-to-waist, arm-to-shoulder), and perceived function of touch (e.g., greeting, playful). The toucher's and recipient's names and institutions were recorded whenever possible, as was the color code of each person's name tag. Because tag color is a rough indicator of standing within the organization, this variable serves as an index of status. To facilitate interpretation of tag color as a status variable, only individuals who wore red tag (student) or blue tag (member, fellow, or associate) were included in the analyses reported below. Other tag colors, comprising a small minority of touches, identified spouses/dependents, exhibitors, foreign affiliates, and high school teachers.

In addition to age by decades and tag color, we included other status measures. These measures were based on variables associated with the individual and with the individual's Ph.D. and current institutions. These were obtained from the membership directory of the organization (American Psychological Association, 1989) in association with Psychological Abstracts and a variety of published rankings of institutional prestige. These other status indices were:

1. Year of birth
2. Year in which Ph.D. was acquired
3. Current academic rank
4. APA membership level (e.g., fellow, member)
5. Reputation ranking of Ph.D. and current institution (Jones, Lindsay, & Coggeshall, 1982)
6. Productivity rank of Ph.D. and current institution (Howard, Cole, & Maxwell, 1987)
7. Social achievement rank order of Ph.D. and current institution (basically reflecting the career prominence of the institution's graduates, De la Croix de Lafayette, 1984)

8. Academic prestige rank of Ph.D. and current institution (De la Croix de Lafayette, 1984)
9. Social prestige rank of Ph.D. and current institution (basically reflecting the social class of the institution's graduates, De la Croix de Lafayette, 1984)
10. Admissions selectivity of Ph.D. and current institution (De la Croix de Lafayette, 1984)
11. Faculty citation rank for Ph.D. and current institution (Endler, Rushton, & Roediger, 1978)
12. Faculty publication rank for Ph.D. and current institution (Endler, Rushton, & Roediger, 1978)
13. Total number of authorships listed in Psychological Abstracts 1986 to 1988.

Unfortunately, there were many missing data for some of these status variables. To maximize the amount of data available for analysis, we created a composite index of status from all of our indices in the form of a proportion. For each touch, for each status indicator, we ascertained whether the higher status had touched the lower status or vice versa. Then we calculated, again for each touch, the proportion of indicators that gave higher status to the toucher. Therefore, for a given touch a proportion of 1.0 meant that all available indicators said higher touched lower, while a proportion of 0.0 meant that all available indicators said lower touched higher. Intermediate proportions indicated inconsistency between status indicators.

We do not assume, of course, that each toucher and recipient were aware of all of each other's status attributes. Nevertheless we do assume that participants would consider full members of the organization to have more status than graduate student attendees, would attribute higher status to more senior-looking individuals, would apply rough notions of the prestige of many (though not all) institutions, would associate the names of psychologists with varying degrees of prestige, and would (in some proportion) be aware of the university that had granted an individual's Ph.D. degree. Applying a variety of status indicators enhances the chance that *some* of them were noticed during the touch incident.

Because the population was not likely to change substantially during the course of the convention, and because observers concentrated their efforts on certain divisions of the organization, there was a high probability that the same individual would be sampled more than once. Therefore, we created a separate variable indicating which role, if any, both the toucher and recipient had played in other instances of touch that were included in the sample. Repeated touches between the identical toucher and recipient were excluded from analyses. Touches for which either (or both) members of the dyad changed roles (e.g., an individual who was previously a toucher became a recipient) were retained. The sampling unit therefore is touches, not individuals.[1]

There were 70 mixed-sex touches meeting these stipulations. In mixed-sex dyads, males initiated 40 touches (57%) and females initiated 30 touches (43%). As in the first study, this distribution was not significantly different from the 50% expected under the null hypothesis of no asymmetry ($\chi^2(1) = 1.43$, $p < .30$). Restricting the analysis to touches with the hand, the MF percentage was almost the same, 58% (touches with the hand made up 86% of all touches seen). Even though these results were not significant, the percentage of male-initiated touches is close to that found in our first study for touches with the hand and to that reported by Major, Schmidlin, and Williams (1990), which included only touches with the hand. Because these three studies were conducted in different geographical regions and by different observers, this figure appears to be quite reliable, though lower than the MF asymmetry of 77% found in Henley's original study in her under-30 age group (Henley, 1973).

As was the case with other studies of asymmetry, this analysis did not control for the dyad members' relative status. As described above, we made use of age, tag color, and a composite index of relative status in order to accomplish this.

Age

As discussed previously, age has been treated as an index of status, with older individuals being assumed to have higher status than younger individuals and also being seen to touch younger ones more than vice versa. In our mixed-sex dyads, the mixed-age touches (i.e., those involving people judged to be in different decades) did not show this pattern, though these touches were limited in number. In 13 touches the older touched the younger, compared to 14 touches with the reverse pattern.

To examine asymmetry controlling for age, we looked separately at equal age touches (i.e., both male and female judged to be in the same decade), touches where the male was older than the female, and touches where the female was older than the male. As Table 4.3A shows, in equal age dyads, males initiated 28 touches (65%) and females initiated 15 touches (35%), a significant difference ($\chi^2(1) = 3.93$, $p < .05$). MF and FM touches were in roughly the same proportion whether the dyad was in its 20s, 30s, or 40s and above. When males were the senior members of the dyads, they touched nearly as often as they were touched by the

---

[1] Because individuals could enter the sample more than once, we do not, strictly speaking, have independence of sampling units in the chi-square analyses reported later. We did remove the greatest threat by eliminating repeat touches by the same toucher within one dyad. Nevertheless, some caution may be in order regarding the p values obtained.

TABLE 4.3. Touch asymmetry in mixed-sex dyads, by relative status of dyad members (Study 2).

Status indicator	MF	FM
A. Age (decades)		
Equal	28 (65%)	15 (35%)
Male older than female	9 (45%)	11 (55%)
Female older than male	3 (43%)	4 (57%)
B. Tag color[a]		
Equal	30 (55%)	25 (45%)
Male higher than female	5 (56%)	4 (44%)
Female higher than male	5 (83%)	1 (17%)
C. Professional status[b]		
Equal[c]	6 (60%)	4 (40%)
Male higher than female	10 (48%)	11 (52%)
Female higher than male	5 (42%)	7 (57%)

Note. See Table 4.1.
[a] Blue tags are higher status than red tags (see text).
[b] Composite status variable (see text).
[c] For definitions of equal, higher, and lower status, see text.

younger females in those dyads (9 and 11 touches, respectively) (Table 4.3A). Likewise, when females were the senior members of the dyads, they too touched, and were touched by, the younger males in those dyads about equally often (4 and 3 touches respectively).

Tag Color

The second status index that was most accessible to both observers and attendees was tag color. Overall, tag color did not produce an asymmetry in touching, but the frequencies were extremely low, indicating that cross-color touches were simply not very frequent: in 6 instances blue (member) touched red (student) and in 9 instances red touched blue. Table 4.3B presents the results for mixed-sex dyads with equal and unequal tag colors. When both parties had the same tag color, males initiated 30 touches (55%) and females initiated 25 touches (45%) ($\chi^2(1) = .45, p < .50$). When both status and age were equal, males initiated 24 (65%) touches and females initiated 13 (35%). This distribution was marginally significant ($\chi^2(1) = 3.27, p < .10$). Table 4.3B also shows the sex breakdown for touches in which the male wore the blue tag and those in which the female wore the blue tag. The frequencies are very small.

Composite Status

As described above, we created a composite variable that subsumed all of our status/prestige variables. In the analysis to follow, a touch for which 70% or more of the available status indicators said that the higher status person touched the lower was operationally defined as a higher-to-lower touch; similarly, when 30% or fewer of the available indicators said that higher touched lower, the touch was operationally defined as lower-to-higher. If a touch had an intermediate proportion, meaning that the status indicators were not consistent, then relative status was ambiguous and was operationally defined as "equal." We find sense in this approach because in actual interaction two people whom we consider "equal" in status are often not *literally* equal across a range of status indicators, but rather are inconsistent in status from one indicator to the next (one is better published whereas the other works at a better school, etc.).

Overall, in the mixed-sex dyads, 17 touches were higher-to-lower status and 16 were lower-to-higher. Thus, there was no relation between status and overall touch, but again we acknowledge the small frequencies. Table 4.3C shows asymmetry between the sexes for equal and unequal status touches. In the equal-status dyads, males tended to touch more than females did (60% MF to 40% FM). For both kinds of unequal status dyads, MF touching tended to be less frequent than FM touching. Due to the small numbers, none of these differences was significant.

The notion of "equal" status was operationalized in a different way as well. In this analysis, toucher and recipient were considered to have "equal" status when all status indicators that were available for that touch were literally the same or the "same" codes were more frequent than codes indicating a status asymmetry. Most of these "same" codes pertained to age, tag color, and membership rank in the organization (e.g., member, fellow) because these were broad categories on which it was not uncommon for both toucher and recipient to be coded as same; other prestige variables, such as number of authorships and institutional status rank, were much less likely to be coded as same. In this new analysis, MF touch prevailed over FM touch when touches were coded as "same" by these criteria (18 MF to 9 FM, or 67% to 33%, $\chi^2(1) = 3.0, p < .10$). When the male was higher status than the female, FM touch prevailed but not significantly (9 MF to 12 FM, or 43% to 57%). When the female was higher status than the male, there was no difference (4 MF to 4 FM).

Qualitative Aspects of Touch

Studies of asymmetry have hardly ever examined the actual touches in detail. We attempted to improve on this situation but were hampered by the low frequencies of touch. As mentioned earlier, most touches were done with the hand. When toucher and recipient are equated on age and touches with the hand are examined, the MF advantage approaches significance ($\chi^2(1) = 3.46, p < .10$), and is of a magnitude comparable to earlier studies. When handshakes are removed from the analysis, the proportion of MF touches remains the same.

Mixed-sex touches were also grouped according to the following functions: formal (greeting/departure and introduction), affectionate (e.g., greeting, playful), and attention-getting; controlling touches were also coded but occurred only once. When both participants had equal age, males initiated more formal touches (9 touches) than females did (2 touches) ($\chi^2(1) = 4.45$, $p < .05$), most of which were handshakes. When status was equalized by tag color, there were no significant gender asymmetries either with or without handshakes. When both age and tag color were equal, males were marginally more likely to use formal touches ($\chi^2(1) = 3.60$, $p < .10$). Type of touch was collapsed into two other categories: (a) spot-touch, patting, and rubbing, and (b) holding and hugging. Analysis failed to reveal significant sex asymmetries for these categories.

Conclusions

These new studies add to our understanding of touch asymmetry between the sexes. Both studies indicate that broadly generalized conclusions about asymmetry, inspired by Henley's important early study (Henley, 1973), cannot be supported without many qualifications. Touch asymmetry favoring males is *not* universally found, and when it is, it is usually of quite small magnitude. In our first study it was not present at all when both hand-initiated and other touches were considered, and indeed in older dyads FM touching prevailed by a wide margin. In our second study, asymmetry favoring males occurred to a modest extent but seemed to vary in complex ways with the relative statuses of the individuals in the dyad.

It is also significant that we found no support for Henley's prediction (Henley & LaFrance, 1984) that asymmetry favoring males would be most pronounced when the males enjoy the higher status. Although our sample size was small there was no evidence whatever for this pattern, nor for the logically complementary pattern of no (or greatly reduced) asymmetry when status is equal or when females have the higher status. Indeed, for two of our status variables, age and composite status, asymmetry actually favored females slightly in the unequal status dyads. To find that asymmetry favoring males is greatest in equal-status dyads would be consistent with expectations states theory (Berger, Rosenholtz, & Zelditch, 1980), which defines sex as a diffuse status indicator that influences people's perceptions most strongly in the absence of more pertinent status indicators. In other words, it may be that when status is ambiguous, sex is a determinant of mixed-sex touching, but when status is clear, sex ceases to have much influence over touching patterns (Eagly, 1987). This intriguing notion, quite the opposite of Henley's speculation, is worth pursuing in larger studies.

It is important also to point out one consistency that seems to be emerging in this field of study: males do seem to touch females with the hand more than vice versa. Though in our studies this was not always significant, the trend is consistent with the earlier work of Henley (1973) and Major, Schmidlin, and Williams (1990).

What is needed now is more fine-grained descriptive research that can better identify what these male-initiated touches consist of and what motivates them. In addition, larger studies and in varied settings of both sex differences and status indicators are very important. Though our second study made good use of a variety of status concepts, its small sample size limits conclusions about the role of status in touch asymmetry.

Acknowledgments. This research was supported in part by grant #RR07143 (Biomedical Research Support Grant, Department of Health and Human Services). The authors wish to thank Norman Belanger, Monica Scully, Sabrina Herman, Treniece Lewis, and Cindy Morin, who served as observers, and Denise Marcoux, who helped enormously with the data analysis.

References

American Psychological Association (1989). *Directory of the American Psychological Association, 1989.* Washington, DC: American Psychological Association.

Berger, J., Rosenholtz, S.J., & Zelditch, M., Jr. (1980). Status organizing processes. In A. Inkeles, N.J. Smelser, & R.H. Turner (Eds.), *Annual review of sociology,* Vol.6. Palo Alto: Annual Reviews.

Brown, R., & Ford, M. (1961). Address in American English. *Journal of Abnormal and Social Psychology, 62,* 375–385.

De la Croix de Lafayette, J.M. (1984). *National register of social prestige and academic ratings of American colleges and universities.* Washington, DC: NASACU.

Eagly, A.H. (1987). *Sex differences in social behavior: A social-role approach.* Hillsdale, NJ: Erlbaum.

Edinger, J.A., & Patterson, M.L. (1983). Nonverbal involvement and social control. *Psychological Bulletin, 93,* 30–56.

Endler, N.S., Rushton, J.P., & Roediger, H.L., III. (1978). Productivity and scholarly impact (citations) of British, Canadian, and U.S. departments of psychology (1975). *American Psychologist, 33,* 1064–1082.

Forden, C. (1981). The influence of sex-role expectations on the perception of touch. *Sex Roles, 7,* 889–894.

Goldstein, A.G., & Jeffords, J. (1981). Status and touching behavior. *Bulletin of the Psychonomic Society, 17,* 79–81.

Hall, J.A., & Veccia, E.M. (1990). More "touching" observations: New insights on men, women, and interpersonal touch. *Journal of Personality and Social Psychology, 59,* 1155–1162.

Henley, N.M. (1973). Status and sex: Some touching observations. *Bulletin of the Psychonomic Society, 2,* 91–93.

Henley, N.M. (1977). *Body politics: Power, sex, and nonverbal communication.* Englewood Cliffs, NJ: Prentice-Hall.

Henley, N.M., & Harmon, S. (1985). The nonverbal semantics of power and gender: A perceptual study. In S.L. Ellyson and J.F. Dovidio (Eds.), *Power, dominance, and nonverbal behavior.* New York: Springer-Verlag.

Henley, N.M., & LaFrance, M. (1984). Gender as culture: Difference and dominance in nonverbal behavior. In A. Wolfgang (Ed.), *Nonverbal behavior: Perspectives, applications, intercultural insights.* Lewiston, NY: C.J. Hogrefe.

Heslin, R., & Boss, D. (1980). Nonverbal intimacy in airport arrival and departure. *Personality and Social Psychology Bulletin, 6,* 248–252.

Howard, G.S., Cole, D.A., & Maxwell, S.E. (1987). Research productivity in psychology based on publication in the journals of the American Psychological Association. *American Psychologist, 42,* 975–986.

Jones, L.V., Lindsay, G., & Coggeshall, P.E. (1982). *An assessment of research-doctorate programs in the U.S.: Social sciences.* Washington, DC: National Academy Press.

Jones, S.E. (1986). Sex differences in touch communication. *Western Journal of Speech Communication, 50,* 227–241.

Juni, S., & Brannon, R. (1981). Interpersonal touching as a function of status and sex. *Journal of Social Psychology, 114,* 135–136.

Major, B. (1981). Gender patterns in touching behavior. In C. Mayo and N.M. Henley (Eds.), *Gender and nonverbal behavior.* New York: Springer-Verlag.

Major, B., & Heslin, R. (1982). Perceptions of cross-sex and same-sex non-reciprocal touch: It is better to give than to receive. *Journal of Nonverbal Behavior, 6,* 148–162.

Major, B., Schmidlin, A.M., & Williams, L. (1990). Gender patterns in touch: The impact of age and setting. *Journal of Personality and Social Psychology, 58,* 634–643.

Radecki, C., & Jennings (Walstedt), J. (1980). Sex as a status variable in work settings: Female and male reports of dominance behavior. *Journal of Applied Social Psychology, 10,* 71–85.

Rosenthal, R., & Rosnow, R.L. (1991). *Essentials of behavioral research: Methods and data analysis,* (2nd ed). New York: McGraw-Hill.

Stier, D.S., & Hall, J.A. (1984). Gender differences in touch: An empirical and theoretical review. *Journal of Personality and Social Psychology, 47,* 440–459.

Summerhayes, D.L., & Suchner, R.W. (1978). Power implications of touch in male-female relationships. *Sex Roles, 4,* 103–110.

Veccia, E.M., & Hall, J.A. Status and touch: Empirical observations. Manuscript in preparation, 1991.

Willis, F.N., Rinck, C.M., & Dean, L.M. (1978). Interpersonal touch among adults in cafeteria lines. *Perceptual and Motor Skills, 47,* 1147–1152.

5
Sex Differences in Interaction Style in Task Groups

WENDY WOOD AND NANCY RHODES

Among the many definitions of groups, a common theme is that members of groups interact with one another and are influenced by each other (Forsyth, 1990; Hare, 1976; McGrath, 1984; Shaw, 1981). Conceptual analyses of group dynamics have echoed this emphasis on interaction. The classic input-process-output perspective identifies interaction process as the key mediator between inputs such as member attributes or task requirements and outputs such as task productivity or patterns of influence (e.g., Hackman & Morris, 1975; McGrath, 1964; Shiflett, 1979).

Interactions among group members are multifaceted and complex. The challenge to researchers has been to identify the important features of interaction process that link group inputs with outputs. One of the most successful demonstrations of this linkage has occurred with the input variable of group members' sex. As we shall argue in this chapter, men and women differ in their interaction styles in task groups and these styles have implications for a variety of outcomes, such as group task performance, who emerges as the group leader, and the satisfaction experienced by group members.

Bales's Interaction Process Analysis

The most frequently used scheme for analyzing men's and women's interaction styles in task groups is that developed by Bales (1950, 1970). We will review this approach in some detail because it provides a specific definition of interaction style.

In Bales's (1950, 1953) view, task-performing groups have four main functional problems: adaptation to the external situation, instrumental control over the situation in order to complete tasks and reach goals, management and expression of members' feelings and tensions among members, and preservation of the social integration of members as a collective.

Bales (1950) devised a system for observation of group behavior that estimates the frequency with which members perform each of these func-

97

tions. In this scheme, the different function categories represent two primary dimensions of group process. Behaviors indicative of adaptation and instrumental control reflect the task-oriented aspects of group interaction. Behaviors directed toward these kinds of goals consist of questions (asking for orientation, opinions, and suggestions) and attempted answers (offering suggestions, opinions, and orientation). Expression of emotions and group maintenance reflect the social-emotional aspects of group behavior. Actions directed toward such goals include positive reactions (showing solidarity, showing tension release, or agreeing) and negative reactions (disagreeing, showing tension, and showing antagonism).[1]

In Bales's research, task and social behavior proved to be associated with member roles and status organization in all-male task-performing groups (Bales, 1953; Bales & Slater, 1955). These groups tended to establish two types of leadership roles. The group member nominated as the overall "leader" of the group concentrated on task functions (e.g., initiated the most acts, was rated by others as having the best ideas). The individual ranked second in overall leadership focused on social concerns (e.g., was rated as best liked). On the basis of these findings, Bales concluded that separate leaders are required to address task and social functions.

This dichotomous structure was thought generic to all small groups. Consequently, the leadership structure observed with task groups was generalized to family groups, with women serving as social leaders by maintaining the internal, social equilibrium of the family (Parsons, 1955; Parsons & Bales, 1955). Men supposedly serve as task leaders, directing and structuring interaction with the external world in order to attain family goals. The complementary roles of each sex were thought to stem from the childbearing and nursing activities of women establishing their dominance over expressive roles (Zelditch, 1955). By default, men specialize in the alternative instrumental functions.

This description of task and social roles as incompatible, and the representation of dichotomous family roles for men and women, received extensive criticism (e.g., Aronoff & Crano, 1975; Leik, 1963). A variety of data indicate that specialization in task or in social domains does not require neglect of the other. In cross-cultural investigations of family activities, men have been found to contribute significantly to expressive tasks, such as child rearing, and women to instrumental tasks, such as hunting/gathering (Aronoff & Crano, 1975; Crano & Aronoff, 1978). Similarly, in all-male task groups (Bales & Slater, 1955; Slater, 1955) the interaction profiles of the best-liked man and the idea man reveal con-

---

[1] This distinction between task and social processes in group interaction is also represented in a variety of other conceptual schemes (e.g., Bion, 1961; Futoran, Kelly, & McGrath, 1989; Fiedler, 1967, 1978; Hemphill, & Coons, 1957; Thelen, 1956; Thelen, Stock, et al., 1954).

siderable overlap in the behaviors associated with each role (cf. Lewis, 1972). For both roles, the largest percentage of contributions is in active task behavior. The next most frequent category is positive social activity. The roles diverge in the relative amounts of these activities. Idea generators tend to focus a higher percentage of their behavior on giving suggestions and opinions and a lower percentage on positive and negative social behavior than the most liked group members.

In sum, task and social behavior do not appear incompatible in family or in ad hoc laboratory groups.[2] Furthermore, Bales's claim that in family groups, the sexes specialize exclusively in one or the other of these roles has received little support. However, as we shall discuss in the next section, Bales was correct in his assumption that women focus more than men on group maintenance activities and men more than women on task activities.

Sex Differences in Interaction in Groups

Reviews of research comparing the interaction style of male and female group members have documented consistent patterns of responses associated with each sex (Anderson & Blanchard, 1982; Baird, 1976; Carli, 1982; Lockheed, 1985).

Frequency of Men's and Women's Responses

Carli's (1982) review included the largest number of studies (a total of 21) and employed meta-analytic techniques to estimate the size and direction of the sex differences. The review compared the frequency with which men versus women engage in task behavior as well as the frequency with which the sexes engage in positive social behavior. Interaction effect sizes were calculated for each study outcome in terms of d (Hedges & Olkin, 1985), which represents the mean frequency of a behavior for males minus the mean for females divided by the common standard deviation. The outcomes for individual studies were then aggregated to yield a mean sex difference effect size across all studies in the sample.

For active task behavior, Carli (1982) estimated that the mean effect ranged from $d = 0.35$ to $d = 0.59$, revealing greater task contribution by men than by women. The mean effect for positive social behavior ranged from $d = -0.36$ to $d = -0.59$, indicating that women more frequently engage in positive social behavior than men do. The sex differences in interaction are of moderate size in comparison with many psychological

---

[2] In an extension of this argument, research on leadership has often found that the most effective leaders are those who perform both task and social functions (e.g., Hemphill & Coons, 1957; Stogdill, 1974).

sex differences (Eagly, 1987; Hall, 1984), and in comparison with typical effect sizes in personality and social psychology (Cohen, 1977; Cooper & Findley, 1982). Furthermore, the sex differences appear to hold for mixed-sex as well as same-sex groups.

The interaction styles that characterize men's and women's behavior are notably similar to the styles associated with the "idea man" and "best-liked man" Bales and Slater (1955) identified in all-male groups. Similar to the interaction profiles associated with these two roles, men and women contribute to both task and social activities in groups. According to Carli (1982), both sexes concentrate the highest percentage of their contributions in the category of active task behavior. The next most frequent category for both sexes appears to be positive social activity. Thus, sex differences in interaction do not conform to a pattern of incompatible task and social roles, but rather represent varying emphasis on task and social concerns.

A Dynamic View of Sex Differences in Interaction

Estimates of the frequency with which men and women engage in certain acts provide a static picture of interaction and do not capture the dynamic sequencing of responses among group members. Response sequencing can reveal the patterning of sex differences across interactions.

Early research suggested that the effects of initial acts on later ones depend on whether the later acts are "proactive" or "reactive" (Bales & Slater, 1955). Proactive behaviors reflect continuing acts by the same individual whereas reactive behaviors consist of contributions by a person other than the one who initiated the previous act.

We recently conducted a study to determine if men and women engage in different sequences of proactive and reactive interaction (Rhodes & Wood, 1990). We employed sequential analysis (e.g., Bakeman & Gottman, 1987) to identify the relative frequency of pairs of acts (i.e., single-lag sequences). We evaluated the effects due to sex of the initiator of the interaction as well as sex of the target. Proactive sequences, by definition, occur within sex, whereas sex of initiator and of target can vary independently in reactive sequences.

In the study, college students participated in three-person mixed-sex groups composed of a male majority or female majority. Group members participated in a discussion task for a total of 75 minutes. Because we were interested in the development of interactions over time, behavior in the groups was videotaped for five minutes at the beginning and then again at the end of interaction. We will report here the findings aggregated across these two time periods. The interactions were coded according to a modified version of Bales's (1950) system into positive social behavior (e.g., showing solidarity, agreeing), negative social behavior (e.g., disagreeing, showing antagonism), or active task behavior (e.g., offering suggestions, opinions).

Social behavior most clearly differentiated the pattern of males' and females' interaction in our data, and we will discuss here the sequences initiated by either a positive or a negative social act. Sex differences emerged in the likelihood that these types of social behavior would be followed by an active task response, a positive social response, or a negative social response.

Given that a positive act occurred, the females in our study were more likely to respond with another positive social act than with an active task act. In contrast, when male group members responded to a positive act, they were more likely to engage in task behavior than positive social behavior. This pattern of responses was observed for both proactive sequences (i.e., the same person responding to him- or herself) and reactive sequences (i.e., a different person responding than initiating). For reactive acts, the tendency for women to reciprocate positive social behavior was particularly strong when the initiator of the sequence was also female.

These findings indicate that women build on positive social behavior with the results of maintaining and amplifying good feelings in the group. When the positive affect originates from another woman, a positive act in return reflects the others' emotions and expresses empathy with them, thus plausibly strengthening emotional ties and cohesiveness among group members. For men, positive social acts, whether initiated by themselves or another group member, set the stage for task contributions. Positive feelings serve as a precursor for men to engage in task activity.

A very different picture emerges with the sequences initiated by negative affective behavior. For both proactive and reactive sequences, when negative behavior had been initiated, men were more likely than women to respond with negative behavior. Thus, men were more likely than women to continue in kind with disagreeing or unfriendly acts. The sex of the initiator also proved important; males were likely to reciprocate negative codes initiated by other men to a greater extent than females reciprocated negative codes initiated by other women. In fact, female responses in any category were highly infrequent when another female initiated a negative act.

These findings for negative social behavior suggest that men tend to escalate the level of conflict in a group, particularly when the original negative act is initiated by a man. In contrast, women do not build on conflict, and instead appear to avoid it. For women, this is particularly true when the initiator of the negative social behavior is another woman.

In general, our findings for sequencing of interaction, in conjunction with the research we reviewed on interaction frequency, suggest that men and women possess somewhat different orientations in task groups. Women (in comparison with men) appear to display a more supportive, friendly orientation. They engage in more frequent social behavior than men, and they are more likely to escalate positive acts by responding in kind to their own and others' agreeing/friendly behavior. Men (in comparison with women) display a more critical, performance orientation. They tend to engage in more active task behavior, to respond to positive social acts with task ideas, and to engage in strings of negative social acts.

The pattern of responses associated with male and with female group members in our research is interesting in light of Bales's (1953; Bales & Slater, 1955) ideas of the functions of task and social behavior. In his view, there exists a dynamic tension between these activities; task behaviors build tension within the group which is then dispelled through positive social acts. The women in our groups were more likely than men to elaborate on and continue this tension reduction process, whereas men were more likely to rebuild tension by returning the group's focus to task completion or by escalating conflicts directly.

In the next section of this chapter we will present several explanations for the differential interaction of male and female group members. We will consider the possible origins of these sex differences as well as the likely effects in task-performing groups.

Origins of Sex Differences in Interaction Style

Socialization Theory

A variety of mechanisms might underlie men's and women's interaction in task-performing groups, including socialization processes and social expectations. Socialization theories emphasize the idea that, through a variety of developmental mechanisms, on the average adult men and women differ in the strength with which they possess certain personality attributes. Men possess stronger tendencies toward dominance, assertiveness, and leadership abilities than women do, whereas women possess stronger tendencies toward interpersonal warmth, emotional expressiveness, and concern for others (Bem, 1974; Spence & Helmreich, 1978). The sex differences observed in group interaction are plausibly a result of men and women acting in accord with these sex-typed predispositions.

One version of the socialization argument particularly relevant to sex differences in group interaction was recently articulated by Maccoby (1990). From this perspective, the development of characteristic interaction patterns in children's same-sex play groups, in conjunction with the high frequency of sex-segregation of children, result in adult men and women possessing different orientations toward social interaction. Men are primarily oriented toward dominance, egoism, and avoiding weakness. In contrast, women are oriented toward support or enabling of others, intimacy, and reciprocity.

Although socialization processes and other explanations (e.g., biological factors) are certainly relevant to explaining sex differences, we mention them here only briefly. In this chapter we will focus on accounts that feature social expectations. Expectation theories have been tailored specifically to explain men's and women's responses in task groups. These perspectives also enjoy greater empirical support than other approaches in accounting for sex differences in adult task-performing groups.

Expectation States Theory

According to expectation states theory, group members form expectations concerning their own and other members' task-relevant abilities and these affect members' interaction style (Berger, Fisek, Norman, & Zelditch, 1977; Berger, Wagner, & Zelditch, 1985). The expectation states perspective originated in Bales's (1950; Bales & Slater, 1955) work on homogeneous, all-male task groups. Within these groups, members exhibited differential amounts of task behavior. The differing contribution levels were thought to originate in members' evaluations of their own and others' abilities, based in part on everyone's earlier contributions to the task.

A variety of attributes of group members can inform performance expectations. The most important are those related to task skill; members judged to have the motivation and ability necessary to complete the group's task are accorded high expectations (Berger et al., 1977). In addition, global attributes of a person such as sex, race, and age, can underlie performance expectations (Webster & Foschi, 1988). When one level of such attributes is more highly valued by society than another level, as is thought to be the case with men (vs. women), whites (vs. blacks and Hispanics), and adults (vs. children), the attributes affect expectations in a manner similar to task-related skill. These "diffuse status characteristics" (Berger et al., 1977) are thought to inform performance expectations in a wide variety of circumstances.

According to expectation states theory, performance expectations drive the differential behavior of group members. Given that task groups are oriented to select people to direct the group's functioning who will maximize performance outcomes, group members are likely to treat each other in ways that are consistent with performance expectations. In general, those members who are expected to perform well are given and take more opportunities to contribute to task solution and their contributions are more likely to be valued than those of members who are not expected to perform well (Berger, Wagner, & Zelditch, 1985; Webster & Foschi, 1988).

Indeed, research has documented a variety of differential reactions to men and women in groups. These reactions occur even when the task solutions and ideas of women, and other low-status group members, are of equal quality to those of men, and higher status members. For example, women's ideas, in comparison with men's, receive less attention from others, are judged to be less competent, and are less influential (Ridgeway, 1981, 1982; Shackelford, Wood, & Worchel, 1991). In non-verbal behavior, both male and female group members display less positive and more negative facial responses when women contribute to task performance than when men do (Butler & Geis, 1990). These differential nonverbal reactions toward males and females occur when men and women are high as well as low contributors to task completion.

From this perspective, then, men's more critical, performance orientation in task groups than women's is due to the higher performance expectations accorded men. Men, like other high-status group members, concentrate their contributions in task performance domains (Lockheed, 1985). Women, as lower status group members, do not contribute as actively to the task. Furthermore, for men and others with high status, a positive response from someone in the group establishes the opportunity to direct task completion and to enhance or maintain one's position in the group's power and prestige order (Rhodes & Wood, 1990). Opportunities to compete within the status hierarchy are not as available to women and other lower status members, and consequently supportive behavior is not an opening to task activity.

Our finding that men are particularly likely to initiate strings of negative acts and to continue negative acts initiated by themselves or another male group member (Rhodes & Wood, 1990) can also be explained through this perspective. The escalation of negative behavior among men plausibly reflects competition for higher status positions within the group. One way to maintain or enhance one's status is to respond critically to the ideas of others, particularly when the others are possible competitors for high-status positions, as is the case with other male group members (Eagly, Wood, & Fishbaugh, 1981).

According to expectation states theory, performance expectations also have implications for social activity in a group. Task behavior is un-expected and out-of-role for low-status people, and social activity is one way for those of low status to legitimize task contributions. Women's high frequency of agreement and friendly behavior may establish that their task performance is motivated by group-oriented, rather than self-oriented, concerns and may convince others that performance contributions are legitimate (Meeker & Weitzel-O'Neill, 1977; Ridgeway, 1978, 1982; Shackelford, Wood, & Worchel, 1991). In addition, the finding that women build on positive social behavior (Rhodes & Wood, 1990) suggests that women use the opportunity accorded by an initial positive response to demonstrate their support for the group and commitment to group outcomes. Women also avoid reacting to a negative act, perhaps because critical, negative responses can lead others to question one's group-oriented intentions. From this perspective, then, women and other low-status group members adopt a supportive, friendly orientation in order to increase the success of their influence attempts and the impact of their ideas.

The expectation states account is generally consistent with a number of findings of sex differences in interaction (e.g., Eskilson & Wiley, 1976; Lockheed & Hall, 1976). A study by Wood and Karten (1986) was explicitly designed to test the idea that differential performance expectations for men and women underlie sex differences in behaviors in task groups. Two men and two women individually completed a "general aptitude test," and then participated as a group in a discussion task. In one condition, group members were publicly given false feedback on their aptitude scores before they began the discussion task; one man and one woman in each group were told that they possessed particularly high levels of intellectual and moral aptitude and one man and one woman that they possessed low aptitude. In another condition, no test-score feedback was given. Five minutes of group discussion were coded using Bales's (1950) interaction process analysis. At the end of the session participants completed questionnaires assessing their perceptions of their own and other members' competence.

The judgments of competence varied with sex and with the false test-score feedback as expectation states theory would predict. When no feedback was given, men were judged higher in competence than women (based on an aggregate of self- and other-ratings). In contrast, when some members were identified as scoring well and others poorly on the initial aptitude test, competence judgments varied with this initial status identification. Members labeled high in competency-based status were indeed perceived as more competent than those identified as low status, and no significant sex differences were obtained in this condition.

The interaction style results paralleled these competence judgments. In the conditions in which no aptitude feedback was given, the typical sex differences emerged in interaction style. Women concentrated a higher percentage of their contributions in positive social activity than men did and men devoted a larger percentage of their contributions to active task behavior than women did. However, no significant sex differences were found when the initial information about aptitude was provided. Instead, interaction style varied with members' supposed general ability. Group members who were said to score well relative to their group devoted a higher percentage of their interaction to active task behavior than members who supposedly scored poorly. Those group members supposedly scoring low on this test concentrated a higher percentage of their contributions in positive social behavior than those scoring well.

Wood and Karten's (1986) findings are consistent with the idea that perceived sex differences in competence underlie sex differences in interaction in groups. Competence judgments, whether based on sex or apparent ability, affected interaction style such that higher perceived competence was associated with greater contributions to the task and lesser contributions to maintenance of positive interaction. These findings provide strong support for the expectation states interpretation of sex differences in interaction style.

Social Role Theory

Eagly's social role theory (Eagly, 1987; Eagly & Wood, 1991) also identifies social expectations as a primary determinant of sex differences. Sex-typed expectations, or gender roles, are defined as shared beliefs about appropriate behavior that apply to people on the basis of their socially identified sex. The content of these expectations can be inferred from stereotypes about the sexes (e.g., Broverman, Vogel, Broverman, Clarkson, & Rosenkrantz, 1972; Eagly & Steffen, 1984). Women are expected to be friendly, unselfish, concerned with others, and emotionally expressive. Men are expected to be independent, masterful, assertive, and instrumentally competent.

These sex-role expectations arise from the distribution of women and men into different social roles, especially family and occupational roles. Stereotypes reflect the belief that women and men possess attributes suited for the roles they typically occupy (Eagly, 1987; Eagly & Steffen, 1984; Williams & Best, 1982). In particular, women tend to be primarily responsible for child rearing and other domestic work, and men and women tend to carry out different types of paid employment.

Role theory assumes that behavioral sex differences are in part caused by the tendency of people to behave consistently with gender-role expectations. It also acknowledges that an individual's personal history of enacting social roles is an indirect cause of sex differences because these experiences help define the person's repertoire of skills and attitudes. Sex-differentiated prior experiences cause men and women to have somewhat different skills and attitudes, which then cause them to behave differently. From this perspective, then, the division of labor between the sexes leads to both gender-role expectations and sex-typed skills and beliefs. These in turn are responsible for sex differences in behavior.

Gender-role expectations influence behavior through mechanisms similar to those described earlier for the evaluative beliefs of expectation states theory. Men and others judged high in competence are likely to take opportunities to contribute to task performance, are encouraged by others to do so, and their contributions are highly valued by the group. Women and others of low or average apparent competence are less likely to attempt to contribute to this aspect of group functioning; other members do not pay much attention and may respond negatively when they do so. Thus, men are more likely than women to adopt a critical performance orientation in group interaction.

The Two Perspectives Compared

Expectation states and gender role theory diverge in part because they were designed to perform very different functions. Expectation states theory was developed within the perspective of Bales's work on task groups to account for members' differential participation rates and status. Gender role theory was developed to account for the commonality between sex stereotypes and behavioral sex differences in a variety of social domains.

We will consider four ways in which the theories diverge. First is the nature of the expectation that leads to sex differences. In expectation states work, sex differences are a function of society's more positive general evaluation of men than of women. According to gender role theory, expectations are based on the specific content of stereotypic beliefs concerning men and women. From this perspective, sex differences in behavior obtain only to the extent that the behavior or related dispositions are differentially represented in social stereotypes of men versus women.

It is important to identify clearly the nature of the initial expectations members form about each other because a variety of attributes in addition to competence covary with sex. For example, recent stereotype research reveals that women are liked more than men (Eagly & Mladinic, 1989). People report more positive feelings about the stereotypic woman than the stereotypic man. Thus, in groups designed to establish and promote friendships or other interpersonal goals, women may possess the more favored status. This possibility is recognized by gender-role but not expectation-states perspectives.

Second, the theories diverge in their explanations for sex differences in positive social behavior. According to expectation states theory, women's greater social behavior than men's is a function of the relative positions of the sexes in the group status hierarchy (Ridgeway & Johnson, 1990). Social behavior is a consequence of task performance expectations.

According to gender role theory, the processes governing task and social behavior are highly similar, with sex differences in both domains due to sex-differentiated social expectations, abilities, and attitudes. In this view, sex differences in social behavior are one aspect of a general tendency for women, in comparison with men, to be more socially skilled, emotionally sensitive and expressive, as well as more concerned with personal relationships. Thus our finding that women are more likely than men to respond in kind to positive social acts (Rhodes & Wood, 1990) can be attributed to women's greater concern with fulfilling social goals in task groups. One strength of social role theory is that gender roles can account for sex differences in a variety of social behaviors when task productivity is not the primary focus of interaction (e.g., empathy,

Eisenberg & Lennon, 1983; sending and receiving nonverbal cues, Hall, 1984; intimacy, Reis, Senchak, & Solomon, 1985).

Third, because expectation states was developed to address dynamics in task groups, it offers a particularly clear depiction of the consequences of sex-typed expectations for status organization. For example, the theory has identified the important dimensions of social stereotypes that inform initial performance expectancies and lead to the formation of status hierarchies. That is, men's (vs. women's) higher perceived competence and likelihood of achieving group goals appear to be the critical components of sex-linked expectancies, and not differential dominance or assertiveness (Ridgeway, 1987; Ridgeway & Diekema, 1989). Furthermore, research within this perspective has identified the processes by which status hierarchies are established in newly formed groups. For example, the reactions of group members to others' behavior appear critical to the establishment of stable hierarchies (Ridgeway & Diekema, 1989).

We would like to mention one final point of divergence. Because gender role theory relies on the concept of stereotypes, it allows a more detailed understanding than expectation states of when group members will form sex-differentiated expectancies. According to both theories, expectations will be based on member sex primarily when other, more diagnostic information is unavailable (Berger, Rosenholtz, & Zelditch, 1980; Kreuger & Rothbart, 1988). Stereotype research specifies further that the goals and capacities of group members are important. Stereotypes can represent a simple, efficient means of forming impressions that perceivers rely on when faced with complex or ambiguous information (Bodenhausen & Lichtenstein, 1987) or when they are unwilling or unable to exert the energy necessary to conduct more detailed analyses (Fiske & Neuberg, 1990). These circumstances are likely to emerge and stereotypes inform initial judgments of group members when groups are composed of large numbers of members, when the group task is relatively unimportant, and when the task is novel and yields no clear procedure for solution. In such cases when expectancies for men and women diverge, sex differences in behavior are likely to obtain.[3]

As we noted earlier, the two theories make identical predictions concerning men's and women's interaction style. We are unaware of any research that would allow us to determine the relative value of each perspective in accounting for interaction. We have outlined points of

---

[3] Expectation states and gender role theories also differ in the mechanisms through which sex differences affect group behavior. According to expectation states, sex and other attributes have an effect only through the mediation of members' expectations. In gender role theory, men's and women's abilities and attitudes can have a direct effect on behavior, in addition to an expectancy-mediated effect.

divergence between the two perspectives with the hope of facilitating future theoretical development and empirical investigation.

Sex Differences in Emotional Responsiveness

We would like to mention briefly one possible artifactual explanation for the sex differences obtained with Bales's interaction process analysis. In Bales's coding scheme, the emotional tone of the response determines how it is categorized. Task-oriented behavior that is accompanied by positive or negative affect is classified as positive or negative social activity, and not as task behavior.[4]

This attribute of the coding system might be responsible for the finding that women concentrate a higher percentage of their contributions in the social domain and a lesser percentage of their contributions in task activity than men do. In investigations of emotional responsiveness, women appear to experience and express more extreme emotions than men (Wood & Grossman, 1990; Wood, Rhodes, & Whelan, 1989). It is plausible that women's task contributions typically possess an emotional tone, such as beginning a task suggestion with an expression of agreement with others or accompanying task activity with smiles. These acts would be classified as positive social behavior in Bales's system. The sex differences found in group interaction may thus be primarily a function of women's (vs. men's) greater emotional expressiveness.

From this perspective, the sex differences we have identified in interaction are due to differential expression of social responses. This stands in contrast to the expectation state's notion that sex differences in interaction style stem from the task structure of groups. An explanation centering on emotional expressiveness would, however, be consistent with the gender role perspective.

Consequences of Sex Differences in Interaction

We argued in the introduction to this chapter that interaction process is a key mediator between inputs to a group, such as member sex, and outputs, such as productivity (McGrath, 1964; Shiflett, 1979). The effects of sex on interaction style provide evidence for the first link in this model. In the second link, interaction style should affect important group outputs such as the level of group performance, who emerges as the leader, and members' satisfaction with the group. In this final section of the chapter

---

[4]This issue of the overlap between task and social activity has been raised in the context of how best to categorize acts of agreement or disagreement in response to others' task activity (Ridgeway & Johnson, 1990).

we will consider how sex differences in interaction are associated with these different outcomes in groups for men and for women.

Sex Differences in Performance

Although the performance of men and women in groups has important applied implications for productivity in employment settings, until recently it received little research attention. Investigation of this area has been limited by a lack of theoretical understanding of what might cause sex differences in performance. Men's and women's interaction style provides a means of understanding such effects.

We believe that sex differences in group performance depend on the fit between members' interaction style and the requirements of the group task. Because men engage in proportionally more task behavior than women and women proportionally more social behavior than men, interaction should impact performance primarily for tasks that require high levels of active task or positive social activity for successful completion. Specifically, when performance at the task is maximized by a high level of active task behavior, all-male groups are likely to outperform all-female groups. In contrast, when performance is maximized by a high level of positive social activity, all-female groups are likely to perform particularly well.

A meta-analytic review by Wood (1987) tested these predictions. The review evaluated the findings of 45 experiments that reported productivity scores for all-male and all-female groups. In the review, the task assigned to the group was judged to demand high levels of task-oriented activity if it consisted of solving a problem for which there was only a single correct solution or if it involved generating or recalling lists of solutions. For both kinds of tasks, high levels of task activity by one or all members should result in effective performance and only minimal coordination among group members is required.[5] Tasks were judged to require high levels of social activity if they explicitly involved cooperation, as in a manual dexterity task requiring two persons. Discussion tasks for which there was no "right" answer were also classified as requiring social activity because only one product could be submitted and this should pressure members to be concerned about others' ideas.

---

[5] These tasks were classified as involving high levels of task activity for the following reasons: For problems for which there is only a single solution, effective performance typically results when one members' work on the task results in identification of the solution. High levels of task activity mean that members are working on the task, thereby increasing the likelihood of any one of them achieving a solution. Tasks that involve generating or recalling lists of solutions intrinsically involve task activity; high levels of such behavior should be linked to effective performance.

Because the studies included in this review did not report tests of the effects of interaction style on performance, this possibility was evaluated indirectly. Wood compared individual performance at the assigned task with group performance. A sex difference in individual performance reflects the effects of nongroup-level factors that favor one sex's performance over the other, such as particular research settings and the content of the assigned task (e.g., math problems concerning quarts of motor oil vs. quarts of milk). The effects of interaction style were detected from a comparison of the magnitude of the sex differences in group versus individual performance. In this way the individual effect was considered a baseline score, representing what would happen in groups if interaction among members had no impact on performance. Higher or lower performance scores for groups than for individuals suggest that members' interaction style in the group setting facilitated or impaired performance at the task.

The sex difference in individual-level performance proved to be the same for tasks requiring social and well as those requiring task activity; men outperformed women. At the group level, tasks requiring task-oriented behavior yielded a similar pattern; all-male groups performed better than all-female ones. The sex difference favoring men's performance was of comparable size for both individuals and groups, suggesting that interaction had little effect on performance at these tasks. However, very different effects were obtained for tasks that required high levels of social activity. At the group level, all-female groups tended to outperform all-male ones. This effect favoring all-female groups was significantly different from the individual performance outcomes, suggesting that women's interaction style facilitated performance, in comparison to men's, at these kinds of tasks.

These findings provide partial support for the prediction that sex differences in group performance depend on the fit between members' characteristic interaction style and the interaction requirements of the task. This prediction held nicely for tasks requiring social behavior but was not strongly supported by tasks involving active task responses.

It is possible that men's interaction did not facilitate performance at tasks requiring task behavior because this activity on the part of men is not always directed toward effective performance. If men engage in task activity at least in part to maintain or enhance their own status in a group (Berger et al., 1977), the solutions they propose and the suggestions they make may not necessarily be optimal for task completion.

Although men's and women's interaction style was identified as the most promising explanation for Wood's (1987) group performance findings, the exact aspect of interaction implicated in the effect remains unclear. It may be the simple frequency of positive social and active task behavior that is responsible for the obtained group sex differences. It is also possible that amount of task and social behavior are associated with

other interaction qualities that are themselves responsible for group performance. For example, high levels of social activity could facilitate group
cohesiveness, which might enhance performance when group consensus is
required. It is also possible that high levels of active task behavior are
associated with a centralized power structure, which in turn affects performance. Indeed, male groups have been found more likely than female
groups to develop such a structure, and this organization may impair
performance when the task requires group consensus (Fennell, Barchas,
Cohen, McMahon, & Hildebrand, 1978). Just as plausibly, centralized
organizations might enhance performance when task solution depends on
any single member's performance, because such a structure may facilitate
identification of the most able member.

These findings concerning group interaction and performance have
implications for real-life work groups. Several analyses of discrimination
in the work force have implicitly assumed that women's work style and
consequent productivity in organizations is likely to be different from
and perhaps inferior to men's (e.g., Harragan, 1977; Hennig & Jardim,
1977). Indeed, in Wood's review, individual men outperformed individual
women. If task contents and settings in natural contexts are comparable
to those in the studies in the review, better male than female individual
performance would be expected.

However, when interaction style is considered, somewhat different
findings emerge. With tasks that require high levels of positive social
behavior, facilitative effects of women's interaction style on group productivity are obtained. We speculate that many of the tasks delegated to
groups in natural contexts are of this form. Groups would likely be
required to address tasks that are technically complex, ambiguous, or
politically sensitive and thus dependent on social coordination for effective solution. The more straightforward tasks are likely to be given to
individuals. Thus we guess that, in real-world settings, all-female groups
may often perform better than all-male ones.

Sex Differences in Emergent Leadership

Members' interaction styles in groups also have implications for the
formation of status hierarchies. Groups often organize into a hierarchy
with a single individual occupying a top leadership position. Men and
women differ in the likelihood that they will emerge as leaders in initially
leaderless mixed-sex groups (Bartol & Martin, 1986; Meeker & Weitzel-
O'Neill, 1977).

A recent meta-analytic review by Eagly and Karau (1991) estimated
the size of the sex difference in leadership emergence in terms of d, which
represents the mean frequency of men emerging as leaders minus the
mean frequency of women, divided by the pooled standard deviation
(Hedges & Olkin, 1985). Effect sizes were calculated for each of the 58

studies in the review and then aggregated across studies. The findings for measures of general leadership, $d = 0.32$, revealed that men were significantly more likely to emerge as leaders than women.

The type of leadership position appears to be important in whether men or women become leaders (Eagly & Karau, 1991). Task leadership is reflected in group members' productivity and ratings of their task contribution. Social leadership is reflected in members' social contributions and liking by others. Men appear more likely to be identified as task leaders than women, whereas women seem more likely to emerge as social leaders than men. Men's greater task leadership is plausibly one aspect of their critical, performance-oriented interaction style and women's social leadership is plausibly linked to their supportive, friendly orientation.

The idea that sex differences in interaction style are linked to sex differences in leadership emergence was further supported by an analysis of the kind of tasks assigned to the groups in the studies Eagly and Karau (1991) reviewed. This analysis was conducted only with task and unspecified, or general, leadership. Some tasks in the reviewed research required minimal social activity for completion whereas others required a great deal of complex social interaction. When tasks require a coordinated effort, the ideal leader is likely to be someone who displays a supportive, friendly orientation. Thus, women may emerge as task and general leaders with coordination-type tasks. Indeed, for these tasks, the tendency for men rather than women to emerge as leaders was significantly smaller than the sex difference found with tasks that required very little social activity. These findings echo Wood's (1987) results for group productivity and suggest that leadership emergence depends on the fit between group members' interaction styles and the interaction requirements of the task.

The sex differences in leadership emergence are interesting in light of Parsons and Bales's (1955) notions of sex-typed roles in family groups. The tendency for men in task groups to serve as task leaders and women as social leaders is consistent with the arguments of these early theorists. Contrary to this early view, however, the size of the sex effect suggests that men's and women's roles overlap to some degree and are not dichotomous; men will sometimes serve as social leaders and women as task leaders.

The results of Eagly and Karau's (1991) meta-analytic review are congruent with both gender role theory (Eagly, 1987) and expectation states theory (Berger et al., 1977). From these perspectives, sex-typed expectancies, in conjunction with sex differences in interaction style, are responsible for sex differences in leadership emergence. These expectancies include the belief that men are more competent than women (Berger et al., 1977) and that men possess greater task leadership ability than women whereas women possess greater social leadership ability than men (Eagly, 1987).

Sex-typed expectations are likely to affect a variety of aspects of leadership in addition to assumption of the leadership role. Indeed, ratings of leadership style reveal that women are more likely than men to adopt a democratic, participative style that involves collaborative decision making whereas men are more likely to adopt an autocratic style that involves taking charge in an authoritative manner (Eagly & Johnson, 1990). In addition, evaluations of male and female leaders reveal that women are devalued relative to men, particularly when female leaders adopt an autocratic or directive leadership style (Eagly, Makhijani, & Klonsky, in press).

In real-world contexts, we guess that sex differences in leadership have important implications for men's and women's success. First, because the performance expectancies for women do not identify them as likely task leaders of groups, and because general leadership positions are determined primarily by task contributions (e.g., Stein & Heller, 1979), women are unlikely to be selected to head task groups in occupational or other settings. Indeed, task leadership is highly valued even in roles like managerial ones that require considerable interpersonal skill (Brenner, Tomkiewicz, & Schein, 1989; Schein, 1973). The benefits to group productivity of social leadership may be subtle and indirect, causing supportive and friendly behaviors to be undervalued in task performing groups. If the leadership contributions of women center in social domains, these may not be recognized in work groups.

Satisfaction with Group Interaction

Men's and women's interaction style also has implications for members' commitment to and satisfaction with their group. Much of group research has focused on the task performance outcomes of interaction and less interest has attended affective outcomes such as member satisfaction. These latter concerns have, however, been researched extensively in the context of friendships and social groups. We will briefly review the evidence for sex differences in affective experiences in these nontask groups and then discuss the implications of the findings for groups focused on task performance.

The interaction sex differences in social settings appear comparable to those we documented in task-performing groups. Among friends, women are more disclosing and engage in more intimate conversations than men. In contrast, men's friendships tend to be more oriented toward shared activities than do women's (Aries & Johnson, 1983; Caldwell & Peplau, 1982; Fiebert & Wright, 1989; Winstead, 1986). Furthermore, the topics discussed by women and by men in social settings appear to differ. Women's discussions center on intimate topics such as feelings and relationships to a greater degree than men's do (Aries, 1976).

The sex differences in style and content of interaction in social contexts are associated with greater feelings of satisfaction in contact with women than with men. This is illustrated particularly well in a study in which members met alternately in same-sex and mixed-sex groups (Aries, 1976). On the occasions when the sessions were mixed-sex, men were less likely to miss sessions and expressed more interest than when the sessions were all-male. The opposite pattern was demonstrated for women: women were more interested in the sessions and more likely to attend when the group was comprised entirely of women than when the group also included men. Thus both men and women appeared to value interaction with women more than with men.

Greater satisfaction in interaction with women than with men also emerges in friendships in natural contexts. Men report greater intimacy, enjoyment, and nurturance in friendships with women than in friendships with other men (Sapadin, 1988). Women, however, rate their same-sex friendships (vs. mixed-sex) as higher on these dimensions (Sapadin, 1988). In same-sex friendships, women also rate their interactions as more meaningful than men do (Reis et al., 1985), and females in same-sex friendships appear to be more emotionally supportive than males (Winstead, 1986). Finally, men and women who spend a greater proportion of time with women report less loneliness than those who spend less time with women (Wheeler, Reis, & Nezlek, 1983). Women who spend relatively large amounts of time in the company of men report particularly high degrees of loneliness.

These findings are congruent with predictions of social role theory (Eagly, 1987). Sex-differentiated experiences likely result in women possessing greater social skills and valuing social interaction more than men. Furthermore, gender-role expectations likely to be salient in social contexts specify that women are warmer and more concerned for others' feelings than are men.

Thus, the more intimate, personal quality of interaction with women than with men appears to yield greater satisfaction with socially oriented relationships. Although we are not aware of any data that would allow generalization to task-performing groups, it seems plausible that similar effects occur in task contexts. That is, women's higher levels of positive social behavior might enhance member satisfaction and group cohesiveness. In long-term task-performing groups, such positive social outcomes may be particularly important because they help to maintain members' interest in group goals and commitment to the group.

Summary

In this chapter we have reviewed the evidence for sex differences in interaction style in task groups, discussed several theories that can account for these differences, and then considered several consequences of interaction sex differences.

Our conceptualization of interaction draws heavily from Bales's (1950) definition of task and social activities in groups. Supporting Parsons and

Bales's (1955) idea that men tend to be task specialists and women social specialists, in task groups men appear to engage in proportionally more active task behavior than women, whereas women engage in proportionally more positive social activity than men (e.g., Carli, 1982). However, these roles are not incompatible; both men and women focus the bulk of their contributions in task domains and the next most frequent contribution for both is positive social behavior.

We argued that these sex differences are a function of group members' initial expectancies for men's and women's behavior (Berger et al., 1977; Eagly, 1987). Men are judged by themselves and by other group members as more likely to contribute effectively to task completion than are women. Men thus concentrate their contributions to the group in the task performance domain. Women focus relatively more on social activity because agreeing with others and acting friendly is a way of legitimizing their task contributions (Ridgeway, 1982) or because social expectations identify women as particularly socially skilled and concerned for others' welfare (Eagly, 1987).

The sex differences in interaction were shown to have several consequences. We argued that interaction styles are associated with group performance, leadership emergence, and member satisfaction. Specifically, with tasks that require high levels of social coordination and consensus, the high levels of positive social behavior in all-female groups enhance performance relative to the interaction style of all-male ones (Wood, 1987). Furthermore, men's relatively high levels of task behavior and women's relatively high levels of social behavior can explain why men tend to emerge as overall leaders or task leaders of groups and women emerge as social leaders (Eagly & Karau, 1991). Finally, we argued that female group members' interaction styles are associated with high cohesiveness and satisfaction with the group experience.

References

Anderson, L.R., & Blanchard, P.N. (1982). Sex differences in task and social-emotional behavior. *Basic and Applied Social Psychology, 3*, 109–139.

Aries, E.J. (1976). Interaction patterns and themes of male, female, and mixed groups. *Small Group Behavior, 7*, 7–18.

Aries, E.J., & Johnson, F.L. (1983). Close friendships in adulthood: Conversational content between same-sex friends. *Sex Roles, 9*, 1183–1197.

Aronoff, J., & Crano, W.D. (1975). A re-examination of the cross-cultural principles of task segregation and sex role differentiation in the family. *American Sociological Review, 40*, 12–20.

Baird, J.E., Jr. (1976). Sex differences in group communication: A review of relevant research. *Quarterly Journal of Speech, 62*, 179–192.

Bakeman, R., & Gottman, J.M. (1987). Applying observational methods: A systematic view. In J. Osofsky (Ed.), *Handbook of infant development* (2nd ed.). New York: Wiley.

Bales, R.H. (1950). *Interaction process analysis: A method for the study of small groups*. Reading, MA: Addison-Wesley.

Bales, R.F. (1953). The equilibrium problem in small groups. In T. Parsons, R.F. Bales, & E.A. Shils (Eds.), *Working papers in the theory of action*. Glencoe, IL: Free Press.

Bales, R.F. (1970). *Personality and interpersonal behavior*. New York: Holt, Rinehart, & Winston.

Bales, R.F., & Slater, P.E. (1955). Role differentiation in small decision-making groups. In T. Parsons & R.F. Bales (Eds.), *Family, socialization, and interaction process* (pp. 259–306). Glencoe, IL: Free Press.

Bartol, K.M., & Martin, D.C. (1986). Women and men in task groups. In R.D. Ashmore & F.K. Del Boca (Eds.), *The social psychology of female-male relations* (pp. 259–310). Orlando: Academic Press.

Bem, S.L. (1974). The measurement of psychological androgyny. *Journal of Consulting and Clinical Psychology*, 42, 155–162.

Berger, J., Fisek, M.H., Norman, R.Z., & Zelditch, M., Jr. (1977). *Status characteristics and social interaction: An expectation-states approach*. New York: Elsevier.

Berger, J., Rosenholtz, S., & Zelditch, M., Jr. (1980). Status organizing processes. *Annual Review of Sociology*, 6, 479–508.

Berger, J., Wagner, D.G., & Zelditch, M., Jr. (1985). Expectation states theory: Review and assessment. In J. Berger & M. Zelditch, Jr. (Eds.), *Status, rewards, and influence: How expectations organize behavior* (pp. 1–72). San Francisco: Jossey-Bass.

Bion, W.R. (1961). *Experiences in groups*. New York: Basic Books.

Bodenhausen, G.V., & Lichtenstein, M. (1987). Social stereotypes and information processing strategies: The impact of task complexity. *Journal of Personality and Social Psychology*, 52, 871–880.

Brenner, O.C., Tomkiewicz, T., & Schein, V.E. (1989). The relationship between sex-role stereotypes and requisite management characteristics revisited. *Academy of Management Journal*, 32, 662–669.

Broverman, I.K., Vogel, S.R., Broverman, D.M., Clarkson, F.E., & Rosenkrantz, P.S. (1972). Sex-role stereotypes: A current appraisal. *Journal of Social Issues*, 28, 59–78.

Butler, D., & Geis, F.L. (1990). Nonverbal affect responses to male and female leaders: Implications for leadership evaluations. *Journal of Personality and Social Psychology*, 58, 48–59.

Caldwell, M.A., & Peplau, L.A. (1982). Sex differences in same-sex friendship. *Sex Roles*, 8, 721–732.

Carli, L.L. (1982). *Are women more social and men more task oriented? A meta-analytic review of sex differences in group interaction, reward allocation, coalition formation, and cooperation in the Prisoner's Dilemma game*. Unpublished manuscript, University of Massachusetts-Amherst.

Cohen, J. (1977). *Statistical power analysis for the behavioral sciences* (rev. ed.). New York: Academic Press.

Cooper, H., & Findley, M. (1982). Expected effect sizes: Estimates for statistical power analysis in social psychology. *Personality and Social Psychology Bulletin*, 8, 168–173.

Crano, W.D., & Aronoff, J. (1978). A cross-cultural study of expressive and instrumental role complementarity in the family. *American Sociological Review*, *43*, 463–471.

Eagly, A.H. (1987). *Sex differences in social behavior: A social-role interpretation*. Hillsdale, NJ: Erlbaum.

Eagly, A.H., & Johnson, B.T. (1990). Gender and leadership style: A meta-analysis. *Psychological Bulletin*, *108*, 233–256.

Eagly, A.H., & Karau, S.J. (1991). Gender and the emergence of leaders: A meta-analysis. *Journal of Personality and Social Psychology*, *60*, 685–710.

Eagly, A.H., Makhijani, M.G., & Klonsky, B.G. (in press). Gender and the evaluation of leaders: A meta-analysis. *Psychological Bulletin*.

Eagly, A.H., & Mladinic, A. (1989). Gender stereotypes and attitudes toward women and men. *Personality and Social Psychology Bulletin*, *15*, 543–558.

Eagly, A.H., & Steffen, F.J. (1984). Gender stereotypes stem from the distribution of women and men into social roles. *Journal of Personality and Social Psychology*, *46*, 735–754.

Eagly, A.H., & Wood, W. (1991). Explaining sex differences in social behavior: A meta-analytic perspective. *Personality and Social Psychology Bulletin*, *17*, 306–315.

Eagly, A.H., Wood, W., & Fishbaugh, L. (1981). Sex differences in conformity: surveillance by the group as a determinant of male nonconformity. *Journal of Personality and Social Psychology*, *40*, 384–394.

Eisenberg, N., & Lennon, R. (1983). Sex differences in empathy and related capacities. *Psychological Bulletin*, *94*, 100–131.

Eskilson, A., & Wiley, M.G. (1976). Sex composition and leadership in small groups. *Sociometry*, *39*, 183–194.

Fennell, M.L., Barchas, P.R., Cohen, E.G., McMahon, A.M., & Hildebrand, P. (1978). An alternative perspective on sex differences in organizational settings: The process of legitimization. *Sex Roles*, *4*, 589–604.

Fiebert, M.S., & Wright, K.S. (1989). Midlife friendships in an American faculty sample. *Psychological Reports*, *64*, 1127–1130.

Fiedler, F.E. (1967). *A theory of leadership effectiveness*. New York: McGraw-Hill.

Fiedler, F.E. (1978). The contingency model and the dynamics of the leadership process. In L. Berkowitz (Ed.), *Advances in experimental social psychology* (Vol. 12, pp. 59–112). New York: Academic Press.

Fiske, S.T., & Neuberg, S.L. (1990). A continuum model of impression formation from category-based to individuating processes: Influences of information and motivation on attention and interpretation. In M.P. Zanna (Ed.), *Advances in experimental social psychology* (Vol. 23, pp. 1–74). Orlando, FL: Academic Press.

Forsyth, D.R. (1990). *Group dynamics* (2nd ed.). Pacific Grove, CA: Brooks/Cole.

Futoran, G.C., Kelly, J.R., & McGrath, J.E. (1989). TEMPO: A time-based system for analysis of group interaction. *Basic and Applied Social Psychology*, *10*, 211–232.

Hackman, J.R., & Morris, C.G. (1975). Group tasks, group interaction process, and group performance effectiveness: A review and proposed integration. In L. Berkowitz (Ed.), *Advances in experimental social psychology* (Vol. 9). New York: Academic Press.

Hall, J.A. (1984). *Nonverbal sex differences: Communication accuracy and expressive style*. Baltimore, MD: Johns Hopkins University Press.

Hare, A.P. (1976). *Handbook of small group research* (2nd ed.). New York: Free Press.

Harragan, B. (1977). *Games mother never taught you: Corporate gamesmanship for women*. New York: Rawson.

Hedges, L.V., & Olkin, I. (1985). *Statistical methods for meta-analysis*. Orlando, FL: Academic Press.

Hemphill, J.K., & Coons, A.E. (1957). Development of the Leader Behavior Description Questionnaire. In R.M. Stogdill & A.E. Coons (Eds.), *Leader behavior: Its description and measurement* (pp. 6–38). Columbus, OH: Bureau of Business Research, Ohio State University.

Hennig, M., & Jardim, A. (1977). *The managerial woman*. Garden City, NY: Anchor Press.

Kreuger, J., & Rothbart, M. (1988). Use of categorical and individuating information in making inferences about personality. *Journal of Personality and Social Psychology*, *55*, 187–195.

Leik, R.K. (1963). Instrumentality and emotionality in family interaction. *Sociometry*, *26*, 131–145.

Lewis, G.H. (1972). Role differentiation in small groups. *American Sociological Review*, *37*, 424–434.

Lockheed, M.E. (1985). Sex and social influence: A meta-analysis guided by theory. In J. Berger & M. Zelditch, Jr. (Eds.), *Status, rewards, and influence: How expectancies organize behavior* (pp. 406–429). San Francisco: Jossey-Bass.

Lockheed, M.E., & Hall, K.P. (1976). Conceptualizing sex as a status characteristic: Applications to leadership training strategies. *Journal of Social Issues*, *32*, 111–124.

Maccoby, E.E. (1990). Gender and relationships: A developmental account. *American Psychologist*, *45*, 513–520.

Meeker, B.F., & Weitzel-O'Neill, P.A. (1977). Sex roles and interpersonal behavior in task-oriented groups. *American Sociological Review*, *42*, 92–105.

McGrath, J.E. (1964). *Social psychology: A brief introduction*. New York: Holt.

McGrath, J.E. (1984). *Groups: Interaction and performance*. Englewood Cliffs, NJ: Prentice-Hall.

Parsons, T. (1955). The American family: Its relations to personality and to the social structure. In T. Parsons & R.F. Bales (Eds.), *Family, socialization, and interaction process* (pp. 3–33). Glencoe, IL: Free Press.

Parsons, T., & Bales, R. (1955). *Family, socialization, and interaction process*. Glencoe, IL: Free Press.

Reis, H.T., Senchak, M., & Solomon, B. (1985). Sex differences in the intimacy of social interaction: Further examination of potential explanations. *Journal of Personality and Social Psychology*, *48*, 1204–1217.

Rhodes, N., & Wood, W. (1990). *Sequences of interaction among males and females in task groups*. Unpublished data, Texas A&M University.

Ridgeway, C.L. (1978). Conformity, group-oriented motivation and status attainment in small groups. *Social Psychology Quarterly*, *41*, 175–188.

Ridgeway, C.L. (1981). Nonconformity, competence, and influence in groups: A test of two theories. *American Sociological Review*, *46*, 333–347.

Ridgeway, C.L. (1982). Status in groups: The importance of motivation. *American Sociological Review*, 47, 175–188.

Ridgeway, C.L. (1987). Nonverbal behavior, dominance, and the basis of status in task groups. *American Sociological Review*, 52, 683–694.

Ridgeway, C.L., & Diekema, D. (1989). Dominance and collective hierarchy formation in male and female task groups. *American Sociological Review*, 54, 79–93.

Ridgeway, C.L., & Johnson, C. (1990). What is the relationship between socio-emotional behavior and status in task groups? *American Journal of Sociology*, 5, 1189–1212.

Sapadin, L.A. (1988). Friendship and gender: Perspectives of professional men and women. *Journal of Social and Personal Relationships*, 5, 387–403.

Schein, V.E. (1973). The relationship between sex-role stereotypes and requisite management characteristics. *Journal of Applied Psychology*, 57, 95–100.

Shackelford, S., Wood, W., & Worchel, S. (1991). *Women exert influence in mixed-sex groups: The importance of task skill and behavioral style*. Manuscript under editorial review.

Shaw, M.E. (1981). *Group dynamics: The psychology of small group behavior* (3rd ed.). New York: McGraw Hill.

Shiflett, S. (1979). Toward a general model of small group productivity. *Psychological Bulletin*, 86, 67–79.

Slater, P.E. (1955). Role differentiation in small groups. *American Sociological Review*, 20, 300–310.

Spence, J.T., & Helmreich, R.L. (1978). *Masculinity & femininity: Their psychological dimensions, correlates, and antecedents*. Austin: University of Texas Press.

Stein, R.T., & Heller, T. (1979). An empirical analysis of the correlations between leadership status and participation rates reported in the literature. *Journal of Personality and Social Psychology*, 37, 1993–2002.

Stogdill, R.M. (1974). *Handbook of leadership: A survey of theory and research*. New York: Free Press.

Thelen, H.A. (1956). Emotionality of work in groups. In L.D. White (Ed.), *The state of the social sciences*. Chicago: University of Chicago Press.

Thelen, H.A., Stock, D., et al. (1954). *Methods for studying work and emotionality in group operation*. Chicago: University of Chicago, Hyman Dynamics Laboratory.

Webster, M., Jr., & Foschi, M. (1988). Overview of status generalization. In M. Webster, Jr. & M. Foschi (Eds.), *Status generalization: New theory and research* (pp. 1–22). Stanford: Stanford University Press.

Wheeler, L., Reis, H.T., & Nezlek, J. (1983). Loneliness, social interaction, and sex roles. *Journal of Personality and Social Psychology*, 45, 943–953.

Williams. J.E., & Best, D.L. (1982). *Measuring sex stereotypes: A thirty-nation study*. Beverly Hills, CA: Sage.

Winstead, B.A. (1986). Sex differences in same-sex friendships. In V.J. Derlega & B.A. Winstead (Eds.), *Friendship and social interaction* (pp. 81–99). New York: Springer-Verlag.

Wood, W. (1987). Meta-analytic review of sex differences in group performance. *Psychological Bulletin*, 102, 53–71.

Wood, W., & Grossman, M. (1990). [Men's and women's emotional responsiveness: Normative pressures and physiological responses.] Unpublished data, Texas A&M University.

Wood, W., & Karten, J. (1986). Sex differences in interaction style as a product of inferred sex differences in competence. *Journal of Personality and Social Psychology*, *50*, 341–347.

Wood, W., Rhodes, N., & Whelan, M. (1989). Sex differences in positive well-being: A consideration of emotional style and marital status. *Psychological Bulletin*, *106*, 249–264.

Zelditch, M., Jr. (1955). Role differentiation in the nuclear family: A comparative study. In T. Parsons & R.F. Bales (Eds.), *Family, socialization, and interaction process* (pp. 307–352). Glencoe, IL: Free Press.

6
Gender and Conversational Dynamics

LYNN SMITH-LOVIN AND DAWN T. ROBINSON

Much of what is important in social life is accomplished through talk. Through conversation, we form acquaintances, request and receive services, conduct business, and negotiate family affairs. In such situations, language use creates a social identity. Conversational styles that reflect our group membership and social position serve to maintain those identities in social interaction. They represent the micro-level mechanisms through which structural-level inequality and differentiation are accomplished in everyday interaction. On the other hand, conversational patterns that contrast with those that are expected from group members may be the mechanisms for social mobility (e.g., leadership acquisition or loss). Therefore, language use and conversational style may reinforce a sense of stereotype, or can alleviate stereotypic beliefs (Jupp, Roberts, & Cook-Gumpertz, 1982, p. 234).

Because language use is related to structural inequality, there has been considerable interest in gender differences in language use. Beginning with classic work on small group interaction in the 1950s (e.g., Bales & Slater, 1955; Strodbeck & Mann, 1956), researchers argued that men and women played different roles in task-group discussions. In the 1970s, a new tradition of research stressed the distinctiveness of women's talk and men's talk in all conversational settings. More recently, theoretical writers have argued whether gender differences in talk are socialized, cultural, situational, or structural. In this chapter, we will review the research on men's and women's conversational styles and offer some new theoretical ideas about how gender differences in conversation develop. In the first section, we review the major theoretical orientations to gender and conversational style. We also review the empirical studies developed within these theoretical traditions in an attempt to establish the variables on which men and women systematically differ and the situations in which these differences normally occur. We offer a new, integrative theoretical approach and outline the research that would address the new model. In a brief empirical example, we illustrate some of these points.

122

Theoretical Traditions in Group Discussion, Conversation, and Gender

The Socialization Perspective

In sociology, the socialization perspective on gender differences began with the functionalist theory of Parsons and Bales (Bales, 1950, 1970; Bales & Slater, 1955; Parsons; 1951; Parsons & Bales, 1955). Parsons argued that gender role differentiation within the family was functional for both families and for society as a whole. Because of women's biological role in childbearing (and, implicitly, child rearing), Parsons suggested that women were likely to be other-concerned, relationally oriented, and socioemotionally skilled. Men, with their (default) responsibility for managing activities that connected the family to larger social spheres, were instrumental and task oriented. Because these orientations were argued to be functional for family relations, Parsons thought that these distinct male and female roles were passed through generations through socialization.

Bales generalized Parsons' arguments to small group processes. He reasoned that all social groups had dual functional imperatives: to accomplish group goals and to maintain the group as a unit. Bales argued that gender-role socialization (shaped by functionality in family contexts) led men and women to adopt different specialties in small task-oriented groups. Bales initially suggested that in sex differentiated groups, men were more likely to become task leaders and women were more likely to produce positive, socioemotional behaviors that served the function of maintaining group solidarity while the task was accomplished. However, the relationship of gender to these group processes has been a source of considerable debate over the years. Later reviews (Anderson & Blanchard, 1982; Lewis, 1972; Riedesel, 1974) challenged this view somewhat, indicating that task and socioemotional functions were not clearly separate in Bales's data. Most interactions for both men and women were task oriented (Anderson & Blanchard, 1982); gender differences were quite small. However, small group studies do suggest that within the task domain gender operates as a status differentiating dimension in most groups (see review in Wagner, 1988). Men talk more, give more opinions, make more directive comments and generally receive more respect than women. Women are more likely to make approving comments and to encourage the ideas of others. They do more of the integrative work that allows the group discussion to function. They are more likely to ask others for opinions, relieve tension, and react to others' suggestions with positive comments (see Ridgeway and Johnson, 1990 for a status interpretation of these findings).

A more recent research tradition using linguistic methods rather than group interaction coding has generalized the instrumental/socioemotional distinction to more universal statements about men's and women's talk. These researchers argued that women are socialized to use language differently than men in many contexts other than task-oriented groups. They stressed that women's talk is generally oriented to maintaining relationships and developing intimacy. These researchers concentrated on variables that constitute verbal stroking of conversation partners. They found that women are more likely than men to express agreement or ask for another's opinion (Eakins & Eakins, 1978), to acknowledge points made by the other speaker at the beginning of a turn, to provide back-channel[1] support for other speakers (Hirschman, 1973; McLaughlin, Cody, Kane, & Robey, 1981), to pause to give another the floor, and to use other conversational devices that serve to draw out one's conversational partner (McConnell-Ginet, 1975). Whether in task groups or in everyday conversation, women seem to encourage communication and disclosure on the part of others. They use talk to form and enhance relationships to a greater degree than men.

Other scholars working in this sociolinguistic tradition have highlighted the inequality implied by traditional gender socialization. They emphasized that women's talk is not only supportive of others, but also unassertive. Lakoff (1975), for example, reported that the communication style of women was characterized by tentative, unsure, and deferential patterns of speech, whereas men's conversational style was stronger and more direct. Researchers investigating these gender differences in linguistic features found that women are more likely to use questions (especially tag questions[2]) (Brouwer, Gerritsen, & DeHaan, 1979; Crosby & Nyquist, 1977; Eakins & Eakins, 1978; McMillan, Clifton, McGrath, & Gale, 1977), hedges, qualifiers, disclaimers, and other linguistic forms conveying uncertainty (Bradley, 1981; Crosby & Nyquist, 1977; Eakins & Eakins, 1978). Women also more frequently use hypercorrect grammar including "superpolite" forms, lengthened requests, and modal constructions (Crosby & Nyquist, 1977; Lakoff, 1975; McMillan et al., 1977).

In summary, both the sociological and sociolinguistic branches of the socialization perspective emphasize that males and females are socialized to play different roles in our society. Men are taught to be more instrumental, whereas women are taught to be more socioemotional, supportive, and tentative. The socialization perspective views these learned

---

[1] Short utterances like "mm hmm," "un huh," or "yeah, I see" may be interjected in short pauses of a speaker's turn. Rather than interrupting, these back-channel utterances serve to support the speaker and indicate attention (if not agreement) on the part of the listener.

[2] A tag question is one that ends an otherwise declarative sentence (e.g., "This issue is a tough one to deal with, isn't it?"). Sociolinguists suggest that tag questions convey uncertainty about one's judgments, ask for support or agreement, and encourage other speakers to respond.

behavioral predispositions and expectations as a part of men's and women's personalities by adulthood. As such, the behavioral differences that they imply will be expected in a wide variety of situations.

Male and Female Culture: Speaking with Different Voices

Closely related to the socialization view is a perspective that regards males and females as developing different cultural forms because of sex-segregated interaction in early life. Clearly, any cultural perspective relies extensively on socialization processes for the communication and continuance of cultural forms. The difference between the cultural view and the traditional socialization perspectives is in the developmental process that they see creating the gender differences, and in the circumstances in which these gender differences will be displayed.

The cultural view grows from sociolinguistic work on cross-ethnic communication and from detailed ethnographic studies of linguistic aspects of children's play (see reviews in Maccoby, 1990 and Maltz & Borker, 1982). Instead of viewing males and females as shaped into gender roles by a dominant culture that trains men to be more instrumental and women to be more socioemotional, this new cultural perspective argued that distinctive male and female styles of interaction grew out of sex-segregated peer cultures. Rather than learning different sets of expectations linked to their social positions of male and female, the cultural theorists claimed that taken-for-granted rules about the meaning of various conversational strategies evolve in boys' and girls' play groups. Sharing these conversational forms allows comfortable coordination of talk, a feeling of being understood, and therefore a sense of shared identity (Tannen, 1982, p. 218). Communication between those who have different ways of signaling intentions or exerting influence often leads to misunderstandings and a breakdown in smooth relations. So, for example, a woman might suggest ideas with a question like "Would you like to go to the party?" and a man might respond "No, I don't want to" (interpreting her question as an inquiry rather than a suggestion). Such misinterpretation may be more likely to be encoded in attribution error (she thinks he's inconsiderate, he thinks she's compliant) than to be resolved. In fact, Tannen (1980, 1982, 1983) argued that such conversational strategies are remarkably resistant to intellectual analysis; they represent fundamental understandings about social interaction that may evoke emotional responses in spite of our intellectual awareness of different conversational codes.

The key feature of the cultural approach is that conversational styles—the ways that seem natural to express and interpret meaning in conversation (Tannen, 1982, p. 230)—are learned early through communicative experience. Rather than being taught to talk like "ladies" and "real men," girls and boys learn a conversational style that fits the social situations in which they play as children. Children, the cultural theorists argued, do not learn their styles of talk through modeling adult speech or expressing appropriate gender role behavior that they've learned through socialization. Children learn what style of talk works within play groups in which they most often find themselves.

The most striking fact about young children's play groups is their gender segregation (see reviews in Maccoby 1988, 1990). From the age of three, children are aware of gender similarity or difference, and display a marked preference for same-gender associates (Wasserman & Stern, 1978). This preference for gender homophily seems to be cross-cultural, substantial in magnitude, resistant to attempts to break down gender segregation, and apparent even when not notably reinforced by institutions, organizations, and activities (Maccoby, 1990, p. 514). Gender segregation in playmate choice appears before the age of 3 and continues well into the school years. Although cross-gender contacts increase around puberty, even adolescent and adult life are characterized by high levels of gender segregation in social life (see review in Smith-Lovin and McPherson, 1991, and evidence in McPherson and Smith-Lovin, 1986, 1987).

Maccoby (1990, p. 515) noted that there is little evidence for differential gender socialization in the nuclear family at very early ages. Furthermore, gender segregation in play groups is strongest in the *absence* of adult observation or institutional constraint. Maccoby further remarked that language behavior is unlikely to be modeled from same-sex adults at an age when children have scant recognition that sex is a permanent characteristic. The impetus for early forms of gender segregation is unclear.

Maccoby (1990, p. 515) suggested two reasons why girls and boys play in separate groups after about age 3. First, girls seem to be repelled by boys' rough-and-tumble play and the competitive dominance struggles that such physical contests foster. Boys are more likely to play outside, in larger groups, in more age-differentiated groups and in more long-lasting, organized games than girls (Lever, 1976). Second, girls are not able to influence boys effectively during a stage of development in which children are increasing dramatically their attempts to influence one another (age 3.5 to 5.5). Girls use polite requests to influence, whereas boys use direct demands. Boys become less and less responsive to polite requests during this age period, at exactly the same time that girls are implementing such requests. Therefore, Maccoby (1990) suggested that girls withdraw from play with boys, and concentrate on more rewarding play with other girls (especially when adults are not around to control the boys' behavior).

Once the segregation occurs, it is easy to see how different communicative styles develop. Boys are in larger, more diverse, outdoor groups. Such a social environment would select for direct demands and other assertive forms that are aimed at establishing dominance. Larger groups typically have a greater level of differentiation and structure. The greater noise and lower attention level directed at any individual actor would select for simple, declarative demands. Girls, in their smaller, quieter indoor play, have success in maintaining a small number of close relationships with polite requests and indirect suggestion. The quieter setting and smaller number of participants allows for the more intense attention to subtlety. In their review of this literature, Maltz and Borker (1982) found that boys were more likely to interrupt and to use commands, threats, or boasts. The boys would more often than girls refuse to comply with another child's demand, heckle a speaker, or use conversation as an occasion to put on a performance (tell a joke, tell a story, top someone else's story, give information or heckle someone). Girls in all-girl play groups were more likely to express agreement, pause to give someone else time to speak, etc.

Maccoby (1990) reviewed more recent research that supported the image developed by Maltz and Borker (1982). Girls concentrate their talk on conflict mitigating strategies; they try to be "nice" and sustain social relationships. Boys use talk for largely egoistic functions, to establish and maintain turf.

It is important to emphasize that both all-boy and all-girl groups function very effectively, and that children of both sexes are effective at asserting their desires within same-gender play groups. Boys, for example, can coordinate play for long-term sports games. Girls can pursue their ends very effectively while using collaborative speech acts. Cultural theorists have argued that these patterns carry into adulthood as "distinctive voices" (Gilligan, 1982)[3], with women adopting a more indirect, considerate style supportive of relationships and men adopting a more direct, imperative style centered on issues of hierarchy.

Several issues are left unexplained by this cultural view of gender differences in language use. Cultural theorists have suggested that the conversational styles that are typical of boys and girls are functionally well-suited to their respective play environments, but explanations of the initial sex segregation of play groups and the gender-differentiation of activities in male and female groups are incomplete. Why do boys and girls shun cross-sex interactions? Why do boys play outside in larger, more diverse groups, whereas girls play inside in couples and threesomes? Why do girls adopt politeness and concentrate on rapport, whereas boys make demands and concentrate on hierarchy?

The cultural theorists argue that once gender conversational differences are established in childhood, these stylistic differences generalize to other contexts including cross-gender interactions. Why don't frequent male/

---

[3] Gilligan actually proposes a more psychodynamic model for the development of male and female styles. Still, her emphasis on the interactional environment (in her case, with the mother) shaping basic understandings and values of male and female children is consistent with the cultural viewpoint.

female interactions later in life break them down (or at least foster bicultural speakers with the capacity to use both male and female forms)? The cultural theorists argue that such language forms are so taken for granted that they are resistant to such learning from cross-sex interaction (Maltz & Borker, 1982; Tannen, 1982). Furthermore, the nature of the interaction created when male and female language patterns interact creates a conversational form that reinforces gender stereotypes. Men are more assertive, and women are indirect and accepting. Miscommunication in cross-sex conversations, created by the mix of male and female cultural forms, reinforces gender identities: men think that women are always agreeing with them, and conclude that it's impossible to tell what a woman really thinks; women think that men are insensitive and fail to listen to their requests (Maltz & Borker, 1982, p. 202). Although cultural theorists have suggested that male/female differences may moderate somewhat in adulthood, basic rules for interpreting conversational events are quite resistant to change. They have argued that one of the major advantages of their approach is that " . . . it does not assume that problems [of communication] are the result of bad faith, but rather sees them as the result of individuals wrongly interpreting cues according to their own rules" (Maltz & Borker, 1982, p. 201).

Expectation States: Gender as a Diffuse Status Characteristic

Theorists who have focused on structural gender inequality would argue that the cultural view overlooks the status and power differentials between men and women that are reflected and maintained in cross-sex talk. The most coherent statement of the status approach has been presented by Joseph Berger and his colleagues (Berger, Conner, & Fisek, 1974; Berger, Fisek, Norman, & Zelditch, 1977; Berger, Rosenholtz, & Zelditch, 1980). Berger developed a theory of status organizing processes in small groups from the pioneering work by Bales and his colleagues (Bales, 1950, 1953, 1970, 1980; Bales & Cohen, 1979; Bales & Slater, 1955). Bales observed that task groups of status equals quickly developed differentiation of participation, with some members dominating the task-ralated discussion. When status differences were present at the beginning of a task-group discussion, these statuses structured the groups' conversations such that high-status members talked more, influenced the groups' decisions, received more positive feedback for their ideas, emitted more negative comments about the contributions of others, and in general overshadowed the other group members (Strodbeck & Mann, 1956). Berger, Conner & Fisek (1974) argued that when members of a task group are different on one or more evaluated characteristics, this differentiation leads to expectations about the value of contributions toward mutually desired group outcomes. Differing expectations lead high-status people to contribute more and low-status people to encourage that greater contribution. There is an implicit assumption in the theory that status orders in small groups are *deference* structures rather than *dominance* structures (see discussion by Fisek, 1974, p. 58). Status (as defined within the scope conditions of the theory) is a consensual, functional structure. Both the low- and high-status people agree that the high-status people have more to contribute to the task at hand. Both have an interest (under the condition of a collaborative, mutual-outcome task) in having the more effective contributions of the high-status/high-expectation person over-shadow the lesser contributions of the low-status members.

Researchers in the expectation states tradition find that gender oper-ates as a status characteristic (see recent reviews in Wagner, 1988 and Wagner, Ford, & Ford, 1986).[4] This finding implies that men not only exert leadership in task groups but that women accept and encourage male leadership. For example, interruptions are mechanisms through which these higher expectation participants can gain the floor and restrict the contributions of lower quality group members (Robinson & Smith-Lovin, 1990).

Ridgeway and Johnson (1990) have shown how the socioemotional behavior displayed by women in such task groups can be explained by the status characteristics model. Low-status people would be expected to respond positively to the valued contributions of higher status group members; these positive responses serve to display deference and encour-age the high-status participants to maintain their high level of contri-bution to the group. High-status participants, on the other hand, would be expected to show high levels of both positive and negative comment; they are assumed by group members to have the competence to judge others' contributions.

The status view fits well with both older evidence from the classic small-group studies and with newer evidence that shows that women exercise influence differently in same-sex and mixed-sex groups (Eagly & Johnson, 1990; Ridgeway 1981, 1982; see also Ellyson, Dovidio, & Brown, Chapter 3 in this volume). In mixed-sex groups, men are assumed to be legitimate leaders unless structures operate to elevate women to that position. Women, when their authority is not thoroughly legitimated, use less direct, other-attributed suggestions (Carli 1990; Ridgeway, 1988) and less dominant nonverbal cues to try to influence group outcomes (see Chapter 3.) When they occupy a firmly legitimated leadership role or when they interact with other women in female contexts, however,

---

[4] The theoretical structure does not require, of course, that any particular charac-teristic cause differentiation. It simply makes prediction about how a character-istic will influence group interaction if it *is* differentially evaluated by group members.

women exercise influence in ways that are quite similar to men. This situational flexibility is not easily explained by the cultural or socialization perspectives.

The status/deference view of conversational dynamics also was supported by a dynamic analysis of the timing of interruptions in group discussions (Robinson & Smith-Lovin, 1990). The fact that interruptions did not display local contagion effects that would be generated by a tit-for-tat pattern reinforced an image of a collaborative, consensual structure. The fact that interruptions increased dramatically over the course of the group discussion also indicated that these conversational devices were being used in a positive, task-oriented way as the discussion warmed to its work.

Conversational Analysts and the Power/Conflict View

Conversational analysts within sociology have argued that the hierarchical aspect of language use is not necessarily due to a consensual deference structure. Sacks, Schegloff, and Jefferson (1974) began this research tradition by focusing attention on turn-taking norms in conversation. They pointed out that conversation is organized typically so that one speaker talks at a time. Speakers alternate smoothly in turns to prevent conversations from becoming monologues. People indicate when their utterance is coming to a transition point with a variety of verbal and nonverbal cues, so that turn taking is accomplished with few overlaps and gaps in speech. In this turn-taking model, interruptions are a striking exception to conversational norms. By disregarding the rights and obligations of the speaker, the interrupter exhibits dominance and exercises control in face-to-face interaction.

Conversation analysts typically study small samples of naturally occurring speech, often recorded in public places. Although findings from such nonrepresentative samples may not be applicable to other populations of speakers or conversations, they serve to illustrate the function that interruptions play in conversation. Zimmerman and West (1975) found that men interrupted women much more than women interrupted men, whereas same-sex conversations showed very well-coordinated speech with few interruptions. Later studies showed that doctors interrupted patients (except when the doctor is a "lady") (West, 1984), and that parents interrupted children (West & Zimmerman, 1977). These results led West and Zimmerman to conclude that the use of interruptions constitutes a display of dominance or control; further, interruptions are effective in control since the incursion disorganizes the speech of the other and shifts attention away from the topic of the other's utterance.

Several later studies contested these conclusions by looking in more detail at the process. These studies typically used larger samples of speech and reported almost identical interruption rates for males and females (Beattie, 1982; Kollock, Blumstein, & Schwartz, 1985; Murray & Covelli, 1988; Roger & Nesshoever, 1987; Smith-Lovin & Brody, 1989). Kollock et al. (1985) agreed that interruptions are a device for expressing and maintaining power, but argued that gender was not a clear determinant of conversational power. In their study of heterosexual and homosexual couples, power in the relationship[5] appeared to be much more important than gender in determining interruptive patterns. Power-balanced couples showed lower rates of interruption than power-imbalanced couples. In both homosexual and heterosexual couples, power imbalance led the more powerful spouse to interrupt the less powerful one. Kollock et al. (1985) did not find an overall sex difference for rate of interruption (although males were slightly higher overall). They did, however, find that male-male conversations had a lower rate of interruption (especially successful interruption) than female-female or male-female conversations.

Smith-Lovin and Brody (1989) found that males and females attempt to interrupt at roughly the same rate, but that males discriminated in their interruptions (interrupting females more often than other males) whereas women didn't;[6] men were also more successful at their interruption attempts against women. This result was interpreted as representing some conflict between women and men in the groups, in addition to a status effect favoring the men.

Drass (1986) provided a dynamic[7] analysis of the relationship between gender and the rate of interruptions, emphasizing the importance of identity in shaping verbal behavior. She found that in same-sex conversations between previously unacquainted people, the gender identity of interactants predicted interruption rates. Both men and women with a more masculine identity interrupted more feminine partners. This result is consistent with the Kollock et al. (1985) study above, if one considers that Drass (1986, p. 296) measured masculine identity with adjectives like bold, strong, hard, powerful, aggressive, assertive, dominant, competitive, ambitious, etc. Thus, the more powerful partners identified in the Kollock et al. study would likely have been identified as more "masculine" by Drass. Several psychologists, measuring dominance as an individual

---

[5] As rated by the two people in interviews prior to the conversation.

[6] Stewart (1988) found a similar result in an expectation states study. Men acted like sex is a status characteristic, but women did not.

[7] This analysis was dynamic in that it modeled the *rate* rather than the *frequency* of interruptions and allowed for the possibility of the rate being dependent on time. However, Drass neither predicted nor attempted to model the time dependence.

trait, also found that dominance predicts interruption (Aries, Gold, & Weigel, 1983; Courtwright, Millar, & Rogers-Miller, 1973; Roger & Nesshoever, 1987; Roger & Schumacher, 1983). Still other researchers have found that although dominance predicts assertiveness in same-sex groups, these effects are less pronounced (Fleischer & Chertkoff, 1986), or even nonexistent (Megargee, 1969) when compared to gender itself in mixed-sex groups.

Vuchinich's (1984, 1986) studies of conflict at family dinners contribute an interesting dynamic view of conversation process. He found that gender effects were strongest on sequencing rather than distributional variables. Females were more likely to respond to conflict moves than males were (see also McCarrick, Manderscheid, & Sibergeld, 1981); gender power differences were displayed through an avoidance of unmitigated confrontation with older males and through giving older males control over the boundary defining of the conflict.

Studies in the conversation analysis tradition clearly emphasize the dominance order rather than the deference order of conversational groups. Rather than a functional, consensual feature of group organization, the conversational dominance by one interactant over another is seen as a violation of norms. In both the Kollock et al. (1985) and Vuchinich (1984, 1986) work, we get a strong impression of lower power members making attempts to reassert their conversational rights, once violated. We know that most dominance hierarchies attain an equilibrium that limits direct power contests (Mazur, 1985). Ridgeway (1991) argued that historical power differences between men and women are the source of current status differences in our culture; power differences get legitimated over time to form more consensual structures. Clearly, if cultural change is creating a breakdown in the consensus that women's contributions are less valuable than men's, cross-sex conversations may shift toward more power/conflict dynamics and less consensual status deference.

Although status and power approaches differ markedly in their assumptions, their theoretical predictions are difficult to disentangle empirically (Robinson & Smith-Lovin, 1990). They share an emphasis on inequality as well as differentiation between men and women. Both perspectives stress that men and women will act similarly in situations where they have similar status or power. Gender differences are predicted to occur only when men have greater status or power. Both theories agree that this inequality will occur in most cross-sex interactions, unless there is some legitimating authority structure that gives women status (as in some of Ridgeway's experiments) and/or some structural power in the woman's favor (see Molm and Hedley, Chapter 1 in this volume). But they see the cross-situational stability in male-female speech as a structural feature, rather than a personal predisposition (either socialized or cultural).

Gender Identity as Affect Control:
An Integrative Approach

It seems likely that all of the processes reviewed above—socialization, culture, status, and power—contribute importantly to gender differentials in language use. Here, we propose a theoretical view that incorporates some of these insights into a more general theoretical structure. We will argue that both socialization and peer-group interaction lead boys and girls to develop gender identities with rather different values on status, power, and expressivity. These identities then affect cross-sex interaction (when they are likely to be salient); they may also modify other social positions that males or females come to occupy. On the other hand, when gender identity is not salient (or when another identity is clearly defining the situation), males and females may operate very similarly in carrying out social roles.

To develop this integration, we use affect control theory, a highly formal version of the symbolic interactionist perspective. The theory will be useful to us because it incorporates a multidimensional view of identity (including both status and power) and offers a dynamic model of how identity produces social behavior in interaction. We, therefore, turn to a brief exposition of the affect control model before explaining its relationship to the problem of gender and language use in conversation.[8]

The Affect Control Model

Affect control theory predicts social behavior based on the initial status, power, and expressivity of the people and previous actions in a situation (Heise, 1979; Smith-Lovin & Heise 1988). Status, power, and expressivity are represented in the theory by Osgood, Suci, and Tannenbaum's (1957) dimensions of affective meaning—evaluation, potency, and activity. All aspects of social interaction—identities, settings, behaviors, and emotions—are defined in terms of their position on these three dimensions. Affect control theory assumes that people operate in identities that carry *fundamental sentiments* that they attempt to control. These identities are defined vis-à-vis other identities in the situation in terms of the relative status, power, and expressivity.

The fundamental sentiments associated with identities and behaviors are a part of our culture. Despite widely varying backgrounds, we largely agree that mothers are nicer than mafiosi, that physicians have more

---

[8] Much of the theoretical development linking affect control theory to conversation and small-group discussions is taken from Robinson and Smith-Lovin (1991).

power than patients, and that children are livelier than cripples. Studies on topics ranging from word connotations to occupational prestige to severity of criminal acts find surprising agreement across social strata in affective meanings associated with social identities and behaviors (see review in Smith-Lovin, 1990, p. 240). We suggest that fundamental sentiments about identities (like gender) get built up through early experience. These fundamental cultural sentiments may be communicated through direct comment ("Policemen are nice"), through emotional expression (a facial display of disgust as one passes a homeless person), by direct experience ("my little sister is easier to push around than my parents"), or by indirect observations ("my mother does what the doctor tells her to"). According to the theory, these cultural sentiments become increasingly stable and resistant to change as information about a social category accumulates (Heise, 1979, pp. 14–18).

Of course, once fundamental sentiments are established, social events may change impressions of particular occupants of social categories, making them seem better or worse, stronger or weaker, livelier or quieter than they were expected to be. Events (social interactions) create *transient impressions* due to the nature of the setting, the identities involved, and the behaviors performed. When an actor's transient impression differs from his or her fundamental sentiment, a deflection is produced. In the three-dimensional semantic space, a deflection corresponds to the squared distance between the fundamental sentiment and the transient impression. Deflections prompt actors to create new events that reaffirm the original meanings associated with their identities (i.e., the fundamental sentiments). Therefore, the theory predicts that new events move transient impressions back toward fundamental sentiments in the three-dimensional space.

Affect control theory is represented in a set of equations relating the affective dimensions of elements of the social situation. Within these equations, identities, events, emotions, and settings are characterized by three-number profiles corresponding to their evaluation, potency and

TABLE 6.1. Evaluation, potency, and activity ratings of identities by male and female undergraduates.

	Male sentiments			Female sentiments		
	E	P	A	E	P	A
Male student	0.8	0.5	1.9	0.6	0.0	1.4
Female student	1.6	−0.3	1.7	0.9	0.0	1.4

Note. Sentiments are measured on scales that range from −4.0 to +4.0. Approximately 40 students rated each identity and modifier. Equations for computing the modifier-identity combinations, data collection, and measurement details are reported in Smith-Lovin and Heise (1988) and Heise and Lewis (1988).
E, evaluation; P, potency; A, activity.

activity positions. The model consists of impression-formation equations (Smith-Lovin, 1987a, 1987b) and mathematical transformations of these equations (Heise, 1988) to describe likely behaviors and labeling. The equations predicting impression formation were empirically derived from research using a sample of United States undergraduates to rate a large number of social events (Smith-Lovin, 1987a, 1987b). The equations predicting behavior and labeling are mathematically derived from the former equations, using the assumption that actors create likely events (behaviors) and likely construals of the situation (labeling) so as to minimize deflections.

To illustrate, consider a Female Student[9] and a Male Student engaged in a conversation in the context of an Experiment. The female subject starts out operating in the nice, not-so-powerful, and lively fundamental identity of Female Student. We assume that the modification of the Student identity with the Female marker will be activated by the cross-sex nature of the conversation; Cota and Dion (1986) provide empirical support for the idea that gender heterogeneity will increase the likelihood that a gender-based identity will be spontaneously adopted in a laboratory interaction. Similarly, the male subject operates in the identity of Male Student (a slightly less nice but more powerful identity) (see Table 6.1 for the evaluation, potency, and activity ratings of the two identities).

During the conversation, the Female Student interrupts the Male Student. This event affects the impressions associated with each of their identities. Both actor (the Female Student) and object (the Male Student) lose evaluation as a result of this not very nice act. Figure 6.1 illustrates how the female speaker is deflected drastically downward in evaluation, remaining roughly stable on the power and activity dimensions, whereas the male loses considerably on all three dimensions—status, power, and liveliness. These transient impressions are represented as t_1 in Figure 6.1. The deflection caused by this event is the squared difference of the sentiments associated with the original definition of the situation (a Male Student and a Female Student interacting in an Experiment), and the impressions produced by the behavior (Female Student Interrupts Male Student). The students become aware of this deflection through the experience of emotion. In this case, the Female Student feels Self-Conscious about her act; the Male Student feels Anxious. This deflection prompts both actors to wish to create a new event to restore the original meanings of the situation. For the interrupting Female Student, an appropriate next behavior would be Admire or Speak To the Male Student. This is a relatively nice, powerful, and somewhat active gesture that

---

[9] We use capitalized identities, settings, behaviors, and emotions to indicate inputs to the program INTERACT. These situation elements have been rated previously by an undergraduate population on the evaluation, potency, and activity dimensions.

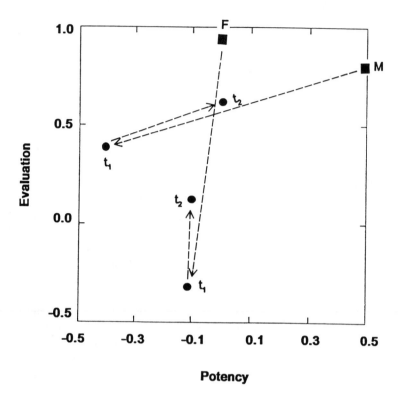

FIGURE 6.1. The effects of the events "Female Student Interrupts Male Student" and "Male Student Talks To Female Student" on transient impressions. ■, fundamental sentiments for Male and Female Students; t_1 •, transient impressions after the Female Interrupts the Male; t_2 •, transient impressions after the Male Talks To Female.

moves both actor and object back toward their fundamental identities. If the Male Student responds to the interruption, the most restorative act— the behavior that, when processed, would move the situational impressions furthest back toward their original identity sentiments—would be for him to Talk To or Excuse the Female Student. Figure 6.1 illustrates the movement that this act would create by plotting the next transient impressions as t_2.

In summary, affect control theory uses information about the setting, actors, and behaviors in a social situation to predict information about impression change. Actors are presumed to resist change in their fundamental sentiments. Such changes produce deflections that are signaled by the experience of emotion (Heise, 1988; Smith-Lovin, 1990; Smith-Lovin & Heise, 1988). For example, the theory predicts that the female would feel Self-Conscious after the interruption; the male would feel Anxious or

Angry. The experience of an emotion communicates to the actor that deflection has occurred and prompts him or her to construct an event that would minimize deflection and move impressions back toward his or her fundamental sentiment. The inputs and results to these equations are three-number profiles representing the ratings of evaluation, potency, and activity, for each of the relevant social elements.

A computer simulation program, INTERACT, contains the equations and a dictionary of identities, settings, behaviors, and emotions that it can match up to the evaluation, potency, and activity profiles (Heise & Lewis, 1988). INTERACT provided the results for the identity changes plotted in Figure 6.1. This simulation program is a useful research tool because it fully contains the theory, and thus provides direct theoretical predictions as its output.

Affect Control as an Integrative Approach

We offer affect control theory as an approach to understanding conversational dynamics both because it helps us consolidate the insights of several earlier theories, and because it explains some of the empirical patterns that have been observed in previous research. The affect control model has a multidimensional conceptualization of identity that allows us to deal with deference, domination, and expressive style. Although status and power are likely to be highly correlated in naturally occurring groups, we can distinguish conceptually between the deference that comes from positive evaluation and the clout that comes from structural control over material resources. Adding the activity/expressivity dimension as a third element incorporates stylistic elements that have been important to sociolinguistic researchers, but not central to the sociological literature. Tannen (1980, 1983), for example, found large differences between high-involvement and high-considerateness style speakers in their use of and interpretation of interruptions; she (personal communication) argued that these stylistic differences are larger and more important than gender differences.

Affect control theory also provides an explanation for an anomalous finding in the status characteristics literature. Two studies have found that males treat men and women differently in ways that indicate a status ranking (with men on top), but women do not (Smith-Lovin & Brody, 1989; Stewart, 1988). This finding is difficult to interpret within the status characteristics approach, since status characteristics are assumed to be widely held cultural evaluations. But if we measure there fundamental sentiments about identities like Man and Woman, we find that young men see Woman as much nicer (by 1.2 units on a scale that ranges from −4 to +4), but also much less powerful than Man (0.7 units difference). Young women's sentiments show the same pattern, but it is much less pronounced (differences between Man and Woman are 0.3 units on each of the evaluation, potency, and activity dimensions). The fact that males' fundamental sentiments about male and female identities are much more differentiated than females' leads us to predict that males' behavior would be much more differentiated by gender of object than would females'. According to the affect control model, males are maintaining very different sentiments when they interact with men and women; females are not.

Within affect control theory, as in all symbolic interactionist theory, the fundamental sentiments that are linked to identities are acquired through social interaction. This postulate has the potential for integrating the socialization and cultural views of language use. We propose that the information that parents communicate to children is often in terms of the three dimensions—evaluation, potency, and activity. Maccoby (1990) noted that there is little evidence that parents directly socialize their children into gender differentiated forms of influence and play. We suggest that parents may be communicating something much more subtle: that girls are nicer but not as powerful and lively as boys. This type of information can be conveyed very efficiently through emotional expressions, which have been characterized in the same three-dimensional structure as we use to characterize identities and behaviors (Ekman, Friesen, & Ellsworth, 1972). If parents display different emotions when looking at boys and girls (communicating that girls are more delicate and pleasant, whereas boys are more robust), these cultural values can be absorbed without direct comment from parents or children.[10] In this way, socialization leading to gender-differentiated behaviors and emotional responses could be accomplished very quickly after the categorization of male and female is achieved cognitively (around age 2 to 3). Parents do not need to have the transmission of cultural knowledge about competence or other behavioral traits to have children develop different fundamental meanings of what boys and girls are like. All parents need to do is to communicate basic sentiments about male and female identities, and the actions will flow from them.

After fundamental sentiments are formed, interaction with peers will be shaped by them and, through a contrast effect, reinforce ideas of gender difference. Boys may come to have a more extreme view of gender differentiation because they are members of larger, more diverse groups. Larger groups with internal differentiation typically lead to stronger in-group bias in evaluation (Ng & Cram, 1988); high-status groups also lead

---

[10] To use a more extreme example, a parent may tell a child that police are nice and helpful, but if the parent's face spontaneously expresses fear and distaste when viewing police in normal circumstances, the child is likely to develop a fundamental sentiment that encodes policeman as powerful, but not very nice. If the parent tells a child that boys and girls should be the same, but treats girls as if they are more sweet and delicate than boys, these subtle affective cues can instill more fundamental values than the direct communication.

their members to a stronger sense of difference between the in-group and out-group (Ellemers, Van Knippenberg, Devries, & Wilke, 1988). The fact that girls are more withdrawn in interaction with boys (Maccoby, 1990) would also lead boys to hold more extreme views. Girls, in social interactions with other girls, would generate behaviors that express and maintain their nice, expressive, but not particularly powerful, gender identities, when these identities are activated. We argue that gender identities (like Girl and Boy) are often activated in same-sex play groups because of the contrast with opposite-sex play groups, and because of the active search of young children for appropriate gender role behaviors. These same-sex interactions will be egalitarian, because there is no difference among the girls on the potency dimension. In interaction with Boys, however, the Girls' greater niceness and lower power would lead to more acquiescent, polite behavior. This inactivity (relative to the boys' more assertive stance) may lead boys to see girls as having even more extreme values on the evaluation and potency dimensions.[11]

The affect control model also encompasses the possibility that males and females might evolve different categorizations and sentiments associated with conversational events in their same-sex interactions. What boys come to view as a Josh may be interpreted by a girl as a Challenge or Tease. Tannen (1980, 1983) has suggested that groups can assign very different meanings to conversational acts like interruption. Murray (1985) pointed out that what defines an interruption can vary from group to group.

A final advantage of the affect control model is that it presents us with a generative view of how identity and social action are linked, and a dynamic model of how social interaction is determined by the definition of the situation. Conversation is not a static series of unrelated events, but this is often the way that quantitative researchers have treated it. Social scientists typically count up speech acts and analyze their distribution disregarding the dynamic processes that underlie their creation. To reveal status and power structures in group conversations, researchers compare the number of participations, positive comments, negative comments, and interruptions emitted by group members without studying the timing and interdependence of these speech acts to describe flow from

---

[11] Note that in same-sex adult groups, a task orientation may repress the gender identities in a same-sex group. Carli (1990) showed that women can be quite assertive in all-female task-oriented groups. We propose that in these groups, the gender identity (Woman) may not be salient; instead, task-relevant status identities may develop from the process of interaction (see Robinson and Smith-Lovin, 1991, or Fisek et al., 1991, for discussion of how such processes might work). This could also explain why competency information can override gender identities and produce assertive behavior from women in mixed-sex groups (as in Wood and Karten, 1986). In these cases, we suggest that information that makes status identities especially salient tends to outweigh any initial gender salience.

one event to the next.[12] Using affect control theory, we can begin to model the interconnectedness of speech events within a discussion. We can see how a group's characteristics affect the flow of talk within it. Our criticism of previous work on conversational events like interruptions is that researchers have used methods that treat conversational turn-taking as if the speaker transitions were either independent of one another, or in some state of equilibrium. The affect control model allows us to assess how such a disruption of normal turn-taking will impact the identities of interrupted and interrupter, and alter the course of the conversation. By avoiding the a priori assumptions of independence and equilibrium, we can more accurately examine how group-level composition and participation features are related to the timing of conversational events like interruptions.

Ideally, research on conversation guided by the affect control model would have three characteristics. First, it would assess the identities that are elicited by the conversational setting, and the fundamental sentiments associated with those identities for the conversational participants. A research design similar to that used by Cota and Dion (1986) to study the salience of gender identities in mixed-sex groups would be appropriate. Second, it would develop highly contextualized definitions of behaviors and their meanings. For example, Murray (1985) had judges code conversation for interruptions using information from the content of the talk before and after the speech transition; he found that what is considered to be an interruption varied a great deal, depending on what was being said and what followed the intrusion. Third, we would want to measure the timing and interdependence of speech events to take advantage of the dynamic predictions from the affect control model. Predictions from other theories about timing and reactions to conversational events are often quite ambiguous (see the attempts by Robinson and Smith-Lovin, 1990, to develop hypotheses about timing from status, power, and stylistic approaches to group discussion).[13] In contrast, affect control theory offers an explicit model of how actors in a conversation will react to speech acts (given knowledge of their identities and how they interpret the behavior).

In this chapter, we offer something far short of this ideal research plan. Below, we present a brief analysis of conversational turn-taking and interruption in six-person task-oriented groups. Here, we must assume that gender identities will be activated in group discussions. We assign these gender identities fundamental sentiments that have been measured

---

[12] For a notable exception, see a new dynamic formulation of the status characteristics/expectation states model by Fisek, Berger, and Norman (1991).

[13] Fisek et al. (1991) and Ridgeway and Johnson (1990) have made substantial progress in this domain with the status characteristics/expectation states theory.

in other undergraduate populations.[14] We define conversational events using conversational analysts' conventions rather than the participants' own definitions of the situation. What we hope to demonstrate is how affect control theory can generate dynamic predictions about the timing and frequency of conversational events, and suggest how data can be linked to these ideas. We turn now to this empirical analysis.

An Empirical Example

In this analysis, we apply an affect control perspective to the study of interaction in small groups. To do this, we assume that conversational interaction is guided by the same processes as other forms of social interaction. We expect actors to produce conversational acts, like other social behaviors, that allow them to construct and maintain a social structure consistent with their definitions of the situation. Like expectation states theorists, we expect status processes to be deferent in nature, but only when actors agree on identities. We also generate expectations for power and expressivity processes.

Suppose we start with the speculation that conversational participation is a valued resource within task-oriented, small-group discussions. Previous researchers noted the relationship between group participation and external status (Berger et al., 1974, 1977, 1980). Behaviors like Speak, Talk, and Explain are relatively good and powerful behaviors—the kind of behaviors to be expected of pleasant, powerful actors. What happens when a female Explains to a male in a group discussion? What happens when a male Explains even more than his powerful identity dictates as socially appropriate?

Figure 6.2 illustrates the results of affect control theory simulations of one-sided conversations between dyads of different gender compositions. The interpretation of the figure is as follows: The "Rounds of Explaining" refers to the number of times Actor 1 Explains to Actor 2 without allowing a reply, before Actor 2 responds by Interrupting Actor 1. When the number of rounds is one, then Actor 1 "Explains" to Actor 2 once, and Actor 2 responds by Interrupting Actor 1. When the number of rounds is two, then Actor 1 Explains to Actor 2, and then Explains to Actor 2 again, without allowing a response. Finally, Actor 2 responds with an Interruption. Deflection reduction refers to the difference in the deflection before and after the interruptive behavioral response, and roughly corresponds to the predicted likelihood of this behavior. The four lines displayed represent the trajectory of deflection reductions experi-

---

[14] Past research has demonstrated that such sentiments are widely shared across different parts of our society (Heise, 1979).

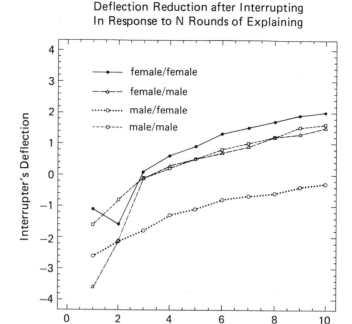

Deflection Reduction after Interrupting
In Response to N Rounds of Explaining

FIGURE 6.2. The results of affect control theory simulations of one-sided conversations between dyads of different gender compositions.

enced by members of four types of dyads: (a) female explainer/female interrupter, (b) female explainer/male interrupter, (c) male explainer/ male interrupter, and (d) male explainer/female interrupter. This figure thus tells us how Actor 2 in the various dyads responds to increasing amounts of conversational dominance.

The identities chosen for the simulations are Male Students and Female Students.[15] Consider, for example, the interaction of two Female Students. As the conversation becomes more and more one-sided, an interruptive response becomes more and more likely. The affect control simulations indicate that when two Female Students are interacting an interruption does not start out as a useful strategy for restoring meaning after only one round of explanation, but becomes more useful as the conversation becomes more and more one-sided. In a conversation between a Male Student and a Female Student, we see that at the beginning of the conversation it is very unlikely that either would interrupt the

---

[15] The simulations are actually run with the identities that corresponded to the composite identities of Male Student and Female Student.

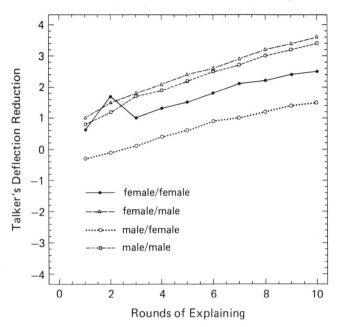

FIGURE 6.3. Evaluations of Talking To, Interrupting, and Explaining as interaction strategies.

other. As the conversation becomes more and more dominated by the Female Student, the Male Student is increasingly tempted to interrupt. In contrast, when a Male Student is Explaining to a Female Student, the interruption becomes less and less unlikely as the length of the male's speech turns increase, but never becomes a particularly likely response (i.e., the curve never gets above the zero point where the interruption creates a deflection *reduction* as opposed to a deflection increase). In other words, the Female Student is more likely to be interrupted by both males and females.. And the Male Student is more likely than a Female Student to interrupt either the Explaining Female or the Explaining male.

We can compare these predictions for interruptions to predictions for noninterrupted turn-taking by doing parallel simulations using the events "Actor 1 Explains to Actor 2; Actor 2 Talks To Actor 1." Talk To is a more positively evaluated behavior than Interrupt, and this shifts the response likelihoods somewhat (see Figure 6.3). However, because the motivation for both responses comes from deflections produced by the overzealous conversation partner, the pattern of deflection reductions is similar. Figure 6.3 shows us that Talk To starts out as a restorative strategy for three of the four dyads. When a Female Student is Explaining, both males and females experience some deflection reduction by Talking To the Female Student in response. As the Female Student retains the floor for longer and longer, the talking response becomes even more effective as a way of restoring fundamental meanings. When two Male Students are in a conversation together the pattern is similar. However, when a Male Student is Explaining to a Female Student, she does not experience any deflection reduction by Talking in response. The longer the Male Student maintains control over the conversation, the more appealing it becomes for the Female Student to Talk To her partner in response, but it never becomes a particularly effective way of reducing deflection.

What predictions can we draw from these results for conversations within six-person task groups? Among conversing dyads, these simulations suggest Female Students should be more probable objects of conversational interruptions. Additionally, Male Students should be more frequent agents of interruptions. Interruptions should be more likely as length of turn increases; this effect should be especially true when a female is speaking. Because both Male and Female Students seem to tolerate longer periods of Explaining from Male Students, we might expect Male Students to have longer lasting conversational turns.

Application of these simulation results to the six-person task groups requires a couple of assumptions. First, dyadic conversation patterns are assumed to be suggestive of small-group discussion patterns. Studies using dynamic processes to model turn-taking in small groups seem to suggest that turn-taking processes actually function at the level of the dyad within small groups (Parker, 1988). Turn-taking opportunities seem to pass among pairs of the interacting group. Thus, as long as there is status variation within the groups, the general predictions generated from these simulated dyads should hold for the six-person discussions.

A second assumption of the simulated conversations is that the identities of the members is known a priori and that it remains constant throughout the interaction. In their analysis of participation in these groups, Smith-Lovin, Skvoretz, & Hudson, (1986, pp. 1001–1002) found that variation in participation did not increase over time in the group discussions; in fact, within sex variations actually decreased slightly. Fisek (1974) also found a very stable degree of participation hierarchy in his groups. Even though they were composed of status equals, over half of the groups began their discussions with substantial participation inequalities and did not increase that differentiation over time. Evidently, group participants use subtle cues like demeanor, dress, and attractiveness to structure initial interaction; this initial structure is then quite stable over time and characteristic of the entire group discussion. Evidence from Mazur and Cataldo (1989) indicates that about 30 seconds of observation are required to make stable, accurate judgments about conversational dominance and influence.

We will explore the implications of affect control dynamics by analyzing the dynamic structure of talk in six-person task-oriented discussion groups. We will examine the pattern of interaction for evidence of identity maintenance processes. Because other aspects of the status structure of these groups have been explored elsewhere (Robinson & Smith-Lovin, 1990, 1991; Smith-Lovin & Brody, 1989; Smith-Lovin et al., 1986), our analyses should not be viewed as hypothesis tests. Rather, we look for consistency between the patterns predicted by affect control theory and the data as analyzed in this new framework. We stress that the simulations we report above are derived formally from affect control theory and thus represent predictions generated directly from the theory.

Data

Data[16] were collected on 29 six-person discussion groups. The subjects were undergraduates enrolled in undergraduate sociology classes. The experiment used only white subjects between the ages of 17 and 25 to minimize variation in status characteristics other than gender. Gender composition of the groups was systematically varied, with approximately four groups in each of seven gender-composition conditions (all female, and one to six males). Group members were seated randomly around a round table.

A gender-neutral collectively oriented task (originally developed by Fisek, 1974) stimulated group discussion. The conversation was videotaped (with the subjects' knowledge) by two cameras; transcripts were later produced from the best of the two tapes, using the secondary tape to clarify problematic passages.

Measurement

The unit of analysis is the spell of talk unbroken by a speaker transition. Three types of events could end a spell. A *normal* transition occurred when the initial speaker completed his or her turn and a speaker change occurred with no overlapped speech. Our definitions of overlaps, successful interruptions, and failed interruptions followed closely the conceptualization used by Zimmerman and West (1975). We coded an *overlap* when the floor changed hands as the result of an interruption, but the original speaker was able to complete his or her utterance to a normal transition point. We coded an *interruption success* when the new speaker broke into another's speech at a place other than a normal transition point and took the floor, preventing the original speaker from completing his or her utterance to a normal transition point. In some analyses, all three types of

---

[16] A more complete description of data collection procedures is available in Smith-Lovin et al. (1986).

abnormal transitions are combined to study all interruption attempts, regardless of outcome. To measure the length of the spells, we counted the number of words spoken between transitions.[17]

There were 5,638 transitions (events) in the 29 conversations. Of these events, 5,040 were normal transitions, 237 were successful interruptions, and 361 were conversational overlaps. (In addition, there were 278 failed interruption attempts.) The final turn in each of the 29 conversations was treated as missing. Because these last spells did not end in speaker transitions, they lacked information about the speaker taking the floor and could not be used in analyses including those variables.

Covariates

Independent variables in the analyses include the dummy variables representing each of the possible gender compositions of the dyad exchanging the floor. These were male-male, female-female, and female-male, compared to a reference category of male-female. Initial analyses also included the gender composition of the groups (coded in six dummy variables), and all two-way interactions between the dyad gender composition and group gender composition variables. We found that the gender of speaker/follower variables did not interact with group gender composition in any analyses. Therefore, these interactions have been dropped from all tables. In addition, we found that the only significant effects involving group gender composition were contrasts that compared single-sex groups to mixed-sex groups. Therefore, the group composition variable is represented as a single variable in the analyses we report here.[18]

Examining the Flow of Conversation

Table 6.2 shows some basic descriptive information on turn length by gender. The average turn was 11 words in length. Thirteen percent of the turns were single-word utterances. Most of these one-word turns were "yes" or "no" responses to questions. Interestingly, turns ending in normal transitions were not any longer than turns ending in interrup-

---

[17] Word counts were used as proxies for time for the two reasons: (a) we feel that the number of words spoken provides a reasonable estimate for the amount of time elapsed between conversational transitions, and (b) the valued resource being shared or competed for is "floor time," which may be better estimated by volume of speech than by real time.

[18] In another paper, we have analyzed the turn-taking dynamics in these data using participation and interruption histories as proxies for status (Robinson & Smith-Lovin, 1991). Interestingly, the gender variables we present here do not interact with the participation and interruption history variables; nor do those conversational process variables eliminate the effects of gender that we describe below. The important aspect of these findings is that gender identities must be operating *in addition to* the process variables, rather than *through* them.

TABLE 6.2. Descriptive data on speaking turns in group discussions by gender.

	Male	Female
Number of turns (Percent of total)	3,066 (54%)	2,601 (46%)
Average length of turn	11.8	10.6
Normal transitions	11.9	10.4
Overlapped transitions	10.6	13.2
Interrupted turns	11.4	11.0

tions and overlaps. Gender influenced frequency of participation in these groups (see also Smith-Lovin et al., 1986), and females kept the floor for slightly shorter utterances than males. The gender difference is largest for normal transitions and overlapped transitions, rather than interruptions. Women, it appears, are not being cut off while speaking to limit their participation. They take shorter turns when exchanging the floor with other speakers through normal transitions.

Methods

Continuous time-event history methods were used to analyze the data. These methods are used to model the effects of covariates on the rate of transitions between states (Tuma & Hannan, 1978, 1984). In the present analyses, the state-space consists of uninterrupted speech, overlaps, and successful interruptions as described in the measurement section.

We denote the state-space as a variable $Y(t)$ which can take on three values indicating the state being occupied by a conversing group at a given time t. To model the rate of transition between these states, we estimate the *hazard* of a transition, which can be described as the probability of a transition from state j to state k during the interval $t + \Delta t$, given the occupation of state j during time t.

To model the waiting time between transitions, we estimate the survival rate of utterances. The survivor function has an exact relationship to the hazard function and can be expressed in terms of the hazard rate integrated over time. In the absence of time dependence, the hazard rate has a linear relationship to the logarithm of the survival function (Carroll, 1983).

However, our present data do exhibit evidence of time dependence. Analyses of spells between interruptions (without regard to speaker turns) by Robinson and Smith-Lovin (1990) indicated that when the dependent variable was length of conversation until an abnormal transition, the rate of interruption increases later in the conversation.[19] Analyzing the tran-

---

[19] The Robinson and Smith-Lovin (1990) analysis studied only the timing of interruptions across the conversation; spells were defined as time between interruptions, rather than speaker turns. Therefore, the earlier data set could not analyze speaker characteristics like gender.

sition between turns, we found the same pattern held for the timing of normal transitions. In addition, Robinson and Smith-Lovin (1991) found spell duration dependence in turn-taking roughly in the form of a log-logistic distribution. The risk of a transition rises across the first five words of a turn and then drops steadily. There is some indication that the risk may increase again toward the tail of the turn-length distribution.

Examining Patterns of Interaction

In addition to assessing the time dependence on the rate of transition between states, event-history methods allow estimation of the effects of covariates on the timing of events. Log-logistic models were estimated for the overall rate of transitions using the LIFEREG procedure in SAS. The final model of covariates influencing the overall rate of transitions is reported in Table 6.3. The dependent variable here is the survival rate, a function of the "waiting time" until an event, and so the coefficients can be interpreted as reflecting a covariate's influence on length of a speaker turn. Because of the noted relationship between the survival rate and hazard rate, the effects of the coefficients can be roughly reversed to consider their effects on the hazard rate, or the risk of an event occurring.

As mentioned previously, smooth transitions were the norm in these conversations, far outnumbering any type of abnormal speaker transition. If we look at all speaking turns, we see that gender composition of the group had no effect on the length of conversational turns. However, males tended to keep the speaking floor longer when followed by other male speakers. Looking at the other equations we see this is not simply due to males failing to interrupt one another. On the contrary, we see both that males are allowed longer turns when followed by other males in normal or overlapped transitions, but there was no such effect on male-male interrupted transitions. In addition, there is a lower risk of over-

TABLE 6.3. The effects of gender on the duration of a turn.

	All turns	Normal turns	Interrupted turns	Overlapped turns
Intercept	1.84**	1.96**	5.24**	4.98**
Single	0.03	0.02	−0.11	0.70**
Female-female	0.00	0.03	0.58**	−0.02
Female-male	0.03	0.01	0.48*	−0.02
Male-male	0.18**	0.14**	0.14	0.65**
Scale	0.62	0.65	0.95	0.92
Log likelihood	−8,542.71	−8,217.84	−1,524.27	−1,071.54

Note. Single is coded 1 = single-sex groups and 0 = mixed-sex groups. The dyad gender variables are coded 1 if true, and 0 otherwise. The reference category is the dyad male-female.
*Significant at the .05 level.
**Significant at the .01 level.

lapping speech in the same-gender conversations. The effects of the dyad variables on the rates of interruptions tell us that females are at a higher risk of being interrupted by both males and females, but that males aren't necessarily more likely to do the interrupting. Finally, by looking at the scale factor on these equations we see that for normal turns, the longer a turn lasts the higher its immediate risk of ending; there is no time dependence for turns ending abnormally.

Maintaining Identities Through Conversation

In this chapter, we have proposed a new theoretical approach as a guide to understanding the role of gender in conversational interaction. This approach has the advantages of being compatible with several earlier theoretical traditions in this area and offering a method of integrating some of their core ideas, as well as providing a much needed dynamic framework from which to analyze social interaction. Affect control theory relies on a simple sociological mechanism—the maintenance of cultural meaning—and the assumption that the important aspects of this meaning are captured within the affective dimensions of evaluation, potency, and activity.

Affect control simulations assessing responses to identity-disconfirming behavior allowed us to predict how actors would use conversational strategies to maintain identities through interaction. Both males and females view Male Students as more powerful and not quite so nice as Female Students. We thus argue that gender (when salient) influences our patterns of interactions by serving as an identity with certain levels of status, power, and expressivity to be maintained. Affect control also allows us to model the fact that there are gender differences in the strength of these sentiments: within an interaction between a Male Student and a Female Student, the Male Student may be striving to maintain a set of sentiments for the Female Student that differ from the sentiments she herself is attempting to maintain. Males' sentiments about gender identities are more extreme than females'; they see females as much nicer and less powerful than males.

To maintain these affective beliefs then, affect control theory predicts that both males and females will be less tolerant of females who dominate a conversational interaction, and that males will be less tolerant of either males or females who attempt to maintain conversational dominance over them. Although the data presented to illustrate these implications were not used for hypothesis-testing purposes, the results were suggestive of identity maintenance processes.

In analyses of conversations within 29 six-person groups, we found that males allowed other males to hold the speaking floor for longer periods than they allowed females to hold the floor. Females made no such distinction, but ran a much higher risk of having the floor yanked from them through an interruption than did their male counterparts. As predicted by affect control simulations, the longer a speaking turn went on, the higher its risk of ending. This was not the case with interruptions. These findings give us the image of interruptions being used not as a form of domination or a method of withholding floor time from lower power speakers, but as a method of maintaining the structure of the conversation. Interruptions and overlaps are used to prevent speakers from monopolizing the conversation to an extent that would be disconfirming to the identities involved.

The most notable difference between affect control predictions and our findings was that males were not more likely than females to interrupt other males. In other words, although affect control simulations predicted that females would be more tolerant than males of male conversational dominance, in fact both genders were extremely patient with long-winded male speakers. One reason for this discrepancy may lie in the determination of "how long is too long" for a male speaker to keep the floor in these group conversations. It may be that males are less tolerant than females when other male speakers dominate the conversation, but that it takes substantially more for the turn of a male speaker to be defined as "too long."

To take full advantage of predictions based on the affect control model, we would need more information about the sentiments actually elicited by the behaviors and the identities within the group interactions. We know that the same behavior can be interpreted as verbally aggressive by one and as lively and involved by another (e.g., Murray, 1985; Tannen, 1983). Further, having access to information about the salient identities of the actors involved should lead to more accurate modeling of their interaction consequences.

To really exploit the modeling capabilities of affect control theory, we would want to measure the emotional responses of the actors as they engaged in interaction. According to our model, such emotional responses would provide to participants as social actors, and to us as researchers, information about how these interactions are confirming or disconfirming the identities involved. Modeling conversational interactions at this level of detail would not only increase the accuracy of our ability to predict the behavior of men and women in interaction, but it would supply a richness to our understanding of these interaction processes that goes beyond the current literature on conversational interaction.

Conclusion

From our review of the literature on gender and language use, we conclude that socialization, sex-segregated peer group culture, status, and power all serve to shape gender-salient interactions. We think that a multidimensional conception of gender identity is necessary to encompass both the nonhierarchical and hierarchical elements of gender interactions.

We also advocate a dynamic approach that allows the explicit modeling of the interconnectedness of events. It is encouraging to see that such dynamic models are developing in approaches focusing on status (Fisek, Berger, & Norman, in press) and on structural power (Molm, 1990). We hope that the affect control approach will provide a model for integrating both the multidimensional view of gender and the dynamic view of social behavior.

One of the most important issues facing affect control theory is the general problem of when gender identities become salient. Clearly, males and females can act very similarly when they are placed in secure, similar roles within a group. Both men and women can be effective leaders or supportive followers. This is a strong indication that other identities can overwhelm gender identities in very structured contexts. On the other hand, gender identities appear to become salient in some circumstances that we might not expect. They are spontaneously aroused in normal, mixed-sex interaction; but they also appear in some same-sex interactions, perhaps when a task, an institutional context, or a developmental stage makes gender an especially salient issue. More careful attention to the issue of when gender identities become salient is necessary for affect control research. This attention to salience issues would also be useful for research in the status characteristics tradition, and in determining when gender will alter behavior within a power structure.

Finally, we urge further attention to developmental issues in early childhood. Affect control theory argues that gender identities must be developed quite early (prior to age 3) to generate the gender differentiated behavior that appears at these early ages. All of the other approaches—culture, socialization, status, and power—also require that *some* social process would differentiate males and females prior to that age (to produce the differences in the behavior). Detailed studies of children during the critical age period from 2 to 3 are necessary to establish what information they come to link with the newly forming categories "male" and "female." Affect control theory predicts a three-dimensional affective meaning, communicated through emotional expression and behavioral interactions. The socialization perspective predicts a set of behavioral expectations associated with the social roles of male and female. The cultural perspective is frankly perplexed by the source of gender homophily in play groups, and implies some sort of essentialist differences in male and female play behavior (perhaps driven by activity differences). Status and power perspectives draw our attention to expectations of competence and power associated with the male and female roles. Only detailed developmental studies can help us distinguish between these possibilities and solve the problem of how gender differences in language use actually arise.

Acknowledgments. The authors thank Annette Lee, Brian Roitman, and Suzanne Ryan for help in coding the data, Arthur Williams for creating transcripts of the videotaped group discussions, and Charlotte Hudson for laboratory assistance in the original data collection. Miller McPherson and Cecilia Ridgeway offered helpful comments at several stages of the project. Preparation of this manuscript was supported by National Science Foundation grant SES 9008951 to the first author.

References

Anderson, L.R., & Blanchard, P.N. (1982, June). Sex differences in task and social-emotional behavior. *Basic and Applied Social Psychology, 3*(2), 109–140.

Aries, E.J., Gold, C., & Weigel, R.H. (1983). Dispositional and situational influences on dominance behavior in small groups. *Journal of Personality and Social Psychology, 44*, 779–786.

Bales, R.F. (1950). *Interaction process analysis: A method for the study of small groups.* Cambridge, MA: Addison-Wesley.

Bales, R.F. (1953). The equilibrium problem in small groups. In T. Parsons, R.F. Bales, & E.A. Shils (Eds.), *Working papers in the theory of action* (pp. 111–161). Glencoe, IL: Free Press.

Bales, R.F. (1970). *Personality and interpersonal behavior.* New York: Holt, Rinehart.

Bales, R.F. (1980). *SYMLOG: Case study kit.* New York: Free Press.

Bales, R.F., & Cohen, S.P. (1979). *SYMLOG: A system for the multiple level observation of groups.* New York: Free Press.

Bales, R.F., & Slater, P.E. (1955). Role differentiation in small decision-making groups. In T. Parsons & P.E. Slater (Eds.), *The family, socialization and interaction processes* (pp. 259–306). Glencoe, IL: Free Press.

Beattie, G. (1982). Look, just don't interrupt. *New Scientist, 95*, 859–860.

Berger, J., Conner, T.L., & Fisek, M.H. (1974). *Expectation states theory: A theoretical research program.* Cambridge, MA: Winthrop.

Berger, J., Fisek, M.H., Norman, R.Z., & Zelditch, M., Jr. (1977). *Status characteristics and social interaction.* New York: Elsevier.

Berger, J., Rosenholtz, S.J., & Zelditch, M., Jr. (1980). Status organizing processes. *Annual Review of Sociology, 6*, 479–508.

Bradley, P.H. (1981). The folk-linguistics of women's speech: An empirical examination. *Communication Monographs, 48*, 73–90.

Brouwer, D., Gerritsen, M., & De Haan, D. (1979). Speech differences between men and women: On the wrong track? *Language in Society, 6*, 313–322.

Carli, L.L. (1990). Gender, language and influence. *Journal of Personality and Social Psychology, 59*(5), 941–951.

Carroll, G. (1983). Dynamic analysis of discrete dependent variables: A didactic essay. *Quality and Quantity, 17*, 425–460.

Cota, A.A. & Dion, K.L. (1986). Salience of gender and sex composition of ad hoc groups: An experimental test of distinctiveness theory. *Journal of Personality and Social Psychology, 50*(4), 770–776.

Courtwright, J.A., Millar, F.E., & Rogers-Millar, L.E. (1979, August). Domineeringness and dominance: Replication and expansion. *Communication Monographs, 46*, 179–192.

Crosby, F., & Nyquist, L. (1977). The female register: An empirical study of Lakoff's hypothesis. *Language in Society, 6*, 313–322.

Drass, K.A. (1986, December). The effect of gender identity on conversation. *Social Psychology Quarterly, 49*, 294–301.

Eakins, B.W., & Eakins, R.G. (1978). *Sex differences in human communication.* Boston: Houghton Mifflin.

Eagly, A.H., & Johnson, B.T. (1990). Gender and leadership style. *Psychological Bulletin, 108*(2), 233–256.

Ekman, P., Friesen, W.V., & Ellsworth, P. (1972). *Emotion in the human face.* New York: Pergamon.

Ellemers, N., Van Knippenberg, A., Devries, N., & Wilke, H. (1988). Social identification and permeability of group boundaries. *European Journal of Social Psychology, 18*, 497–513.

Fisek, M.H. (1974). A model for the evolution of status structures in task-oriented discussion groups. In J. Berger, T. Conner, & M.H. Fisek (Eds.), *Expectation states theory: A theoretical research program* (pp. 53–84). Cambridge, MA: Winthrop.

Fisek, M.H., Berger, J., & Norman, R.Z. (1991). Participation in heterogenous and homogenous groups: A theoretical integration. *American Journal of Sociology, 97*, 114–142.

Fleischer, R.A., & Chertkoff, J.M. (1986). Effects of dominance and sex on leader selection in dyadic work groups. *Journal of Personality and Social Psychology, 50*(1), 94–99.

Gilligan, C. (1982). *In a different voice: Psychological theory and women's development.* Cambridge, MA: Harvard University Press.

Heise, D.R. (1979). *Understanding events: Affect and the construction of social action.* New York: Cambridge University Press.

Heise, D.R. (1988). Affect control theory: Concepts and model. In L. Smith-Lovin & D.R. Heise (Eds.), *Analyzing social interaction: Advances in affect control theory* (pp. 1–34). New York: Gordon and Breach Science Publishers.

Heise, D.R., & Lewis, E. (1988). *Introduction to INTERACT.* National Collegiate Software Clearinghouse, Box 8101, North Carolina State University, Raleigh, NC 27695.

Hirschman, L. (1973). *Female-male differences in conversational interaction.* Paper presented at Linguistic Society of America, San Diego.

Jupp, T.C., Roberts, C., & Cook-Gumperz, J. (1982). Language and disadvantage: the hidden process. In J.J. Gumpertz (Ed.), *Language and social identity* (pp. 232–256). New York: Cambridge.

Kollock, P., Blumstein, P., & Schwartz, P. (1985). Sex and power in interaction. *American Sociological Review, 50*, 34–47.

Lakoff, R. (1975). *Language and women's place.* New York: Harper and Row.

Lever, J. (1976). Sex differences in the games children play. *Social Problems, 23*, 478–483.

Lewis, G.H. (1972). Role differentiation. *American Sociological Review, 37*, 424–434.

Maccoby, E.E. (1988). Gender as a social category. *Developmental Psychology, 26*, 755–765.

Maccoby, E.E. (1990). Gender and relationships: A developmental account. *American Psychologist, 45*(4), 513–520.

Maltz, D.N., & Borker, R.A. (1982). A cultural approach to male-female miscommunication. In J.J. Gumpertz (Ed.), *Language and social identity* (pp. 196–216). New York: Cambridge University Press.

Mazur, A. (1985, December). A biosocial model of status in face-to-face groups. *Social Forces, 64*(2), 377–402.

Mazur, A., & Cataldo, M. (1989). Dominance and deference in conversation. *Journal of Social Biological Structures, 11*, 377–402.

McCarrick, A.K., Manderscheid, R.W., & Sibergeld, S. (1981). Gender differences in competition and dominance during married-couples group therapy. *Social Psychology Quarterly, 44*, 164–177.

McConnell-Ginet, S. (1975). Our father tongue: Essays in linguistic politics. *Diacritics, 4*, 44–50.

McLaughlin, M.L., Cody, M.J., Kane, M.L., & Robey, C.S. (1981). Sex differences in story receipt and story sequencing behaviors in dyadic conversations. *Human Communication Research, 7*, 99–116.

McMillan, J.R., Clifton, A.K., McGrath, D., & Gale, W.S. (1977). Women's language: Uncertainty or interpersonal sensitivity and emotionality? *Sex Roles, 3*, 545–559.

McPherson, M., & Smith-Lovin, L. (1986). Sex segregation in voluntary associations. *American Sociological Review, 51*, 61–79.

McPherson, M., & Smith-Lovin, L. (1987). Homophily in voluntary organizations: Status distance and the composition of face to face groups. *American Sociological Review, 52*, 370–379.

Megargee, E.I. (1969). Influence of sex roles on the manifestation of leadership. *Journal of Applied Psychology, 53*, 377–382.

Molm, L.D. (1990). Structure, action and outcomes: The dynamics of power in social exchange. *American Sociological Review, 55*, 427–447.

Murray, S.O. (1985). Toward a model of members' methods for recognizing interruptions. *Language in Society, 14*, 031–040.

Murray, S.O., & Covelli, L.H. (1988). Women and men speaking at the same time. *Journal of Pragmatics, 12*, 103–111.

Ng, S.H., & Cram, F. (1988). Intergroup bias by defensive and offensive groups in majority and minority conditions. *Journal of Personality and Social Psychology, 55*(5), 749–757.

Osgood, C.E., Suci, G.C., & Tannenbaum, P.H. (1957). *The measurement of meaning*. Urbana: University of Illinois Press.

Parker, K.C.H. (1988). Speaking turns in small group interaction: A context-sensitive event sequence model. *Journal of Personality and Social Psychology, 54*(6), 965–971.

Parsons, T. (1951). *The social system*. Glencoe, IL: Free Press.

Parsons, T., & Bales, F.F. (1955). *Family, socialization and interaction process*. Glencoe, IL: Free Press.

Ridgeway, C.L. (1981, June). Nonconformity, competence and influence in groups: A test of two theories. *American Sociological Review, 46*, 333–347.

Ridgeway, C.L. (1982, February). Status in groups: The importance of motivation. *American Sociological Review, 47*(1), 76–88.

Ridgeway, C.L. (1988). Gender differences in task groups: A status and legitimacy account. In M. Webster Jr. & M. Foschi (Eds.), *Status generalization:*

New theory and research (pp. 188–206). Stanford, CA: Stanford University Press.

Ridgeway, C. (1991). *The social construction of status value: Gender and other nominal characteristics*. *Social Forces*, 70.

Ridgeway, C., & Johnson, J. (1990). What is the relationship between socio-emotional behavior and status in task groups? *American Journal of Sociology*, 95, 1189–1212.

Riedesel, P.L. (1974). Bales reconsidered: A critical analysis of popularity and leadership differentiation. *Sociometry*, 37(4), 557–564.

Robinson, D.T., & Smith-Lovin, L. (1990). Timing of interruptions in group discussions. In E.J. Lawler, B. Markovsky, C. Ridgeway, & H. Walker (Eds.), *Advances in group processes: Theory and research* (Vol. 11). Greenwich, CT: JAI Press.

Robinson, D.T., & Smith-Lovin, L. (1991). *Identity maintenance and affect control in group discussions*. Paper presented at the American Sociological Association meetings, Cincinati, Ohio.

Roger, D.B., & Nesshoever, W. (1987). Individual differences in dyadic conversational strategies: A further study. *British Journal of Social Psychology*, 26, 247–255.

Roger, D.B., & Schumacher, A. (1983). Effects of individual differences on dyadic conversational strategies. *Journal of Personality and Social Psychology*, 45, 700–705.

Sacks, H., Schegloff, E., & Jefferson, G. (1974). A simplest systematics for the organization of turn-taking for conversation. *Language*, 50, 696–735.

Smith-Lovin, L. (1987a). Impressions from events. *Journal of Mathematical Sociology*, 13(1–2), 35–70.

Smith-Lovin, L. (1987b). The affective control of events within settings. *Journal of Mathematical Sociology*, 13(1–2), 71–102.

Smith-Lovin, L. (1990). Emotion as confirmation and disconfirmation of identity: An affect control model. In T.D. Kemper (Ed.), *Research agendas in emotions*. New York: SUNY Press.

Smith-Lovin, L., & Brody, C. (1989). Interruptions in group discussions: The effects of gender and group composition. *American Sociological Review*, 54, 425–435.

Smith-Lovin, L. & Heise, D.R. (Eds.), (1988). *Analyzing social interaction: Advances in affect control theory*. New York: Gordon and Breach Science Publishers.

Smith-Lovin, L., & McPherson, J.M. (1991). You are who you know: A network perspective on gender. In P. England (Ed.), *Theory on gender feminism on theory*. New York: Aldine.

Smith-Lovin, L., Skvoretz, J., & Hudson, C. (1986). Status and participation in six-person groups: A test of Skvoretz's comparative status model. *Social Forces*, 64, 992–1005.

Stewart, P. (1988). Women and men in groups: A status characteristics approach to interaction. In M. Webster Jr. & M. Foschi (Eds.), *Status generalization* (pp. 69–85). Stanford: Stanford University Press.

Strodbeck, F.L., & Mann, R.D. (1956). Sex role differentiation in jury deliberations. *Sociometry*, 19, 3–11.

Tannen, D. (1980). *Toward a theory of conversational style: The machine-gun question*. Sociolinguistics Working Paper No. 73. Austin, TX: Southwest Educational Development Library.

Tannen, D. (1982). Ethnic style in male-female conversation. In J.J. Gumpertz (Ed.), *Language and social identity* (pp. 217–231). New York: Cambridge.

Tannen, D. (1983). When is an overlap not an interruption? One component of conversational style. In R.J. DiPietro, W. Frawley, & A. Wedel (Eds.), *The first symposium on language studies: Selected papers* (pp. 119–129). Newark: University of Delaware Press.

Tuma, N.B., & Hannan, M.T. (1978). Approaches to the censoring problem in analysis of event histories. In K.F. Schuessler (Ed.), *Sociological methodology 1979*. San Francisco: Jossey-Bass.

Tuma, N.B., & Hannan, M.T. (1984). *Social dynamics*. New York: Academic Press.

Vuchinich, S. (1984). Sequencing and social structure in family conflict. *Social Psychology Quarterly*, *47*(3), 217–234.

Vuchinich, S. (1986). On attenuation in verbal family conflict. *Social Psychology Quarterly*, *49*(4), 281–293.

Wagner, D.G. (1988). Gender inequalities in groups: A situational approach. In M. Webster Jr. & M. Foschi (Eds.), *Status generalization: New theory and research* (pp. 55–68). Stanford, CA: Stanford University Press.

Wagner, D.G., Ford, R.S., & Ford, T.W. (1986, Febraury). Can gender inequalities be reduced? *American Sociological Review*, *51*, 47–61.

Wasserman, G.A., & Stern, D.N. (1978). An early manifestation of differential behavior toward children of the same and opposite sex. *Journal of Genetic Psychology*, *133*, 129–137.

West, C. (1984). When the doctor is a "lady": Power, status and gender in physician-patient exchanges. *Symbolic Interaction*, *7*, 87–106.

West, C., & Zimmerman, D.H. (1977). Women's place in everyday talk: Reflections on parent-child interaction. *Social Problems*, *24*(5), 521–529.

Wood, W., & Karten, S.J. (1986). Sex differences in interaction style as a product of perceived sex differences in competence. *Journal of Personality and Social Psychology*, *50*(2), 341–347.

Zimmerman, D.H., & West, C. (1975). Sex roles, interruptions and silences in conversations. In B. Thorne & N. Henley (Eds.), *Language and sex: Difference and dominance* (pp. 105–129). Rowley, MA: Newbury House.

7
Are Gender Differences Status Differences?

CECILIA L. RIDGEWAY AND DAVID DIEKEMA

Are gender differences in interaction a result of women's lower status and power in society as a whole? A number of researchers have argued that they are (Berger, Rosenholtz, & Zelditch, 1980; Fishman, 1978; Hall, 1972; Henley, 1977; Lockheed, 1985; West & Zimmerman, 1977; Zimmerman & West, 1975). To anyone whose motive for studying gender differences is to understand gender inequality, status explanations are powerful and appealing. They promise to explain how inequality in society structures interaction and how the resulting inequalities in interaction perpetuate gender stratification in society. The consequence is an increase in our understanding not only of interaction, but of the larger process of gender inequality.

Recently, however, the status approach to gender and interaction has been attacked on both conceptual and empirical grounds. The central conceptual criticism is that status and power explanations are too narrow in focus and, in a sense, too simple to account for gender's diverse effects on interaction (Eagly, 1987; Hall, 1984; Maltz & Borker, 1982). The empirical criticism arises from recent evidence that some gender differences are actually smaller in mixed-sex interaction than they are between male and female same-sex interaction (Carli, 1989, 1990; Hall, 1984; Piliavin & Martin 1978). As some have noted, the status approach does not provide a clear explanation for such results (Carli, 1989; Hall, 1984).

This chapter examines complaints against the status approach and makes a case for its continuing importance as an explanation for gender differences in interaction. In the first section we describe the status approach to gender differences and criticisms against it, using expectation states theory (Berger, Conner, & Fisek, 1974; Berger, Fisek, Norman, & Zelditch, 1977) as the exemplar of the approach. The next section examines two alternatives, the gender subcultures explanation (Maccoby, 1990; Maltz & Borker, 1982) and Eagly's (1987) role theory. Contrasting these alternatives with the status approach reveals important strengths in the status explanation. The third section of the chapter attempts to meet the criticisms against the status approach. We link expectation states theory to concepts from other approaches to provide an expanded account that preserves the advantages of a status explanation while offering a broader and empirically more adequate account of gender differences in interaction.

Gender Differences and the Status Approach

Evidence has accumulated for several decades that men talk more, are talked to more, and are more influential over group opinion than women (Becker, 1986; Eagly & Carli, 1981; Eagly & Wood, 1985; Hall, 1984; Meeker & Weitzel-O'Neill 1977; Strodtbeck & Mann, 1956). Men are also more likely than women to become group leaders (Bartol & Martin, 1986; Brown, 1979; Eagly & Karau, 1991; Strodtbeck & Mann, 1956). In task-oriented discussions, men devote a somewhat higher proportion of their speech to task concerns (e.g., giving or asking for information, suggestions, or opinions) and a lower proportion to positive socioemotional behavior (e.g., showing support, satisfaction, understanding, giving help, and agreeing) compared to women (Anderson & Blanchard, 1982; Borgatta & Stimson, 1963; Carli, 1982, 1989; Piliavin & Martin, 1978). Men interrupt more than women and are less likely than women to yield to an interrupter (Kollack, Blumstein, & Schwartz, 1985; Smith-Lovin & Brody, 1989; West, 1984; Zimmerman & West, 1975). Women, on the other hand, are more nonverbally expressive than men and more skilled at reading nonverbal cues (Hall, 1984). They also smile and gaze more at other people than men and are gazed at more in return (Hall, 1984).

The traditional explanation for these differences holds that men and women have different stable personality traits acquired as a result of gender-typed socialization. The evidence, however, suggests that men's and women's assertive behavior is highly variable from situation to situation which is inconsistent with the stable dispositions argument (Meeker & Weitzel-O'Neill, 1977; Wagner, 1988). Furthermore, efforts to test this explanation have not been successful. Wood and Karten (1986), found no relationship between masculinity or femininity of personality and behavior in interaction. A number of studies have shown that the personality trait of dominance, often considered a male stereotypic trait, cannot account for gender differences in leader selection. Even when a high-dominance woman is paired with a low-dominance man, the man still is more likely to be selected leader than the woman (Carbonell, 1984; Fleischer & Chertkoff, 1986; Megaree, 1969; Nyquist & Spence, 1986).

Status explanations address these inadequacies by pointing out that many gender differences in interaction are related to the exercise of power and influence within the interactional setting. A person who talks more, contributes more task suggestions and is more influential obviously has more power and prestige in the interaction than someone who is lower on these behaviors (Berger et al., 1980; Hall, 1972; Meeker & Weitzel-O'Neill, 1977). Similarly, although interruptions can serve many functions, they are clearly related to control of the conversation (Kollack et al., 1985; Smith-Lovin & Brody, 1989; West & Zimmerman, 1977; Zimmerman & West, 1975). And it is just these behaviors on which gender differences favor men. Henley (1977) further argues that many gender differences in nonverbal behavior reflect men's exercise of power over women.

The fact that many of the behaviors on which gender differences occur are those by which power and prestige is exercised in interaction suggests that they reflect power dynamics rather than gender dynamics per se. That is, these interactional differences are not produced by any gender-based differences in personality or ability. They are caused by men's greater power and status in society as a whole, which induces men to enact greater power and prestige in interaction as well. Because these interactional differences between men and women reflect power dynamics rather than processes unique to gender, they should be similar to the interactional differences produced by other power differences, such as that between parents and children or doctors and patients. Furthermore, since these behaviors are caused by situational power and prestige, a given individual's behavior should vary from context to context as his or her situational power and prestige changes. As will be seen, this is generally consistent with the evidence.

Status and power approaches provide a better account of the situational variability of men's and women's assertive behavior than traditional personality explanations. Just as important, they shift the explanatory focus from individual characteristics to the dynamics of interpersonal power and prestige and its relationship to gender stratification in society.

Several different versions of the status and power explanation have been proposed (e.g., Fishman, 1978; Hall, 1972; Henley, 1977; Meeker & Weitzel-O'Neill, 1977; West & Zimmerman, 1977). However, by far the most conceptually developed and empirically documented is the version offered by expectation states theory (Berger et al., 1974; Berger et al., 1977; Berger et al., 1980; Hall, 1972; Pugh & Wahrman, 1983; Wagner, Ford, & Ford, 1986). Because we will use the expectation states version as the exemplar of the status approach to gender and interaction, a brief summary is in order.

Expectation States Theory

Expectation states theory limits its analysis to situations where interactants are oriented toward a collective goal or task. This restriction is not too severe since most of the evidence about gender differences we seek to explain comes from task-oriented discussion or decision-making groups.

Also, much interaction that is goal oriented has significant consequences for social inequality.

The theory argues that power and prestige in task-oriented interaction is determined by the performance expectations formed for one interactant compared to another (Berger et al., 1974). A performance expectation is an anticipation of how useful a person's contributions to the task are likely to be. It is roughly equivalent to inferred task competence. The higher the performance expectation held for one interactant compared to another, the more opportunities that person will be given to speak, the more assertive and confident the person's nonverbal cues are likely to be, the more task suggestions the person will make, the greater the likelihood that these suggestions will be positively evaluated, and the more influential the person will be compared to the other (Berger et al., 1974; Ridgeway, Berger, & Smith, 1985). In this way, rank-ordered performance expectations held for self and others drives interactants' behavior in such a way as to confirm these expectations. This produces a behavioral hierarchy of power and prestige that reflects the order of performance expectations.

According to expectation states theory, gender shapes interactional behavior by affecting the performance expectations formed for women compared to men (Berger et al., 1977; Berger et al., 1980). Gender is a status characteristic in our society in that widely held beliefs attach more esteem, honor, and importance to men than women. Like other status characteristics such as race or occupation, gender status carries beliefs that those with the higher state of the characteristic (men) will be diffusely more competent than those with the lower state (women). When gender is made salient in the situation, either by differentiating among the members or by being relevant to the task, these diffuse competence beliefs are activated and affect the performance expectations formed for men and women. Once activated, gender status will affect performance expectations even when irrelevant to the task. However, its impact is stronger when it is made relevant by a sex-typed task.

In addition to status characteristics, performance expectations are affected by interactants' reputations for specific abilities, the reward levels they receive, feedback on performance, and their behavior in the situation (Berger et al., 1974; Berger & Zelditch, 1985). The effects of these factors, each weighted by its task relevance, combine to produce aggregate performance expectations for the interactants. As a consequence, the effect of gender status on power and prestige will be conditioned by other factors also operating in the particular situation.

The expectation states formulation addresses complaints leveled at the "oppression hypothesis," as some versions of the status approach have been called (Eagly, 1987; Hall, 1984; Maltz & Borker, 1982). First, because it specifically argues that gender combines with other determinants of power and prestige in interaction, it does not predict that any man will have power over any woman or that women will never have power over men. Second, it describes a clear mechanism by which men's dominance in the social system affects interactional behavior rather than merely assuming that this must occur. Finally, it explains men's greater influence and prestige in interaction without necessarily assuming that men intend to dominate women in interaction (or that women intend to defer). The hierarchy develops out of interactants' shared interest in the task independently of their other intentions toward one another. Since performance expectations are often implicit, out-of-awareness assumptions, interactants are frequently unaware of the processes by which the power and prestige order emerges.

In addition to these conceptual strengths, the expectation states formulation does an excellent job of predicting task-related behavior in mixed-sex interaction. Consistent with the evidence, it predicts that, other factors equal, women in mixed-sex interaction will speak less, offer fewer task suggestions, receive fewer agreements from others, be interrupted more, and be less nonverbally assertive and less influential than men (Anderson & Blanchard, 1982; Carli, 1982; Dovidio, Brown, Heltman, Ellyson, & Reating, 1988; Eagly, 1983; Hall, 1972; Major, Schmidlin, & Williams, 1990; Meeker & Weitzel-O'Neill, 1977; Ridgeway et al., 1985; Smith-Lovin & Brody, 1989). In addition, as the theory proposes, there is evidence that gender does create differential expectations for competence and that these mediate gender differences in task-related behaviors (Berger et al., 1980; Wood & Karten, 1986). Altering the competence expectations held for men and women in mixed-sex interaction alters their behavior and influence accordingly (Piliavin & Martin, 1978; Pugh & Wahrman, 1983; Wagner et al., 1986; Wood & Karten, 1986). Finally, the theory provides an account of women's lesser tendency to emerge as leaders in mixed-sex settings (Eagly & Karau, 1991) independent of personality dispositions such as dominance.

Expectation states theory makes some unique predictions about mixed-sex interaction whose empirical confirmation is especially telling. It predicts that when the task is male-typed, men's advantage in task behaviors and influence will be exaggerated. However, when the task is female-typed, the competence implications of gender status are reversed, and women should actually have an advantage over men in task behavior and influence. Evidence indicates that both these patterns actually do occur (Dovidio et al., 1988; Wentworth & Anderson, 1984; Yamada, Tjosvold, & Draguns 1983). In a striking confirmation, Dovidio et al. (1988) found that men in mixed-sex dyads showed a higher verbal and nonverbal power style than women, and when the task was male-typed, these behavioral differences became even stronger. Men spoke even longer, initiated more speech, gestured more, and looked less while listening than their women partners, all behaviors previously related to power and assumed competence. Then, when the same dyads turned to a female-typed task, these patterns of behavior *reversed*. Women spoke more, initiated more speech, gestured more, and looked more while speaking and less while listening than their male partners. That the hierarchy actually reverses is strongly supportive of the expectation states explanation.

Expectation states theory provides a thorough and accurate account of gender's impact on power and prestige in mixed-sex encounters. It is an account that explicitly and elegantly connects the development of gender inequality in interaction with women's lesser status value in society as a whole. Yet despite these strengths, shortcomings have become evident that have increasingly called into question the status approach to gender and interaction.

Recent Criticisms

Two major criticisms have developed around the status approach, as exemplified by expectation states theory. First, it has been criticized for limiting its scope to task-related behavior and the power dynamics they engender. Several of the behaviors more characteristic of women in interaction bear an uncertain relation to power. Women's greater non-verbal skill and expressiveness, smiling, and positive socioemotional behavior may have a power component, but the data suggest that more is involved (e.g., Carli, 1990; Hall, 1984). To most they reflect a separate socioemotional dimension to interaction that cannot be explained by a simple status approach (Eagly, 1987; Hall, 1984).

The second criticism of the status approach arises from certain contradictory evidence in same-sex groups. Expectation states theory predicts that gender status will not be salient and affect performance expectations in same-sex groups unless the task is sex-typed. Recently Ridgeway (1988) has suggested that gender may also become salient if the organizational authority structure that delegates the group task is disproportionately of the opposite sex from the members of a same-sex group. This could account for the activation of gender status in all-female groups within a predominantly male organizational structure. Except for these special activation conditions, however, the theory predicts greater gender effects in mixed-sex groups than same-sex groups.

The problem is that evidence indicates certain behavioral differences are actually greater between men and women in same-sex groups than they are in mixed-sex groups. Although men generally devote a higher percentage of their speech to task behaviors unaccompanied by affect than women and women show higher rates of positive socioemotional behavior than men, these differences are actually smaller in mixed-sex interaction than between same-sex groups (Carli, 1989, 1990; Piliavin & Martin, 1978).[1] Because Carli (1989, 1990) used a gender-neutral task,

---

[1] Wood and Rhodes (Chapter 5, this volume) note that the coding scheme on which these results are based scores a behavior as socioemotional if it contains

her results cannot be explained by the task activation of gender status in same-sex dyads.[2] Hall (1984) argues that because there is a tendency for one to receive more of the same nonverbal behavior one engages in, greater gender differences in same- rather than mixed-sex groups may also characterize certain nonverbal behaviors. In its present formulation, expectation states theory offers no clear explanation for these results.

These problems of scope and empirical adequacy have caused some to question the entire status approach to gender differences in interaction (Eagly, 1987; Hall, 1984; Maltz & Borker, 1982). Hall (1984), for instance, suggests that something entirely apart from status may be affecting interaction among and between women and men. In response to such dissatisfaction, two major alternative explanations have been offered. The first argues that gender-segregated cultural norms of communication account for interactional differences between women and men (Maltz & Borker, 1982). The second proposes that social roles acting in the situation, which include but are not limited to gender roles, account for gender differences in interaction (Eagly, 1987). We will consider each of these alternatives in turn.

Alternative Explanations

The Cultural Approach

Maltz and Borker (1982) argue that people learn rules for interacting with "peers" (those who are not formal superiors or subordinates) from peer-group interaction in childhood. Childhood peer groups are gender segregated. Furthermore, because it is a period of gender-role learning, the

---

any affect. If women accompany a task behavior with affect (e.g., smiling or laughing), it is classified as socioemotional rather than task oriented. Consequently, it is possible that women do not actually devote any less of their speech to the task than men but rather, perform less task behavior that is *unaccompanied* by affect.

[2] Although Carli (1989) clearly shows greater differences between same-sex groups than within mixed-sex groups, she actually finds no gender differences in mixed-sex groups. Given the number of studies using the same coding scheme that do show gender effects in mixed-sex groups (Anderson & Blanchard, 1982; Wood & Karten, 1986), these results are anomalous. They may be due to the fact that, unlike previous studies, Carli used dyads. The pressure of maintaining conversation in dyads usually produces less differentiation in speech patterns than in larger groups. Because Carli only reports types of behaviors as a percentage of a subject's speech acts, there are no total participation or unconfounded influence measures that could indicate gender status effects in her mixed-sex dyads.

In a more recent study, Carli (1990) did find differences in mixed-sex groups—women used more tentative speech than men in mixed-sex groups but not in same-sex groups. But she also found that women used more intensifiers and verbal reinforcers (socioemotional behaviors) than men in same-sex groups but not in mixed-sex groups.

subcultures children develop in peer groups actively accentuate gender differences. As a result, the cultural rules of interaction men and women learn are different. Boys learn to use speech to assert positions of dominance and compete for attention. Girls learn to use speech to maintain relations of closeness and equality, to criticize in nonchallenging ways, and to accurately interpret each other's speech (see Maccoby, 1990).

In adulthood, argue Maltz and Borker, these different subcultural norms produce substantial differences between male and female same-sex interaction. Male groups focus around task and power concerns, female groups focus more on relationships. In mixed-sex interaction, men's and women's different cultural goals lead to substantial miscommunication. In response, men and women modify their behavior somewhat to deal with the other, producing less extreme behavioral differences than in same-sex groups.

Maltz and Borker's cultural explanation has not been directly tested or elaborated in any conceptual detail, although it has attracted considerable attention (see Maccoby, 1990). It is certainly intriguing and may prove informative about same-sex friendships. On the other hand, as a broad account of gender differences in interaction, particularly task-oriented interaction, it has several shortcomings. Most problematic is its assumption that gender-segregated rules for interaction learned in childhood remain unchanged through adulthood, despite the problems they cause in mixed-sex interaction. In our society, the rate of mixed-sex interaction in adulthood is very high. For example, even though jobs are highly sex segregated in terms of formal position or title, very few work environments are sex segregated in terms of actual interaction and social contact. How could separate cultures be maintained in the face of such repeated contact? Why wouldn't men and women continue to learn and change their expectations for interaction? Because men and women are hypothesized to adjust their behavior to one another, why do they not also take on one another's goals and expectations in mixed-sex interaction? Is it likely that the gender segregated subcultures of childhood persist as the primary determinant of mixed-sex interaction in adulthood?

A second problem is the content of male and female subcultures. No explanation is offered for why segregation in childhood peer groups would lead to such universal gender differences in talk, play, and interactive styles. Why wouldn't we see more random variation across different groups of boys and girls?[3] Why does it happen that male subculture

---

[3] On Maltz and Borker's (1982) and Maccoby's (1990) accounts, both boys and girls learn what it takes to influence others in many different contexts. Consequently, they learn the same interactive skills and, hence, have the same individual skills and behaviors available to them (Maccoby, 1990, p. 514). Yet Maccoby argues that gender segregation in childhood occurs because girls find it difficult to influence boys. If they have the same repertoire of skills, why should girls find it

focuses on power and inequality and female culture doesn't? Inequality is certainly a basic problem in female groups as well, just as male groups must grapple with closeness. Why then does the culture of one gender focus on one rather than the other? Proponents of the cultural approach must develop an answer to this question. Otherwise the approach risks devolving into an explanation based on stable gender-typed personality differences, even though cultural proponents themselves find this undesirable (Maccoby, 1990).

As we have already noted, stable personality traits such as dominance do not provide a good account of gender differences in interaction, but the cultural approach has a difficult time explaining the evidence in this regard. Male subculture should teach men to be concerned with dominance in interaction. But what if an individual female develops a high concern for dominance and an individual male a low interest in dominance? As Maltz and Borker (1982) note, this is a possibility for girls who play with boys or boys who play with girls. From the cultural approach, high-dominance females should demonstrate the same status concerns, tendencies to dominate, and interactive styles typical of males, whereas males low in dominance should show the socioemotional concerns typical of females. If these interactional styles mediate influence, a high-dominance female should gain status over a low-dominance male when they interact. But the evidence does not support this (Fleischer & Chertkoff, 1986; Megaree 1969; Nyquist & Spence, 1986). In a mixed-sex group with a low-dominance male and a high-dominance female, it is the male who is most likely to become the leader. Although high-dominance females in these studies do tend to display more dominance behaviors (Nyquist & Spence, 1986) and express a greater interest in leadership than low-dominance females (Fleisher & Chertkoff, 1986), they nevertheless are more likely to end up in the role of follower, not leader, in mixed-sex groups. Although these studies do not consititute a direct test of the cultural approach, they pose difficulties for it that are not raised for a status or social role interpretation.

Finally, the cultural approach does not give a very good account of women's behavior in task-oriented situations. In these situations, women in both same- and mixed-sex groups devote more than half of their behavior to giving and asking for task suggestions. In fact, their rate of

---

so difficult to influence boys unless they also learn that gender is differentially valued in society. Boys and girls may learn early on through direct experience and indirectly from authority figures that being a boy is more highly valued than being a girl. These different valuations become translated into expectations and behaviors that favor boys and disfavor girls in mixed-sex interaction and that frustrate girls' attempts to achieve influence in these contexts. What children learn, then, and what may contribute to the observed sex segregation of boys and girls, is that the paths to influence are different for boys and girls.

such behavior (unaccompanied by affect) is only about 8% lower than men's (Carli, 1982, 1989; Piliavin & Martin, 1978). The cultural approach tells us little about the majority of women's behavior in task groups. This is a serious shortcoming because many of the interactional differences we are seeking to explain are derived from task groups. In our view, then, the cultural approach as presently formulated does not provide a more adequate alternative to the status account of gender and interaction. It may, however, contain ideas that could be used to develop a more adequate account.

Eagly's Social Role Approach

Eagly (1987) has proposed a broad theory of gender differences that, although incorporating some ideas from the status approach, focuses on the situational roles men and women play rather than power dynamics as the cause of differences in their interactional behavior. She argues that people act in accord with the requirements of the roles they are assigned in a given situation. Our society's division of labor assigns the home-maker role almost exclusively to women and the role of paid worker, particularly well-paid worker, disproportionately to men. People form their gender role expectations from observing the actual activities that men and women engage in. What they see is men, because of their work roles, engaging in more *agentic* behaviors (task-oriented, directive be-haviors) than women, and women, due to their homemaker roles, en-acting more *communal* (interpersonally oriented) behaviors than men. Besides creating different gender role expectations, society's sexual divis-ion of labor creates gender-typed skills and beliefs by providing men and women with different experiences.

Eagly incorporates status by noting that the roles men play are higher status and wield more power in society than those assigned to women. Enacting high-status, superordinate roles requires more agentic behaviors than enacting low-status, subordinate roles. As a result, status differences contribute to stereotypes of women as less agentic than men.

With other recent analyses of gender and behavior (Deaux & Major, 1987), Eagly (1987) emphasizes the importance of *proximate* causes. Thus she argues that when a male lawyer interacts with his female secretary, it is their work roles that explain their behavior, not gender per se. In similar roles men and women act similarly. Gender role expectations determine behavior directly only when other roles in the situation are ambiguous. However, gender may indirectly affect the way people enact their roles by affecting the skills and beliefs one acquires.

Because roles assigned to research subjects are usually ambiguous, Eagly argues that gender role expectations are likely to be salient, causing men to engage in more agentic behavior and women in more communal behavior. If the subjects are assigned a task, this proximate demand will make both women and men primarily task oriented, but gender differences will occur within that context. In same-sex groups, whether or not gender expectations are specifically activated, women's and men's different skills and beliefs will produce gender differences in interaction. In this fashion, Eagly accounts for the evidence on gender and interaction.

Clearly, Eagly's theory is a much stronger contender to replace the status approach than is the gender subcultures argument. It gives an account of task- and power-related (agentic) behavior as well as socioemotional (communal) behavior, and it incorporates the effects of women's lower status in society. Eagly's is a broad-based theory of behavioral gender differences whereas expectation states theory is a broad-based theory of status processes that only deals with gender effects in influence- and status-related behaviors. Furthermore, despite differences in focus and approach between the two theories, many of their predictions about gender and interaction are compatible. Why then should a person interested in gender rather than status per se bother with the status approach? This is the next question we wish to address.

Roles Versus the Dynamics of Power and Prestige

Like Eagly, we believe that gender's impact on interaction is best explained in terms of proximate causes. We contend, however, that expectation states theory draws attention to an important cause of behavior in the situation that is even more proximate than Eagly's social roles. This more proximate cause is the emerging power and prestige hierarchy itself. That both women and men form power and prestige hierarchies after only minutes of interaction is well documented (Anderson & Blanchard, 1982; Bales, 1950; Fisek & Ofshe, 1970). The powerful impact of these hierarchies on the interactants' subsequent behavior is also well known (Berger et al., 1974).

Naturally, if the participants begin interaction with formally ordered roles (boss and secretary) these chiefly determine the interactional hierarchy. Even then, however, the interactional order must be enacted in the situation. It is the particular characteristics of that emergent order that govern future interaction, so that some secretaries, for instance, have much more influence over their bosses than others. When there are no preassigned roles, as in most research on gender and interaction, the emergent hierarchy is a particularly important determinant of behavior.

Because expectation states theory focuses on a more proximate cause of behavior in the situation, it is able to make more precise predictions about women's and men's task- and influence-related behavior than role theory. In particular, it can make important predictions about the way influence-related behavior will be constrained by proximal performance expectations independently of any gender-typed individual skills and concerns. This allows expectation states theory to predict some important power dynamics that Eagly's theory cannot.

Such a difference between the two theories' predictions can be seen most clearly when a mixed-sex group deals with a feminine task. In this situation, expectation states theory predicts that gender will be activated and, because of its task relevance, will become the basis for differentiated performance expectations and power and prestige behaviors favoring women. These specific task-based expectations will override the diffuse competency-based expectations favoring men and women will have the advantage over men in the developing hierarchy. We have seen that these predictions are consistent with the evidence (Dovidio et al., 1988; Wentworth & Anderson, 1984).

Although Eagly discusses mixed-sex groups working on a stereotypically female task, predictions of women's advantage over men are elusive in her social role interpretation because it does not incorporate the proximate effects of the emerging power and prestige hierarchy. On Eagly's account, gender should be salient in these situations and, unless other more specific situational roles are present, diffuse gender role expectations should guide behavior (see Eagly, 1987, p. 24).[4] And because situational norms for task orientation make everyone, both males and females, task directed, there should be no expectation for women to be more task directed, more agentic, or more directive of others than men.

In fact, Eagly's theory only predicts that females will be more agentic when (a) the task specifically requires agentic skill for completion and (b) the particular agentic skill required is more likely to be possessed by women due to their previous occupation of particular social roles. But even on a feminine task that requires agentic skills, Eagly's theory does not necessarily predict either that females will be more agentic *than males*, who should also be influenced by both situational norms and diffuse gender role expectations, or that women will clearly dominate in procedural/directive task activities.[5] Her theory only predicts that females will be more agentic than in other settings.

---

[4] If a more specific role in the situation is salient (e.g., manager vs. employee), the expectations associated with this role will tend to overwhelm the diffuse effects of gender. It is not clear, however, that this is the case in a task group where the only discriminating characteristic is gender. If one defines "role" broadly, then it is possible that being an "expert" constitutes a role, but there is no indication that this is how "role" is being defined by Eagly. And even so, it is not clar that Eagly's theory predicts that an "expert" female (by virtue of the feminine nature of the task) will be more agentic and directive than any males in the group.

[5] Without incorporating the proximate cause of the developing power and prestige order, the social role interpretation offers no reason to believe that the skills necessary to complete the task (whether agentic or socioemotional) will overlap

More interestingly, on a feminine task that requires communal behaviors or socioemotional skills for successful completion, Eagly's theory should actually predict that women will engage in more socioemotional behaviors and fewer agentic behaviors than in mixed-sex groups working on a masculine task.[6] In this situation, both situational task requirements and diffuse gender role expectations would be in favor of increased communal behaviors from women. On the other hand, in a mixed-sex group working on a masculine task, diffuse gender role expectations would encourage communal behaviors from women, but the situational norms would encourage agentic behaviors. Hence, while Eagly's (1987, p. 110) social role interpretation predicts women to be greater task contributors and more task oriented on feminine tasks, it does not necessarily predict women to be higher than males on procedural/directive behaviors.

It is clear that expectation states theory is a better predictor of gender's impact on power and prestige dynamics in interaction than is Eagly's role theory. This is not surprising given the different goals of the two theories. Eagly's theory focuses on gender differences and is only indirectly concerned with power and prestige dynamics. In Eagly's theory, such dynamics are only one of many contexts in which gender differences may occur. Furthermore, Eagly's theory has its own distinctive strengths in that it can make predictions about gender differences across a broader range of contexts than can expectation states theory.

However, to a person whose primary interest is in gender inequality, expectation states theory's superior analysis of gender's role in power and prestige dynamics is an important advantage. A clear analysis of the development of influence hierarchies is crucial to understanding the role of interaction in maintaining women's disadvantaged position in society. Face-to-face interaction (e.g., job interviews, performance evaluations, networking) is a key mediator of individuals' distribution into positions of greater or lesser power and status in our society. Access to such positions is in turn an important determinant of income. Thus, understanding how gender affects the influence dynamics of face-to-face interaction is important to explaining women's difficulty in achieving levels of power, status, and income equivalent to those of men. It is interesting to note that such mediating interaction is usually task oriented and, thus, falls under the scope of expectation states theory.

---

with the agentic type of behavior necessary to attain a status advantage in the group.

[6] Of course, Eagly (1987, p. 112) clearly recognizes that on the molecular level many traditionally female roles require considerable agentic behaviors and many traditionally male roles require considerable socioemotional behaviors. But this observation simply suggests that both males and females have a large repertoire of both task and socioemotional behaviors available to them. It remains to be explained why we find the differences we do in task groups.

In effect, expectation states theory shows more clearly than role theory how women are maintained in their low-status positions in interaction and, through that, in society. By demonstrating the proximal power of performance expectations created by gender status independently of actual abilities, it offers more insight into the mechanisms by which women's oppression occurs.[7] For those interested in explaining gender inequality, then, there are good reasons for continuing to use the status approach represented by this theory. However, the conceptual and empirical shortcomings of the approach must be addressed. This can be accomplished by linking the theory with concepts from Eagly's role theory and the cultural approach to account for both socioemotional behavior and differences between same- and mixed-sex groups.

Broadening the Expectation States Account

Gender Status in Same- and Mixed-Sex Groups

Of the two criticisms against the expectation states approach, accounting for differences between same- and mixed-sex groups is the most critical. Expectation states theory argues that gender status only affects performance expectations and behavior when it is activated in the situation. This activation assumption is essential to the theory's situational approach to interpersonal power and prestige, an approach that has given the theory its distinctive explanatory power. Yet this is the assumption that is called into question by results comparing mixed- and same-sex groups.

Expectation states theory assumes that status characteristics like gender are activated either by task relevance or by contrast, as in a mixed-sex group or between a female same-sex group and a male organizational authority structure. Since differences between same- and mixed-sex groups have been obtained with gender neutral tasks, it is really the contrast assumption that is at issue here. In fact, evidence indicates that gender is much more salient when a contrast exists than when it does not (Cota & Dion, 1986), suggesting that the contrast assumption itself is basically sound.

Could it be that some situational contrast is activating gender status in same-sex groups under the conditions in which they have been studied? If this were the case, we would expect members of female groups to all act in a low-status manner and members of male groups to all act in a high-status manner. This would indeed create greater gender differences in task behaviors between same-sex groups than within mixed-sex groups.

---

[7] A good example is expectation states research demonstrating that gender status creates double standards for performance such that people require a better performance from a woman than a man to decide that they have the same level of ability (Foschi, 1988, 1990).

Ridgeway (1988) argues that this is exactly what is happening under the conditions in which all-female groups have been studied. The relevant studies of female groups (Anderson & Blanchard, 1982; Carli, 1989) have all been conducted in university settings which typically have male-dominated authority structures. When an all-female group engages in an official activity of the university, as in a research study, Ridgeway proposes that women's low gender status is salient in contrast to their knowledge that the organization is run by males. This occurs even if the actual experimenter is female.

All-male groups in the same studies are in a different situation. There is no gender contrast between them and the authority structure of the university and, consequently, there should be no situational activation of gender status. If the task is gender neutral, there is no relevance activation either. Is gender status operating in these all-male groups? We suggest that it is not. We argue that the men in these groups are not aware of themselves as men. It is expected, taken for granted, that people in such a setting will be men. It is only noticeable when they are not.

If gender is not salient in the situation, then it is not gender per se that is producing interaction patterns in these all-male groups. We argue, instead, that these patterns are caused by cultural norms for interaction in achievement-oriented settings such as universities and businesses. These *setting norms* prescribe highly task-oriented, fairly competitive, and emotionally cool behavior as appropriate to interaction in such organizational settings. Norms for interaction in different types of settings have been demonstrated to affect people's behavioral expectations in the setting (Smith-Lovin, 1988). People learn these norms as part of societal culture and use them as "blueprints" that define the kinds of goals and behaviors appropriate to established social contexts (Ridgeway, 1983). For all-male groups within an achievement-oriented organization, these setting norms are sufficient to produce a pattern of highly task-directed interaction in which members strive to gain approval through task contributions rather than socioemotional behavior. Gender status need not be activated to produce such effects.[8]

The concept of setting norms is similar to the cultural approach to gender and interaction, but with one important difference. Instead of different cultural norms characterizing men and women, we argue that different cultural norms characterize common settings for interaction.

---

[8] It is possible, of course, that the cultural norms for achievement settings have the content that they do because these settings have historically been dominated and controlled by men. As a consequence, behavioral norms within them reflect the orientations and concerns of men rather than women, as these have been socially constructed in our society. However, this is an indirect effect of gender through its prior impact on cultural setting norms rather than a direct effect of gender activated and operating in the actual situation of interaction.

Setting norms are held similarly by both men and women. As a result they also affect interaction in all-female and mixed-sex groups in achievement settings. This is why both women's and men's behavior in such groups is primarily task directed. However, in mixed-sex and all-female groups within most achievement organizations, gender status is also activated, creating low performance expectations that proportionately reduce women's task contributions.

The concepts of setting norms and the situational activation of gender status in all-female groups can account for differences in task behavior between men and women in mixed- and same-sex groups. The situational activation assumption is an extension of expectation states theory itself. Setting norms, on the other hand, are outside of the theory. They are, in a way, a further specification of the scope condition of task-oriented interaction under which expectation states theory is assumed to apply. As such, they form a cultural argument that can be used in combination with the theory to give a fuller account of task behavior in interaction.

The Problem of Socioemotional Behavior

The problem remains of accounting for gender differences in socioemotional behavior, which we will call *social behavior* for brevity. Because expectation states theory focuses on power dynamics, it can only predict social behavior to the extent that it interacts with the power and prestige hierarchy. In task groups, social behavior is not central to the power and prestige order, but it is not entirely independent of it either (Ridgeway, 1982, 1988; Ridgeway & Johnson, 1990). A partial explanation of women's higher level of social behavior compared to men may be the pressure of low status expectations when gender is activated in all-female or mixed-sex groups. After discussing how this can occur, we will further suggest nonstatus sources of women's greater social behavior.

A number of writers have suggested that, when gender status is activated, women in task groups face not only the pressure of low performance expectations, but also a sense that they are not legitimate candidates for high influence and prestige in the group (Fennell, Barchas, Cohen, McMahon, & Hildebrand, 1978; Meeker & Weitzel-O'Neill, 1977; Ridgeway, 1988). In an expectation states account, Ridgeway and Berger (1986) argued that these legitimacy issues are created by widely held beliefs that women are less likely than men to hold valued status positions in society. When gender is activated, women expect others to share these beliefs and to view their efforts to achieve power and prestige as illegitimate. To assuage the resistance this illegitimacy arouses (e.g., Butler & Geis, 1990), women may attempt to portray their efforts to gain influence as cooperative and group-oriented in intent rather than merely self-interested (Meeker & Weitzel-O'Neill, 1977). One way to do this is by accompanying task-oriented influence attempts with positive social behaviors. There is, in fact, evidence that when women do this in mixed-sex groups, they can achieve higher influence than otherwise (Ridgeway 1982; Shackleford, Wood, & Worchel, 1989). It is possible, then, that anxiety over others' reactions to their efforts to gain influence may be one source of women's "nicer" behavior. This can occur in all-female as well as mixed-sex groups as long as gender is activated.

The pressure of low status when gender is activated may affect women's social behavior in another way as well. Most people try to create a positive identity in a situation as a way of gaining approval, respect, or other rewards (Alexander & Wiley, 1981). In a task group, the primary way to do this is to gain influence and prestige through task-related behavior. But what if low performance expectations cause a woman to feel that this primary means of identity affirmation is blocked? It is possible that she would try to be especially supportive of others as an alternative way of gaining their approval and creating a positive situational identity.

Such social behavior is, in effect, ingratiating behavior. That people in low-status positions show higher rates of ingratiating behavior is well established (Jones, 1964; Jones & Pittman, 1982). In a task group, such behavior will not affect the person's influence and prestige directly. However, it could have an indirect positive effect if it gives the impression that the person is helpful and group oriented or an indirect negative effect if it seems self-interested and manipulative (Ridgeway, 1978). Such impressions affect the group's willingness to trust the person with power, all other factors being equal (Hollander & Julian, 1970; Ridgeway, 1982).

Because of the difficulties created by low status and legitimacy, then, expectation states theory suggests some reasons for women's higher rates of social behavior, even though it offers no formal account of such behavior. On the other hand, it is unlikely that low status alone accounts for women's greater social behavior (see Carli, 1990). After all, some members of all-male groups are in positions of low influence and prestige. Although low-position men may have higher rates of positive social behavior than those in high positions, the overall rates of such behavior are lower in these groups than in mixed-sex groups. This suggests that something more than status dynamics is involved.

To more fully account for women's social behavior, the expectation states account can be linked with concepts from Eagly's role theory. Eagly is surely right that the almost exclusive assignment of women to caretaking roles in our society creates stereotypic expectations that women will engage in more positive social or communal behaviors than men (Hoffman & Hurst, 1990). We argue, slightly at variance with Eagly, that these stereotypic expectations are only activated when gender is salient in the situation.[9] Furthermore, the effect of these expectations is less powerful than that of the more situationally relevant setting norms for task direction. In mixed-sex and all-female groups where gender is salient, these activated stereotypic expectations will exert pressure on women to engage in some positive social behavior, although in the main, their behavior will be task directed.

An Expanded Account

When expectation states theory is linked to the concept of cultural setting norms and a recognition that the activation of gender brings forth both stereotypic expectations for women's social behavior and status expectations, it produces the following account of gender differences in interaction. In all-male task groups in a male-run organization, gender is not activated when the task is gender neutral. However, setting norms dictate high rates of task-related, emotionally neutral behavior for all members. As each member tries to fulfill these norms, a pattern of high task activity is established which becomes the norm in the group. Furthermore, because members are peers in external status, no one has an immediate reason to defer to the others and the influence and prestige hierarchy is established through a slower, more competitive behavioral process (Berger & Conner, 1974). This too raises the average rate of task activity over the period of interaction.

In an all-female group in a male-run organizational setting, gender is situationally activated. This evokes low performance expectations for all members combined with a concern that efforts to exercise influence may appear illegitimate. Gender stereotypic expectations for positive social behavior are also activated. Yet the more relevant setting norms require high task activity. The effect of these conflicting expectations is to make women's behavior primarily task directed but studded with positive social behaviors to assuage illegitimacy and give some obeisance to gender stereotypic expectations. Because all members face pressures of low performance expectations and forced illegitimacy, each is likely to model for the others a behavioral pattern with a relatively low level of affectively neutral task behavior and high level of social behavior. As a result, such a pattern is likely to become normative in the group even after an influence hierarchy emerges and some members become more task directive than others. When this happens, neutral task behavior is lower and social behavior higher for women in all-female groups where gender is activated than for women in mixed-sex groups.

---

[9] If stereotypic expectations for men's greater agency are also activated, these are redundant with diffuse performance expectations and are in effect, part of what makes gender a status characteristic.

In mixed-sex groups, gender status and stereotypic expectations are activated and setting norms are present. Driven by setting norms and their expected greater competence and legitimacy, men jump in with task behaviors that quickly gain them influence. The early achievement of influence reduces the status pressure on men so that they do not have to remain as highly task competitive as in all-male groups. Low performance expectations keep women's task behaviors and influence below that of men's. Ironically, however, women face fewer problems of illegitimacy than in all-female groups because women are not allowed, let alone required, to exercise as much influence as some of them must in all-female groups. This reduces women's need to surround their task behaviors with quite as much agreeing, joking, laughing, or supportive comments. As a result, although stereotypic expectations produce a moderate rate of positive social behavior from women, the rate is not as high as in all-female groups. Women's positive behavior in turn encourages men to reciprocate with more positive behavior than occurs in all-male groups. Consequently, in mixed-sex groups, men have more influence and prestige and are more task active and less social than women, but less task active and more social than men in all-male groups. Women are more task active and less social than in all-female groups but are subject to men's power and influence unlike in all-female groups.

Conclusion

Despite recent criticisms, a status approach to gender differences in interaction continues to provide more theoretical insight into gender inequality and more predictive power over behavior than other available approaches. This is true, in any case, if we employ the sophisticated status explanation offered by expectation states theory and focus on goal-oriented interaction. The expectation states account of gender status and interaction has the advantage of greater conceptual clarity and validity than explanations in terms of gendered subcultures. In comparison to Eagly's role theory, the expectation states account offers greater predictive precision because it incorporates an additional, more proximate cause of behavior in interaction than roles. This more proximate cause is the power and prestige order created by the formation of performance expectations. Finally, by focusing on the relationship between interactional power dynamics and gender, expectation states theory provides a clearer account of the interactional means by which women are maintained in a disadvantaged position in society.

Despite these strengths, there is validity to recent criticisms that a status explanation alone cannot account for gender differences in socioemotional behavior or for the magnitude of gender differences between women and men in same-sex groups compared to mixed-sex groups.

However, these criticisms can be met if the expectation states account is employed in association with concepts borrowed from other theories. Specifically, the concept of cultural setting norms, such as those defining appropriate behavior in achievement settings, can be combined with expectation states assumptions about the activation of gender status to explain men's greater task behavior and lesser social behavior in all-male compared to mixed-sex task groups. As well, acknowledging that the activation of gender evokes stereotypic expectations for women's social behavior in addition to status and legitimacy expectations provides an explanation for women's higher level of social behavior as well as the differences between women's behavior in all-female and mixed-sex task groups. We used these ideas to construct an expanded account of gender and interaction that preserved the strengths of the status explanation while offering a broader scope and greater empirical adequacy than a status account alone provides.

Our account and most empirical studies focus on task-oriented interaction. Although such interaction is both common and especially important in its consequences for gender inequality in society, in does not cover all interaction. Systematic accounts of gender's effects on less focused or more intimate interaction are also needed. Although different mechanisms may be involved, it is our belief that women's lower status in society will be an important factor in this interaction as well. One may study gender differences in interaction, for many reasons. However, if an understanding of women's inequality in society is one of these, then status approaches will continue to have powerful explanatory strengths.

References

Alexander, C.N., & Wiley, M.G. (1981). Situated activity and identity formation. In M. Rosenberg & R. Turner (Eds.), *Social psychology: Sociological perspectives* (pp. 269–289). New York: Basic Books.

Anderson, L.R., & Blanchard, P.N. (1982). Sex differences in task and social-emotional behavior. *Basic and Applied Social Psychology*, *3*, 109–139.

Bales, R.F. (1950). *Interaction process analysis*. Cambridge, MA: Addison-Wesley.

Bartol, K.M., & Martin, D.C. (1986). Women and men in task groups. In R.D. Ashmore & F.K. Del Boca (Eds.), *The social psychology of female-male relations: A critical analysis of central concepts* (pp. 259–310). Orlando, FL: Academic Press.

Becker, B.J. (1986). Influence again: Another look at studies of gender differences in social influence. In J.S. Hyde & M.C. Linn (Eds.), *The psychology of gender: Advances through meta-analysis* (pp. 178–209). Baltimore, MD: Johns Hopkins University Press.

Berger, J., & Conner, T. (1974). Performance expectation and behavior in small groups: A revised formulation. In J. Berger, T. Conner, & M.H. Fisek (Eds.), *Expectation states theory: A theoretical research program* (pp. 85–110). Cambridge, MA: Winthrop.

Berger, J., Conner, T., & Fisek, M.H. (1974). *Expectation states theory: A theoretical research program.* Cambridge, MA: Winthrop.

Berger, J., Fisek, M.H., Norman, R.Z., & Zelditch, M., Jr. (1977). *Status characteristics and social interaction.* New York: Elsevier.

Berger, J., Rosenholtz, S., & Zelditch, M., Jr. (1980). Status organizing processes. *Annual Review of Sociology, 6,* 479–508.

Berger, J., & Zelditch, M., Jr. (1985). *Status, rewards, and influence.* San Francisco: Jossey-Bass.

Borgatta, E.F., & Stimson, J. (1963). Sex differences in interaction characteristics. *Journal of Social Psychology, 60,* 89–100.

Brown, S.M. (1979). Male versus female leaders: A comparison of empirical studies. *Sex Roles, 5,* 595–611.

Butler, D., & Geis, F.L. (1990). Nonverbal affect responses to male and female leaders: Implications for leadership evaluations. *Journal of Personality and Social Psychology, 58,* 48–59.

Carbonell, J.L. (1984). Sex roles and leadership revisited. *Journal of Applied Psychology, 69,* 44–49.

Carli, L.L. (1982). *Are women more social and men more task oriented? A meta-analytic review of sex differences in group interaction, reward allocation, coalition formation, and cooperation in the Prisoner's Dilemma game.* Unpublished manuscript, University of Massachusetts, Amherst.

Carli, L.L. (1989). Gender differences in interaction style and influence. *Journal of Personality and Social Psychology, 56,* 565–576.

Carli, L.L. (1990). Gender, language, and influence. *Journal of Personality and Social Psychology, 59,* 941–951.

Cota, A.A., & Dion, K.L. (1986). Salience of gender and sex composition of ad hoc groups: An experimental test of distinctiveness theory. *Journal of Personality and Social Psychology, 50,* 770–776.

Deaux, K., & Major, B. (1987). Putting gender into context: An interactive model of gender-related behavior. *Psychological Review, 94,* 369–389.

Dovidio, J.F., Brown, C.E., Heltman, K., Ellyson, S.L., & Keating, C.F. (1988). Power displays between women and men in discussions of gender-linked tasks: A multichannel study. *Journal of Personality and Social Psychology, 55,* 580–587.

Eagly, A.H. (1983). Gender and social influence: A social psychological analysis. *American Psychologist, 38,* 971–981.

Eagly, A.H. (1987). *Sex differences in social behavior: A social-role interpretation.* Hillsdale, NJ: Erlbaum.

Eagly, A.H., & Carli, L.L. (1981). Sex of researchers and sex-typed communications as determinants of sex differences in influenceability: A meta-analysis of social influence studies. *Psychological Bulletin, 90,* 1–20.

Eagly, A.H., & Karau, S.J. (1991). Gender and the emergence of leaders: A meta-analysis. *Journal of Personality and Social Psychology, 60,* 685–710.

Eagly, A.H., & Wood, W. (1985). Gender and influenceability: Stereotype versus behavior. In V.E. O'Leary, R.K. Unger, & B.S. Wallston (Eds.), *Women, gender, and social psychology* (pp. 225–256). Hillsdale, NJ: Erlbaum.

Fennell, M.L., Barchas, P., Cohen, E.G., McMahon, A.M., & Hildebrand, P. (1978). An alternative perspective on sex differences in organizational settings: The process of legitimation. *Sex Roles, 4,* 589–604.

Fisek, M.H., & Ofshe, R. (1970). The process of status evolution. *Sociometry*, *33*, 327–346.

Fishman, P. (1978). Interaction: The work women do. *Social Problems*, *25*, 397–406.

Fleischer, R.A., & Chertkoff, J.M. (1986). Effects of dominance and sex on leader selection in dyadic work groups. *Journal of Personality and Social Psychology*, *50*, 94–99.

Foschi, M. (1988). Status characteristics, standards, and attributions. In J. Berger, M. Zeldich, and B. Anderson (Eds.), *Sociological theories in progress: New formulations* (pp. 58–72). Newbury Park, CA: Sage.

Foschi, M. (1990). *Double standards in the evaluation of men and women*. Paper presented at the Annual Meeting of the Canadian Sociology and Anthropology Association, Victoria, B.C., May, 1990.

Hall, J.A. (1984). *Nonverbal sex differences*. Baltimore, MD: Johns Hopkins University Press.

Hall, K.E. (1972). *Sex differences in initiation and influence in decision-making among prospective teachers*. Unpublished doctoral dissertation, Stanford University.

Henley, N.M. (1977). *Body politics: Power, sex, and nonverbal communication*. Englewood Cliffs, NJ: Prentice-Hall.

Hoffman, C., & Hurst, N. (1990). Gender stereotypes: Perception or rationalization. *Journal of Personality and Social Psychology*, *58*, 197–208.

Hollander, E.P., & Julian, J.W. (1970). Studies in leadership legitimacy, influence, and innovation. In L. Berkowitz (Ed.), *Advances in experimental social psychology* (Vol. 5, pp. 33–69). New York: Academic Press.

Jones, E.E. (1964). *Ingratiation: A social psychological analysis*. New York: Appleton-Century-Crofts.

Jones, E.E., & Pittman, T.S. (1982). Toward a general theory of strategic self-Presentation. In J. Suls (Ed.), *Psychological perspectives on the self*. Hillsdale, NJ: Erlbaum.

Kollack, P., Blumstein, P., & Schwartz, P. (1985). Sex and power in interaction. *American Sociological Review*, *50*, 34–47.

Lockheed, M.E. (1985). Sex and social influence: A meta-analysis guided by theory. In J. Berger & M. Zeldich (Eds.), *Status, rewards, and influence* (pp. 406–429). San Francisco: Jossey-Bass.

Maccoby, E.E. (1990). Gender and relationships: A development account. *American Psychologist*, *45*, 513–520.

Major, B., Schmidlin, A.M., & Williams, L. (1990). Gender patterns in social touch: The impact of setting and age. *Journal of Personality and Social Psychology*, *58*, 634–643.

Maltz, D.N., & Borker, R.A. (1982). A cultural approach to male-female miscommunication. In J.J. Gumperz (Ed.), *Language and social identity* (pp. 196–266). New York: Cambridge.

Meeker, B.F., & Weitzel-O'Neill, P.A. (1977). Sex roles and interpersonal behavior in task-oriented groups. *American Sociological Review*, *42*, 91–105.

Megaree, E.I. (1969). Influence of sex roles on the manifestation of leadership. *Journal of Applied Psychology*, *53*, 377–382.

Nyquist, L.V., & Spence, J.T. (1986). Effects of dispositional dominance and sex role expectations on leadership behaviors. *Journal of Personality and Social Psychology*, *50*, 87–93.

Piliavin, J.A., & Martin, R.R. (1978). The effects of sex composition of groups on style of social interaction. *Sex Roles*, *4*, 281–296.

Pugh, M.D., & Wahrman, R. (1983). Neutralizing sexism in mixed-sex groups: Do women have to be better than men? *American Journal of Sociology*, *88*, 746–762.

Ridgeway, C.L. (1978). Conformity, group-oriented motivation, and status attainment in small groups. *Social Psychology Quarterly*, *41*, 175–188.

Ridgeway, C.L. (1982). Status in groups: The importance of motivation. *American Sociological Review*, *47*, 76–88.

Ridgeway, C.L. (1983). *The dynamics of small groups*. New York: St. Martin's.

Ridgeway, C.L. (1988). Gender differences in task groups: A status and legitmacy account. In M. Webster and M. Foschi (Eds.), *Status generalization: New theory and research* (pp. 188–206). Stanford, CA: Stanford University Press.

Ridgeway, C.L., & Berger, J. (1986). Expectations, legitimation, and dominance behavior in task groups. *American Sociological Review*, *51*, 603–617.

Ridgeway, C.L., Berger, J. & Smith, L. (1985). Nonverbal cues and status: An expectation states approach. *American Journal of Sociology*, *90*, 995–978.

Ridgeway, C.L., & Johnson, C. (1990). What is the relationship between socio-emotional behavior and status in task groups? *American Journal of Sociology*, *95*, 1189–1212.

Shackleford, S., Wood, W., & Worchel, S. (1989). *How can low status group members influence others? Team players and attention getters*. Unpublished manuscript, Texas A & M University.

Smith-Lovin, L. (1988). The affective control of events within settings. In L. Smith-Lovin & D. Heise (Eds.), *Analyzing social interaction: Advances in affect control theory* (pp. 71–102). New York: Gordon and Breach.

Smith-Lovin, L., & Brody, C. (1989). Interruptions in group discussions: The effects of gender and group composition. *American Sociological Review*, *54*, 424–435.

Strodtbeck, F.L., & Mann, R.D. (1956). Sex role differentiation in jury deliberations. *Sociometry*, *19*, 3–11.

Wagner, D.G. (1988). Gender inequalities in groups: A situational approach. In M. Webster and M. Foschi (Eds.), *Status generalization: New theory and research* (pp. 55–68). Stanford, CA: Stanford Press.

Wagner, D.G., Ford, R.S., & Ford, T.W. (1986). Can gender inequalities be reduced? *American Sociological Review*, *51*, 47–61.

Wentworth, D.K., & Anderson, L.R. (1984). Emergent leadership as a function of sex and task type. *Sex Roles*, *11*, 513–524.

West, C. (1984). When the doctor is a "Lady": Power, status and gender in physician-patient exchanges. *Symbolic Interaction*, *7*, 87–106.

West, C., & Zimmerman, D.H. (1977). Women's place in everyday talk: Reflections on parent-child interaction. *Social Problems*, *24*, 521–529.

Wood, W., & Karten, S.J. (1986). Sex differences in interaction style as a product of perceived sex differences in competence. *Journal of Personality and Social Psychology*, *50*, 341–347.

Yamada, E.M., Tjosvold D., & Draguns, J.G. (1983). Effects of sex-linked situations and sex composition on cooperation and style of interaction. *Sex Roles*, *9*, 541–553.

Zimmerman, D.H., & West, C. (1975). Sex roles, interruptions, and silences in conversation. In B. Thorne & N. Henley (Eds.), *Language and sex: Difference and dominance* (pp. 105–129). Rowley, MA: Newbury House.

8
Gender and Double Standards for Competence

MARTHA FOSCHI

Gender inequality in interaction takes many forms and is maintained by various processes. For example, men and women frequently differ in the amount of competence that is assigned to them and in the emotional reactions they receive when they attempt to occupy leadership positions. Moreover, women who do achieve such positions often have difficulties exerting influence. For instance, they tend to be perceived as aggressive whereas men exhibiting the same behavior are seen as decisive. In addition, there are usually differences in the types of personality characteristics that men and women are expected to exhibit (e.g., women are expected to be more sensitive than men). There are also gender differences in the rules specifying what degree of informality is acceptable in a given situation.

This chapter focuses on gender effects in the assignment of competence in task groups. In my opinion, the process of competence assignment is at the core of the difficulties women experience in such settings. For although there is a price to be paid for not being liked or for not being considered to be a good team player, the consequences of not being deemed competent are even more serious. In other words, although the attribution of positive personality characteristics and its accompanying emotional reactions are clearly important conditions for effective participation in task groups (particularly for the exertion of influence), the assignment of competence is a necessary one.

It is common to observe that the sex[1] of the performer biases the evaluation of performances in achievement contexts, so that men's con-

---

[1] As generally agreed upon in the social psychological literature, I use the term "sex" to refer to biological differences between males and females, and "gender" to cultural aspects of these differences. Thus, beliefs about the relative competence of men and women are social products and therefore a gender issue, whereas what activates these beliefs is usually nothing more than the mere perception of the performers' sex. When the evidence available involves only such perceptions, or when the only intention is to identify participants in a study as either men or women, I use the term "sex."

tributions to the task solution are judged to be better than women's. How does this happen and what are its effects? The chapter begins with an account of this process. Next, it focuses on a class of situations in which the operation of such biases should be *blocked*, namely, when the quality of the performance has been assessed as either good or poor through the use of objective criteria. Can gender still affect perceived competence in those cases? I argue that it can, through the operation of a double standard of ability evaluation, stricter for women than for men. The chapter outlines a theory of such double standards and reviews empirical support for its predictions. A number of promising areas for future research are examined at the end.

Status, Expectations, and Biased Evaluations

Heider (1944) noted that the evaluation of an act and the evaluation of the person who did it are seldom independent. This observation is particularly appropriate for situations where the act in question is the performance of a task and where criteria for success are ambiguous. In those cases, attributes of the performer such as sex, ethnicity, social class, and record of prior performance tend to bias the evaluation of the outcome. If the performer is positively evaluated regarding one of these attributes, so too is the performance. The opposite holds for the negatively evaluated performer. Early demonstrations of this phenomenon appear in Harvey (1953); Sherif, White and Harvey (1955); and Zander and Cohen (1955). For a recent study of an organizational setting, illustrating how workers underevaluate their peers and overevaluate their managers, see Humphrey (1985). Biased evaluations which result from labeling the performer as "good" are often described in the social psychological literature as "halo effects." For the "poor" performer, these are referred to as "negative halo" or "forked-tail" effects (see, for example, McArthur, 1985; Sears, Freedman, & Peplau, 1985, Chapter 3).

A substantial amount of research provides evidence of how *gender* biases the evaluation of performances. A study by Goldberg (1968) has now become a classic in this area. Female undergraduates were asked to assess the quality of professional articles in different fields. Pretests had established that these fields were perceived to be either sex-linked (male or female) or sex-neutral. Articles were presented to the subjects as having been written by either a man or a woman. Male authors received more favorable ratings than female authors in all occupational fields, particularly in those defined as masculine. Subsequent research has increased the understanding of the conditions under which this phenomenon occurs. For example, in addition to sex linkage of the task, level of performance, amount of available information about the performers, and motivation to make correct evaluations, have all been found to be important factors. (See Paludi & Strayer, 1985, for a recent study on this topic; for reviews of research, see Lott, 1985; Nieva & Gutek, 1980; Wallston & O'Leary, 1981.)

Status characteristics theory offers a sound, comprehensive account of how biased evaluations occur. The theory investigates how status differences determine levels of assigned competence and corresponding performance expectations. The latter, in turn, affect the power and prestige order of a task group. This order is defined as a set of interrelated behaviors: unequal distribution in the offer and acceptance of opportunities to perform, the type of evaluations received (either positive or negative), and the rates of influence exerted among group members.

A "status characteristic" is any valued attribute implying task competence. Such characteristics are viewed as having two levels or states (e.g., being either high or low in mechanical ability, being either black or white), one carrying a more positive evaluation than the other. They are also defined as varying from specific to diffuse, depending on the range of their perceived applicability. For example, mechanical ability is relatively specific, or associated with well-defined performance expectations. Ethnicity, on the other hand, tends to be diffuse, or to carry both limited and general performance expectations. The "diffuseness" refers to the fact that since there is no explicitly set limit to the expectations, the characteristic is viewed as relevant to a large, indeterminate number of different task situations. In most societies, gender is a powerful diffuse status characteristic: women are not only expected to be inferior to men in a number of tasks requiring specific abilities, but they are also expected to be of inferior competence in a general, undefined way.

Status characteristics theory has been extensively tested, and results provide it with strong empirical support. This theory is part of expectation states theory, a research program on status-organizing processes in small, task-oriented groups (see Berger, Fisek, Norman, & Zelditch, 1977; Berger, Rosenholtz, & Zelditch, 1980; Berger, Wagner, & Zelditch, 1985; Webster & Foschi, 1988; for assessments, see Deaux, 1985; Wiley, 1986). Status characteristics theory offers two particular strengths for the study of gender effects on evaluations (and on the assignment of competence in general): (a) Because the theory assumes that the key variable is status, not gender, the explanation of biased evaluations that it provides has a wider range and is therefore more powerful than one that would account only for gender effects.[2] (b) Similarly, because the theory treats biased evaluations as *one* of the various components of the power and prestige order of a group, it offers a more thorough understanding of

---

[2] Such a generalizing approach is reflected in the organization of this chapter. Although the theoretical background, based on status characteristics theory, treats gender as one of several status variables, the discussion and the examples focus on gender.

status effects. This strength becomes apparent when the theory is used to develop propositions regarding double standards. As proposed later in the chapter, such standards can be viewed as another component of the power and prestige order of the group.

For the most part, biased evaluations have been treated in this theory as an unobservable construct mediating the relationship between status and influence (Berger et al., 1977; Moore, 1969). As a result, most empirical studies have focused on measuring how different status variables affect influence rates. For example, Moore (1968) and Webster and Driskell (1978) demonstrated how influence is affected by the status variables of academic attainment and ethnicity, respectively. Webster and Entwisle (1976), on the other hand, conducted one of the few studies originating in this theory that measures biased evaluations directly. The basis for status in that study is ability at schoolwork, and results confirm the predicted effect on evaluations.

Let us now present the theory's predictions regarding status effects on evaluations in more detail and with special reference to gender. The theory is formulated from the point of view of a person p ("self"), who performs a task with a partner o ("other").[3] Several scope conditions apply. There is a single ability required for successful task performance and the two persons are task oriented (i.e., they value the ability and are trying to do the task well). They are also assumed to be motivated to form correct (i.e., accurate) expectations about each other's task ability. There are no objective criteria with which to evaluate task outcomes, and sex is a diffuse status characteristic for p. For simplicity, let us assume that opportunities to perform are not allowed to vary with status, but are instead equally distributed. The theory predicts that if p knows that self and other are of the *same sex*, and the situation does not provide any information about differences in their respective levels of task competence, p will conclude that the two persons are of equal ability. (Sex linkage may still affect the *absolute* levels of competence inferred by men and women, but that level would nevertheless be the same for both members of a pair if no other factors point to a difference.)

On the other hand, if p knows that the other person is of the *opposite sex*, the expectations formed by p on the basis of this information will vary depending on the type of existing association between sex and the task in the culture under consideration. There are three possible situations: (a) the task may have a sex linkage (i.e., either men may be expected to be better at it than women, or vice versa), (b) there may be a known dissociation between sex and competence at the task, or (c) the

---

[3] If the group consists of more than two persons, the theory views it as a network of dyadic interactions in which each person takes turns at being the focal actor p, and interacts with every other member of the group one at a time.

two may be neither associated nor dissociated. If the task is sex-linked, then that association will dictate the performance expectations that are formed. These expectations will in turn bias the evaluations so that a man's performance at a masculine task will be assessed as better than the same performance by a woman. The opposite will occur if the task is defined as feminine. Sex, however, will not have such effects if it has been explicitly dissociated from competence at the task. Finally, if the possibility of a relationship between sex and task competence is left open, the diffuse nature of the former characteristic will still enable the formation of higher expectations for the man than for the woman. These will then bias the evaluations so that the man's performance will be seen as the better of the two. Because the onus is placed on the woman to prove equal ability, the process is known as "burden of proof."

Moreover, if the two persons are involved in a collective task (i.e., each is prepared to accept the partner's solution if it is believed to be correct), the biased evaluations will result in different rates of acceptance of influence. These, in turn, will contribute to the maintenance of the initial expectations. (See Foschi, 1990; Lockheed & Hall, 1976; Pugh & Wahrman, 1983; Wagner, Ford, & Ford, 1986 for empirical tests of these predictions; for status accounts of sex effects in task groups and for reviews of research on this topic, see Lockheed, 1985; Meeker & Weitzel-O'Neill, 1977; Ridgeway, 1988; Wagner, 1988.)

There are two important points to note regarding the status characteristics formulation. First, it is a *situational* approach. Differences in evaluations and in acceptance of influence rates reside in features of the situation, not in attributes of the individuals. As a result, the same person is predicted to behave differently depending on the partner's sex (or any other status characteristic that is seen as relevant to the task at hand). Other situational factors also affect the person's behavior, such as the value attached to the task. The second point, closely related to the first, is that propositions are *conditional* in nature. In particular, it is assumed that p treats sex as a diffuse status characteristic. It follows that if p does not, then the theory does not apply. Because of the inclusion of such scope conditions, the theory is sensitive to cultural, historical, and individual differences. Thus, it incorporates the fact that although sex is a diffuse status characteristic in most societies, it is more so in some than in others. The extent to which sex is a status characteristic may also vary within a given society from one historical period to another. In addition, the theory reflects the fact that even in strongly sexist societies, there are always individuals who are less sexist than the majority, and maybe even some who are not sexist at all. (This may be due, for example, to variations in socialization practices within a given culture, or to various degrees of success of such practices.)

Two recent studies utilizing this framework and carried out in Canada (Foschi, Lai, & Sigerson, 1991; Stewart, 1988) suggest that the strength of sex effects in task groups may be diminishing. However, other recent experiments in this tradition, two from Canada and one from the United States (Foschi, 1990; Foschi & Freeman, 1991; Wagner et al., 1986), do not show such a decrease. All five studies had undergraduates as subjects. The reasons for the difference in these results may be traced to the following. The theory assumes that women *as well as* men may treat sex as a diffuse status characteristic and thus devalue women's performances. However, as with most status systems, those persons who benefit from the existing order should be expected to be more supportive of it than those who do not, socialization practices notwithstanding. Although Foschi (1990) and Wagner et al. (1986) did not find such a difference by sex of subject, Foschi and Freeman (1991), Foschi et al. (1991) and Stewart (1988) did. The results from these five studies, considered together, indicate that sex role stereotypes in North America may not be as ingrained as they used to be and that, not surprisingly, the change originates in those defined as having lower status: although men still tend to believe in the association between sex and competence, women are no longer accepting it to the same extent. In other words, these studies suggest that this scope condition is more likely to be met by men than by women.

Biased evaluations and ensuing differences in acceptance of influence are thus a status-maintenance mechanism, because they protect higher status actors and penalize lower status ones. What happens, however, if the operation of biased evaluations is blocked by the use of objective criteria, that is, if the quality level of the performance is *not* under question? Let us assume that two performances, one by a man and the other by a woman, have been judged by a third, objective party to be of the same quality (either equally good or equally poor). Will sex of performer still affect the power and prestige order of such a group? I argue here that this will indeed be the case, and that a double standard of ability evaluation will be the status-maintenance mechanism through which this occurs.

Standards, Performance Evaluations, and Competence

Before discussing double standards, however, the relationship between standards, evaluations, and the inference of ability should be examined. In general terms, "standards" are defined in this chapter as rules providing performance requirements for the inference of both ability or lack of ability. Such standards play a major role in how performance evaluations are processed: for example, depending on the standards used, the same level of success may be interpreted as either conclusive or inconclusive evidence of ability. Performance scores provide a useful illustration: a score of 70% is usually a sufficient indication of ability if the standard is

60%, but the same score becomes an unconvincing performance if the standard is 80%. The same is true for the interpretation of failure.

Although couched in various other labels and defined somewhat differently, the concept of "standards" has appeared in a variety of research contexts in the social psychological literature. It can be traced to the writings of William James (1981 [originally published in 1890], p. 296), who defined "self-esteem" as the ratio of successes to pretensions. The concepts of "level of aspiration" and "goal setting" also have some similarity to that of "standards" as defined here. However, work on those two topics has dealt mostly with the level of performance that a person who values success will strive for, or would prefer to achieve, rather than with requirements for ability inference. Furthermore, and also as a result of such emphasis, the work has not been concerned with standards for *lack* of ability. Finally, this literature has tended to concentrate on the effects of goal setting on performance (e.g., in directing attention, mobilizing effort, and increasing persistence) and on the affective consequences of performing above or below one's aspirations, rather than on ability attributions. For a classical examination of the relationship between level of aspiration, inferred competence, and self-esteem, see Lewin, Dembo, Festinger, and Sears, 1944; for reviews on goal setting and task performance see Latham and Yukl, 1975; Lee, Locke, and Latham, 1989; Locke, Shaw, Saari, and Latham, 1981. A review by Higgins, Strautman, and Klein (1986) deals specifically with standards. But although these authors' definition of the concept is quite close to the one adopted here, their focus is again different. They are interested in emotional reactions to performances that either meet or do not meet a given standard, and the relationship between evaluations, standards, and ability is assumed rather than investigated.

That relationship has also been assumed in work on formal organizations. This research is of interest because it serves to underscore the practical implications of the topic. Dornbusch and Scott's (1975) theory of evaluations and organizational authority is of particular interest. Because it utilizes a generalizing approach, it offers the advantage of applying to evaluation processes in *any* type of formal organization. Furthermore, although the theory is not directly concerned with the question of how different standards affect inferences of ability (or lack of ability), the assumption of such a relationship is nevertheless central to its arguments. The theory examines how organizational standards may prevent performers from receiving evaluations at their acceptance level (i.e., the minimum level satisfactory to them). In formal organizations evaluations are, of course, the major basis for decisions regarding assignment of competence and resulting rewards. Workers may be prevented from receiving the evaluations they want by standards that are too high, or in conflict with each other, or not clearly formulated (Dornbusch & Scott, 1975, Chapter 9).

A program of research has applied the theory to school settings (McDill, Natriello, & Pallas, 1986; Natriello & Dornbusch, 1984; Natriello & McDill, 1986). This work has examined what characteristics of high school teachers, students, and their interactions result in unchallenging standards, and the interest has been in how to raise standards without increasing dropout rates. It is proposed, for example, that more challenging standards will bring about better performances only if students are provided with the resources and the assistance to attain them. The relative influence of various standard-setters (teachers, parents, peers) on students' performances is also an important factor that has been examined in this research.

Theoretical and empirical work on standards done within the status characteristics tradition is of most relevance to this chapter. Foschi and Foddy (1988) propose a conceptualization of "standards for ability" and "standards for lack of ability." Their proposal is particularly well suited to the study of double standards. Foschi and Foddy assume a situation involving p and o, who are both task oriented and motivated to form correct expectations about each other. Several tasks are involved, each requiring either a single ability or a number of abilities related to it. The proposal concerns the standards used by p to infer that a person has or does not have the ability in question. Each of the tasks consists of a series of trials and each trial has the same level of difficulty. The standards may be either imposed by a third party, or generated by p. Five dimensions of standards are included in the proposal: (a) the degree of difficulty of the trials in one of the tasks requiring the ability, (b) the proportion of correct responses in that series of trials, (c) the number of times the series has to be repeated, (d) the number of additional tasks requiring the ability, and (e) the number of additional tasks requiring related abilities.

Each of these dimensions is conceptualized as having two values, one more demanding than the other. These values, in turn, are used to construct "standards for ability" differing in strictness. For example, a standard for ability of at least 80% correct responses requires more evidence and is therefore stricter than a standard of at least 65%. A similar definition is proposed for "standards for lack of ability." Thus, a standard that defines "lack of ability" as 35% or fewer correct responses is more lenient than one that sets that figure at 55%.

Such standards are, in turn, used to define various "expectation states" differing in strength depending on whether or not p and o meet the standards imposed on their respective performances. For example, if p's performances meet the standard for ability and o's performances meet the standard for lack of ability, p is said to form higher expectations for self than for other that are "strong" (i.e., definite or conclusive). If p performs better than o but neither person meets the imposed standards, p will still form expectations of superior competence relative to the partner, but these will be "weak" (i.e., less definite). Intermediate degrees of strength result if one standard (either for ability or for lack of ability) is met by self but not by other, and vice versa.

Other work within this tradition involves modeling the relationship between standards, evaluations, and the inference of competence. Utilizing an earlier version of the above definition that conceptualizes "standards" only in terms of the proportion of correct responses over a single series of trials, Foschi and Foschi (1976) developed a Bayesian model for the formation of expectations on the basis of evaluations. A Bayesian model specifies how an ideal person would process information, and predicts the confidence that each new piece of evidence adds to each of two or more alternative hypotheses. Such models are useful tools in investigating the extent to which real subjects follow normative values.

In the Foschi and Foschi model, evaluations of the performances by self and other are the evidence to be processed, whereas three types of expectations (higher, lower, or equal for self relative to other) become the hypotheses that self has to assess. Standards are the key parameter of this model, as it is assumed that each person's individual standards regulate his/her own definitions of what constitutes superior, inferior, or equal ability (and the corresponding expectations). It is further assumed that each person brings his/her own standards to the interaction with the partner and maintains them throughout the performance of the task. The amount of confidence in a given hypothesis that may be extracted from the evidence is directly related to how that hypothesis has been defined in terms of standards. For example, if the standard for superior ability is strict, a single instance of superior performance adds less confidence to that hypothesis than if the standard is lenient. The model has been extended (Foschi & Foschi, 1979) to include situations in which self is not one of the two interactants, but is instead an observer evaluating the performances of two others. This extension, in turn, has been used to formulate and test hypotheses regarding differences in the expectations formed by actors and observers (Foschi, 1986).

Two experiments provide direct evidence on the role of standards in ability inference. Both utilized the earlier version of the conceptualization. In the first, by Foschi, Warriner, and Hart (1985), two types of expectations (either superior or inferior competence for self relative to the partner) were created. Each type, in turn, was made either strong or weak through variations in the imposed standards. The study tested hypotheses on the relationship between the various expectations and the degree of acceptance of influence from the partner. For example, a person believing to be definitely better at the task than his/her partner was predicted to accept less influence than a person considering this superiority to be uncertain. The hypotheses were tested with male and female dyads. Results show that the manipulations created either strong or weak expectations, as intended, for the females. Men, however, tended not to differentiate between the treatments, particularly when they received lower scores than their partners. The hypotheses were clearly supported in those cases in which the manipulations had been successful. However, since gender was not the focus of this study, there was not a sufficient number of subjects of each sex to determine fully the effects of this variable.

A subsequent study by Foschi and Freeman (1991) was specifically designed with that objective. Only lower expectations for self than for other were investigated, since these were the conditions where sex differences had been most pronounced in the earlier experiment. Strength of expectations (through variation in standards) and sex of dyad were the two independent variables. The possible effects of motivation, seriousness about task performance, task importance, and control over performance were also explored. The results confirmed those obtained in the corresponding conditions of the earlier study: whereas women formed either strong or weak expectations, as intended, men formed weak expectations regardless of the standards assigned to them. Furthermore, none of the four additional factors accounted for the findings.

The authors conclude that in both studies, male and female subjects were reacting differently to the evaluations and standards received from the experimenters, with females accepting them as a basis for expectations more than males. This, in turn, is seen as reflecting the status difference betwteen subject and source of expectations. Because the female experimenter communicated but did not generate the evaluations, it is proposed that she alone was not the source of expectations. Rather, these were shaped by the combination of experimenter, faculty project, and laboratory setting, all of which communicated both competence to evaluate and authority to do so.

The study illustrates the strength of gender effects: even when a single standard is set by an authoritative source, sex of subject results in different levels of acceptance of that standard. It is interesting to notice that this is, in fact, a form of a double standard in ability inference. However, this is not the double standard that is of central interest in this chapter. Rather, the focus here is on how a difference in sex between the performers results in the activation of a double standard when none has been set. This is discussed next.

Double Standards for Competence

Let us now return to the situation outlined at the end of the first section, and specify its scope conditions in more detail. There is a task group consisting of two persons, a man and a woman. Only a single ability is required for task performance. Both persons are task oriented and motivated to form correct expectations about each other's competence. Sex is a diffuse status characteristic for both and, at this stage of the interaction, it constitutes the only cue available regarding their relative levels of competence. Thus, from the man's point of view, p's competence is superior to o's; from the woman's point of view, the opposite is true. Each person performs the task individually and then receives evaluations for the performances of both self and partner. These evaluations, which are made by a source outside the dyad and are accepted by p to be objective, show the two persons to be either equally successful or equally unsuccessful. There are, however, no previously set and agreed-upon standards on how to infer either ability or lack of ability from these performances.[4]

At this stage, then, each person has two cues to task competence: sex of performers and actual outcomes. There may be a third cue if sex and task are *either* linked *or* neither associated nor dissociated from each other. Under these circumstances, what are the relative effects of these cues on assignment of competence? In particular, does task outcome overrule sex effects? Both attribution theory and status characteristics theory deal with this situation, and both predict that sex will still be a factor.

Let us now examine some of these predictions. Attribution theory investigates the process through which individuals, acting as "naive psychologists," assign causes to events. (For reviews and formulations, see Harvey & Weary, 1984; Kelley & Michela, 1980; Olson & Ross, 1985; Ross & Flechter, 1985.) A major area within this theory has focused on attributions for the causes of performance outcomes in achievement contexts. The effects of sex of performer have received special attention. According to attribution theory, the man's success in the situation described above will be seen as due to ability, whereas the same performance by the woman will tend to be attributed to other factors, such as good luck or additional effort. The opposite pattern of attributions is predicted for failure.[5] Furthermore, for both success and failure, the more masculine the task is perceived to be, the stronger the pattern.

---

[4]Notice that the definition of an outcome as a "success" is not necessarily equivalent to the standard used to infer ability from it. For example, a successful outcome could be defined as *either* at least 60% *or* at least 75% of the task correctly completed. Let us assume that the latter has been agreed upon as the definition of "success." Such an outcome, in turn, may or may not meet the standard for ability. That standard could be a performance at least 75% correct (i.e., the same as the definition of "success"), but it could also be a performance of at least 80% correct, or a score of at least 80% in a specified number of repeated performances. A corresponding comment applies to the definition of "failure" and standards for lack of ability.

[5]In some of the more recent attribution literature, sex of performer has been treated as a social category, and the hypotheses about sex and task outcome have accordingly been extended to other factors such as ethnicity and social class (see, for example, Deaux, 1984; Deschamps, 1983; Hewstone & Jaspars, 1982; Howard, 1990). The concept of "social category" has of course much in common with that of "diffuse status characteristic."

These hypotheses have been extensively tested; however, for the most part the results provide only weak support. (See Foschi & Plecash, 1983; Hansen & O'Leary, 1985; Sohn, 1982; Whitley, McHugh, & Frieze, 1986, for reviews of work on gender, outcome, and attributions.)

Status characteristics theory utilizes a graph-theoretic model to derive predictions about this same situation (Berger et al., 1977). According to this model, an actor is said to "possess" a given state of a characteristic and to be linked through "paths of relevance" to other components of the situation, such as expectations for competence (general as well as specific) and actual performance outcomes. Thus, in our case, the female actor is linked to both specific and general expectations of poor performance on the basis of her sex, but only to specific expectations of a successful performance on account of her actual outcome. Paths of relevance between an actor and an expected outcome may vary in length. For example, an actor may be linked *directly* to an expected outcome because an actual performance has occurred, or linked *indirectly* through a burden-of-proof process, as discussed earlier. The first constitutes a shorter path of relevance than the second. An actor may also be consistently connected to a given expected outcome (that is, either success or failure) through alternate paths, or there may be some paths linking the actor to expected success whereas others lead to expected failure. The model calculates the lengths of these various paths, as well as the number of consistent and inconsistent ones. The shorter the paths and the larger the number of consistent paths, the stronger the resulting expectations for succcess (or failure). Thus, when a man does well at a masculine task, a stronger expectation for success is formed than when a woman does equally well at the same task. Experimental tests by Pugh and Wahrman (1983) and Wagner et al. (1986) have resulted in clear support for these hypotheses.

As mentioned earlier, the attribution hypotheses have been only weakly supported by the evidence. It should be noted, however, that many of the studies do not do full justice to the attribution ideas. The quality of the research in this area varies widely, both in terms of the designs used and in the extent to which the relevant variables have been incorporated. Because the attribution ideas are sound and insightful, this situation suggests that what is needed is to reformulate them. Foschi (1989) has proposed an account of sex effects in performance contexts that incorporates the attribution hypotheses. This account is based on status characteristics theory and elaborates on it by including the notion of standards as well as ideas from other parts of the expectation states program, namely, work on expectations and evaluations, and on source of expectations. (See Berger, Wagner, & Zelditch, 1989, for a recent review of research on the various branches of this program.)

Foschi's (1989) account applies to situations involving performers who differ with respect to any status characteristic. This section, however, summarizes the proposal as it applies to the case of gender. The scope of the proposal is defined by the situation described at the beginning of this section. Before any performance takes place, the two persons form expectations for each other regarding task outcomes. For example, if the task is perceived to be masculine the man will expect that he will do well at it and that his partner will do poorly; the woman, in turn, will hold the opposite expectations. Foschi proposes that, in addition, the actors will activate standards for ability and for lack of ability with which to interpret the outcomes *once* these occur. There will be a double standard for each type of outcome, and these standards will be consistent with the status difference. The standard for ability will be stricter (i.e., will require *more* evidence of *ability*) for the woman than for the man. Similarly, the standard for lack of ability will be stricter (i.e., will require *less* evidence of *lack of ability*) for the woman than for the man.

Once the performances occur and are evaluated, these standards will be applied to them. In other words, standards will act as filters through which the outcomes are assessed.[6] Notice that if sex is a diffuse status characteristic for both persons, the woman as well as the man is predicted to activate such a double standard. Let us consider the case of an equally successful performance by the two actors at a task considered by both to be masculine. The man will be more likely to meet the more lenient standard applied to him than the woman will be to meet the stricter standard imposed on her. As a result, his performance will be seen as a sufficient indication of ability, whereas hers will be attributed to non ability factors such as good luck or additional effort. This, in turn, will lead to expectations for future success that will differ in strength: strong for the man, weak for the woman.

A similar argument may be used in the opposite case, namely, when different standards for lack of ability are applied to the two actors' unsuccessful performances. For both types of outcome, if the persons are subsequently involved in a collective task, rates of influence will be determined by the strength of the expectations. Thus, double standards for success and for failure are key contributors to the maintenance of the power and prestige order of the group when biased evaluations cannot occur.

If the task is seen as feminine, its sex linkage will activate a double standard of the opposite type (that is, more lenient for the woman) both in success and in failure. If sex and the task are neither associated nor dissociated from each other, the two will become associated through a burden-of-proof process, as discussed earlier. The strictness of each ac-

---

[6] It should be mentioned that it is not assumed that p goes through these steps in a conscious manner. In particular, p is not necessarily seen as explicitly formulating standards and calculating their effects. Rather, the proposal is a model to be used to predict p's behavior. To that end, it is convenient to think of p *as if* this person performed the specified operations.

tivated standard will be a function of sex of performer and of partner, but this relationship will not be as strong as in the case of a masculine task. Finally, no double standards are expected to be activated if sex and task have been clearly dissociated from each other.

Foschi's (1989) formulation also incorporates an extension to situations in which p forms expectations without being a performer. In that case, p receives objective evaluations from an outside source regarding the performances of two others, o_1 and o_2. These two performers differ with respect to a diffuse status characteristic. The same characteristic may also be used to describe p. Thus, in the case of sex, p is either a man or a woman evaluating a male o_1 and a female o_2. This extension is of theoretical interest because it allows for the investigation of the relative extent to which three variables affect assignment of task ability: self's role as either performer or nonperformer, the state of the diffuse status characteristic possessed by self, and the states of that same characteristic possessed by the two performers. Moreover, the extension is clearly of considerable practical interest, as there is a large class of concrete, everyday situations meeting its abstract conditions. These include, for example, the assessment of job applicants, promotion decisions, and teachers' evaluations of students.

In addition, Foschi's model includes an extension to those cases involving more than one characteristic. Of special relevance to the present discussion are those in which the male and the female performers are known to have one or more additional characteristics, and their states are consistently evaluated with the sex difference: for example, the man is white and the woman is black. This extension predicts that in that case an even stricter standard would be applied to the woman.

Foschi's model on double standards for competence is an elaboration of the graph-theoretic formulation of status characteristics theory. An alternative account of such double standards has been proposed by Foddy and Smithson (1989). Their model, based on the same theory, uses fuzzy sets rather than graphs and paths of relevance. Like Foschi's model, it includes situations in which the performers are differentiated with respect to either one or several status characteristics, and is equally applicable to p and o as to p, o_1, and o_2. A feature of special interest in the Foddy and Smithson formulation is that the concept of "double standard" is extended to include the rules through which status and performance information are combined. That is, it is not only that performance requirements (such as the number of correct responses and the number of tasks to be successfully completed) will be stricter for the woman. In addition, even if these have been met, the rules for combining performance and status information will give less weight to her success and more weight to her failure, than to the respective performances by her male counterpart. Although they propose different accounts for the operation of double standards, both models treat them as an order-preserving mechanism, and make compatible predictions. Because the models are quite recent, both have yet to be thoroughly tested and their differences assessed. The next section discusses the available evidence on double standards.

But before turning to that discussion, an important point should be made. There are also some situations in which women are told that their performances are a sufficient indication of ability when in fact they are not. It should be noted that this is another type of double standard in ability inference, namely, one that is more lenient to the lower status person even when the status characteristic and competence at the task are either directly linked or associated through burden of proof. Such patronizing standards deprive the performer of the learning experience that an accurate assessment supplies; furthermore, those who proclaim them seldom go on to actually use them to infer ability.

Patronizing standards for ability are thus an important additional mechanism for the maintenance of the status quo. They are commonly used when the assessor wants to avoid communicating a poor appraisal, and are more likely to occur when this person expects no negative consequences to him/herself for making (or at least communicating) incorrect assessments. They are of course also used when legislated quotas have to be met, or when the hiring of certain groups such as women and minorities is perceived as either the moral or the politically correct course of action. In any of these situations, it is again often the case that a lower level of ability is inferred nevertheless. There are also corresponding patronizing standards for lack of ability. This chapter focuses on those situations in which stricter standards are imposed on the lower status person. The use of more lenient standards for this individual merits a separate discussion in its own right, and more research into the conditions for its occurrence. (See Epstein, 1970a, 1970b for a discussion of patronizing standards for women; for a discussion of such standards in the assessment of the academic ability of blacks, see Blalock, 1979.)

Evidence Regarding Double Standards

The expression "double standards" is often used in everyday language and in a variety of contexts. In most cases, the words appear to be well understood and to refer to a phenomenon that is clearly recognizable to the speaker. Although that use is more general than the one adopted here, there is no contradiction between the two. In fact, double standards for competence may be seen as just one type in a family of double standards. For example, the expression is often used to describe discrepancies, affecting various categories of individuals, in the administration of criminal justice and in decisions regarding immigration requirements.

As to men and women in particular, in addition to double standards applied to the inference of competence, the practice has been reported regarding beauty, aging, codes of morality (particularly regarding sexual behavior), and mental health. (For examples involving these other types, see Deutsch, Zalenski, & Clark, 1986; Lips, 1988, pp. 145–146 and 214–215; Maslin & Davis, 1975; Sontag, 1979; Tudor, Tudor, & Gove 1979.)

All of these double standards have in common the idea that a decision is being made as to whether or not a person has a certain trait or property (e.g., is moral or immoral, competent or incompetent) on the basis of certain evidence, and that the evidence required varies depending on the characteristics of that person (e.g., sex, race, presence or absence of a criminal record, country of origin, social class). It should also be noted that if these characteristics have more than two levels or states, then the possibility of multiple, rather than just double standards, occurs. In general, when different standards are applied to different types of people, the situation may be described as one in which particularistic rather than universalistic criteria are being applied.

Although double standards of several types appear to be common in a variety of settings, and some authors have presented valuable descriptions of them (as noted above), in general social scientists have not given the practice the attention it deserves. One of the few exceptions is Eichler (1977, 1980), who explicitly uses the expression "double standard" to refer to "all norms, rules and practices which evaluate, reward and punish identical behavior of women and men differently" (1977, p. 14). Her work is of special interest because she examines this practice from a perspective that includes several of its varieties. Thus, although her primary concern is with other types of double standards, her work does include ability inference. Furthermore, she notes that double standards may be based on categories other than gender (Eichler 1988).

Let us now concentrate on gender-based double standards for competence and on the empirical evidence of their operation. The work in this area is limited but may be classified into three groups: descriptions, indirect experimental evidence, and direct experimental evidence. In the first group, the writings of Kanter and Epstein provide insightful descriptions of particular interest. Although these authors do not always use the expression "double standards," it is clear that they are referring to this practice. Thus, Epstein (1970a, Chapter 5; 1970b; 1981, Chapters 1 and 3) reports that professional women often express the belief that they must be better than a man, and Kanter (1977a, 1977b) describes the increased performance pressures felt by women in token positions. For discussions in which the terms "double standards" (as well as "multiple standards") are used explicitly, see Epstein 1973, 1975.

The second group consists of three experiments from the status characteristics tradition. Although the words "double standards" are not used in this work, the results may be interpreted as indirect evidence of the practice. In all three cases, the experimental instructions describe the task to be completed as valuable, and motivate the subjects to collaborate with the other group member(s) in achieving its correct solution. All three studies investigate sex differences in acceptance of influence. The first two utilize the standardized setting common in expectation states research, the third employs a more open interaction context.

The study by Pugh and Wahrman (1983) has opposite-sex dyads and consists of two phases. In the first, each person performs the task individually and then receives scores for his or her performance and for that of the partner. The effects of these scores are measured by the amount of influence that is accepted from the partner in the second phase, where a series of prearranged disagreements between the two participants occurs. Claims by the experimenter that the task is sex-neutral are not sufficient to make the two subjects equally influential, nor are scores indicating that both persons have performed equally. It is only when the woman outperforms her male partner that she achieves the same level of influence as he does.

The second study, by Wagner et al. (1986), was designed to assess the effects of different types of performance information on initial expectations. Again, groups consisted of opposite-sex dyads, and subjects received scores that either confirmed (the woman performed worse than her partner) or contradicted (the woman performed better than her partner) those impressions. This was followed by a series of prearranged disagreements designed to measure acceptance of influence from the partner. As predicted, disconfirmation had a more pronounced effect on expectations (and corresponding influence rates) than did confirmation, and this was the case regardless of sex of subject. Moreover, among subjects who outperformed their opposite-sex partner, men *rejected more* influence than women; on the other hand, when subjects were outperformed by the partner, men *accepted less* influence than women. In other words, men were assigned ability (and denied lack of it) more readily than were women. Such findings suggest that different standards are being used to process performance information, depending on whether or not this information is in line with status-based expectations.

The third experiment is by Ridgeway (1982) and investigates perceptions of competence and acceptance of influence in four-person groups. Each group consists of either three male or three female subjects and a confederate who is either male or female. At each trial, the confederate is the last person to propose a solution to the group task and, by design, this choice is different from the one(s) suggested by the other three individuals. Furthermore, the confederate has been instructed to behave in either a self-oriented or a group-oriented manner when arguing for his or her choice. The results from the mixed-sex groups are of particular interest. Those findings show that although the group-oriented male confederate was only moderately more influential than his self-oriented counterpart, adopting the former attitude enabled the female confederate to be significantly more influential than did exhibiting the latter. It should be noted, however, that a group-oriented man stilll exerted more influence than a group-oriented woman. The results may be interpreted in terms of the operation of a double standard whereby the woman had to be seen as group oriented before she could attain a level of influence comparable to that of the self-oriented man.

These three status characteristics studies are of particular significance because of the consistency among their results. As a set, the three suggest that performance information is processed through a different standard depending on sex of the performer: women either have to perform better than men, or they have to exhibit additional qualities above those required of men, before both sexes exert comparable levels of influence.

The third group consists of studies that have been specifically designed to test propositions on the operation of double standards. To my knowledge, only the work by Foddy and Smithson (1989), Foschi (1989) and Foschi and Foddy (1988) comprises a systematic treatment of double standards for competence. Some of the propositions derived from this work have now been tested, with results providing direct evidence of this practice.

Foddy and Graham (1987) investigated standards for ability and lack of ability (as set by the subjects themselves) in same-sex and opposite-sex dyads. The task involved "pattern recognition," a specific, valued competence described to the subjects as either masculine or feminine, or of no known sex linkage. Scores received were prearranged to indicate that the subject had performed either definitely better or definitely worse than the partner; the effects of these scores on acceptance of influence were measured in a subsequent phase. The results regarding standards for ability imposed on self in the mixed-sex dyads are particularly interesting. Foddy and Graham found that when the task was defined as masculine, women set a stricter standard for themselves than did men. This effect was larger when the female subjects had performed worse than their male partner than when they had performed better than him. A double standard was again found when the task was defined as neutral, with the effect still being stronger in failure than in success. On the other hand, and as predicted, there was no evidence of a double standard when the task was defined as feminine. Results on acceptance of influence are consistent with those on standards, that is, the higher the standard for ability imposed on self, the less competence inferred relative to the partner and the greater the influence accepted from this person.

Although an experiment by Foschi (1990) investigated a similar situation to that studied by Foddy and Graham (1987), there were, however, some noteworthy differences. Foschi's central interest was on standards for ability applied to either self or partner in a task defined as masculine.

Furthermore, the study included control as well as experimental conditions. Two of the latter are of special interest. Subjects were told that self and partner had performed at an ordinary level, with the partner marginally outperforming the subject. The small difference between the two scores was introduced to provide subjects with the largest possible range in setting their standards. As expected, male subjects with a female partner reported a stricter standard for their teammate than did female subjects with a male partner. As in Foddy and Graham (1987), acceptance of influence results were again in line with those on standards. It is worth noting that the findings from these two experiments, taken together, indicate that double standards are activated by the sex difference between the performers *regardless* of both target of standard (self or other) and level of advantage (minimal or substantial) of one performer over the other.

The third study in this group is by Foschi, Lai, and Sigerson (1991). The work investigates double standards in a setting that replicates various key features of the hiring process in a professional context. Subjects were male and female undergraduates who were led to believe that they were members of a university-wide committee making recommendations for summer jobs. Each subject had to assess three files, each containing information about "short-listed candidates" for a position in one engineering field. The critical file consisted of a man and a woman applying for a job in nuclear engineering. In addition to sex of candidate, the only information differentiating the applicants were the grades obtained in relevant university courses. These grades were unexceptional for both candidates, but in one condition the man slightly outperformed the woman whereas in the other this situation was reversed. The subjects had three options for their recommendations: to hire either the man or the woman, or to hire neither. In my opinion, this measure is a key strength of the study. That is, subjects were not explicitly asked about the standards they were using, but revealed them through the choices they made (see footnote 6). In this way, a behavioral measure of their standards was obtained. Subjects were also asked to evaluate both candidates in terms of competence and suitability for the job.

Results show that a double standard was in operation in the decisions made by the male subjects. When the better performer was a man, he was chosen by these subjects significantly more times than they chose the woman when she was the better performer. Conversely, the subjects recommended either the worse performer or neither candidate significantly more often when the better performer was a woman than when this person was a man. The female subjects, however, did not show any of these tendencies. Furthermore, for subjects of both sexes, measures of competence and suitability were consistent with the choice measures. As mentioned earlier in this chapter, the authors interpret these results as an indication that men and women differed in the extent to which they treated sex as a status variable. It is also likely that the effects of that difference were heightened because p was an assessor but not a performer.

Suggestions for Further Research

As the previous section indicates, research on double standards has just begun. In this section I outline two directions that I think would be most fruitful to pursue in the future.

The studies by Foddy and Graham (1987) and by Foschi (1990) use the standardized experimental setting common to expectation states research, and extend it to include the measurement of subjects' standards. Together, the two studies investigate the effects of sex of subject, sex of partner, sex linkage of task, and level of performance. Both indicate that the design works well for the study of double standards. Thus, a first direction to pursue would be to use the same design to investigate the effects of other variables on double standards. This strategy would have the advantage of ensuring cumulativeness in the research.

In my opinion, two areas are of particular interest. The first involves studying the effects of a second status variable. For example, apart from sex, performers could be differentiated in terms of their ethnicity, educational background, or social class. What are the effects of such an addition? States of the second variable may be either consistently or inconsistently associated with states of sex. For example, either the man is white and the woman is black, or the man is black and the woman is white. According to Foschi's (1989) model (and the graph-theoretic formulation on which it is based), the state of each characteristic and the degree of consistency between the two determines the expectation advantage that one person has over the other. For example, a white man would have a larger expectation advantage over a black woman than over a white woman. The model also includes situations with more than two status characteristics. For any number of these characteristics, the prediction regarding standards is that the larger the expectation advantage of p over o, the stricter the standards for both ability and lack of ability imposed on o. The existence of such multiple standards has not yet been tested, however. The prediction is of special interest because of its consistency with work on the formation of performance expectations in multicharacteristic situations.

Another area where research is needed is that of the effects of extraordinary levels of performance (either successful or not) on the application of standards. Let us assume again that the situation involves two actors, a man and a woman. Let us also assume that, at those performance levels, each meets the respective standards applied to them. Therefore, under such circumstances, both should be assigned competence (or incompetence). But are they? Is it not often the case that, instead, yet other requirements are imposed on the successful female performer *ex post facto*? Conversely, when both perform at a definitely poor level, is not the man's perceived competence preserved by making the standard for lack of ability more lenient? Informal evidence suggests that, in success as well as in failure, the double standard is maintained by re-definition after the fact. I think of this process as "the Hydra phenomenon." The conditions under which it occurs, however, still need to be clearly identified. Because the redefined standard should be the one applied to the *next* performance, a thorough understanding of this process involves extending the current theoretical work on double standards to include more than one performance. A discussion of such an extension appears in Foschi (1989, p. 70).

Finally, research on double standards will also benefit from pursuing a second direction. This would involve attempting to link this practice at the interactional level to processes occurring at the structural level. For example, in both Canada and the United States, there are well-documented work-related gender inequalities at the latter level, such as the gender gap in earnings and related rewards, and the different rates at which men and women are hired and promoted (Colwill & Lips, 1988; Nielsen, 1990, pp. 65–75). Thus, women earn approximately two thirds of every dollar earned by men and have, in general, lower returns from their educational achievements than do their male counterparts (Calzavara, 1988; Giele, 1988).

I propose that a double standard for competence at the interactional level is a major factor contributing to those structural inequalities. One promising way of linking the two levels would be to design and carry out laboratory experiments replicating aspects of organizational settings (Evan, 1971; Zelditch, 1969). Thus, the informal task groups would become units in formal organizations, and the experimental tasks would be replaced with duties assigned by a supervisor. In this way, processes occurring in those units could be studied with the advantages of the experimental method. The investigation of the setting of standards for competence in formal organizations appears to be particularly suited to such a methodology, as standards easily translate into requirements for hiring and promotion. Although the approach is rich with possibilities, these have not yet been fully explored in the status characteristics tradition. The work by Foschi, Lai, and Sigerson (1991), however, is an experiment that attempts to do just that.

Conclusion

This chapter examines gender effects on the assignment of competence in task groups from the perspective of status characteristics theory. When there are no objective criteria for performance evaluation, men's contributions to the task solution are often judged to be better than women's. In some situations, however, objective criteria are available and women's performances can be clearly demonstrated to be as good as those of men. But even in those cases, gender often results in the devaluation of women's contributions. I propose that the mechanism through which this occurs is a double standard of ability inference, stricter for women than for men. For a better understanding of double standards, two areas are discussed first in the chapter: the operation of biased evaluations, and the effects of a single standard on ability inference. This discussion is followed by an outline of theoretical work on double standards for competence and a review of empirical evidence. Because research on this topic is only in its initial stages, there is yet much that needs to be learned. Nevertheless, only a clear understanding of how double standards operate will provide the means necessary to prevent their use. The chapter concludes with a discussion of the most promising areas for future research in this area.

Acknowledgment This chapter was prepared with the assistance of a research grant from the Social Sciences and Humanities Research Council of Canada (#482–88–0015, Strategic Grants Division, Women and Work Theme). This support is gratefully acknowledged.

References

Berger, J., Fisek, M.H., Norman, R.Z., & Zelditch, M., Jr. (1977). *Status characteristics and social interaction: An expectation-states approach.* New York: Elsevier.

Berger, J., Rosenholtz, S.J., & Zelditch, M., Jr. (1980). Status organizing processes. *Annual Review of Sociology, 6,* 479–508.

Berger, J., Wagner, D.G., & Zelditch, M., Jr. (1985). Introduction—expectation states theory: Review and assessment. In J. Berger & M. Zelditch, Jr. (Eds.), *Status, rewards, and influence: How expectations organize behavior* (pp. 1–72). San Francisco: Jossey-Bass.

Berger, J., Wagner, D.G., & Zelditch, M., Jr. (1989). Theory growth, social processes, and metatheory. In J.H. Turner (Ed.), *Theory building in sociology: Assessing theoretical cumulation* (pp. 19–42). Newbury Park, CA: Sage.

Blalock, H.M., Jr. (1979). *Black-white relations in the 1980's: Toward a long-term policy.* New York: Praeger.

Calzavara, L. (1988). Trends and policy in employment opportunities for women. In J. Curtis, E. Grabb, N. Guppy and S. Gilbert (Eds.), *Social inequality in Canada: Patterns, problems, policies* (pp. 287–300). Scarborough, Ont.: Prentice-Hall Canada.

Colwill, N., & Lips, H.M. (1988). Issues in the workplace. In H.M. Lips (Ed.), *Sex and gender: An introduction* (pp. 292–315). Mountain View, CA: Mayfield.

Deaux, K. (1984). From individual differences to social categories: Analysis of a decade's research on gender. *American Psychologist, 39,* 105–116.

Deaux, K. (1985). Sex and gender. *Annual Review of Psychology*, *36*, 49–81.

Deschamps, J.C. (1983). Social attribution. In J. Jaspars, F.D. Finchman, & M. Hewstone (Eds.), *Attribution theory and research: Conceptual, developmental and social dimensions* (pp. 223–240). London: Academic Press.

Deutsch, F.M., Zalenski, C.M., & Clark, M.E. (1986). Is there a double standard of aging? *Journal of Applied Social Psychology*, *16*, 771–785.

Dornbusch, S.M., & Scott, W.R. (1975). *Evaluation and the exercise of authority*. San Francisco: Jossey-Bass.

Eichler, M. (1977). The double standard as an indicator of sex-status differentials. *Atlantis*, *3*, 1–21.

Eichler, M. (1980). *The double standard: A feminist critique of feminist social science*. London: Croom Helm.

Eichler, M. (1988). *Nonsexist research methods: A practical guide*. Boston: Allen and Unwin.

Epstein, C.F. (1970a). *Woman's place: Options and limits in professional careers*. Berkeley, CA: University of California Press.

Epstein, C.F. (1970b). Encountering the male establishment: Sex-status limits on women's careers in the professions. *American Journal of Sociology*, *75*, 965–982.

Epstein, C.F. (1973). Bringing women in: Rewards, punishments, and the structure of achievement. *Annals of the New York Academy of Sciences*, *208*, 62–70.

Epstein, C.F. (1975). Tracking and careers: The case of women in American society. In E.L. Zuckerman (Ed.), *Women and men: Roles, attitudes and power relationships* (pp. 26–34). New York: Radcliffe Club.

Epstein, C.F. (1981). *Women in law*. New York: Basic Books.

Evan, W.M. (Ed.). (1971). *Organizational experiments: Laboratory and field research*. New York: Harper and Row.

Foddy, M., & Graham, H. (1987). *Sex and double standards in the inference of ability*. Paper presented at the Annual Meeting of the Canadian Psychological Association, Vancouver, B.C.

Foddy, M., & Smithson, M. (1989). Fuzzy sets and double standards: Modeling the process of ability inference. In J. Berger, M. Zelditch, Jr., & B. Anderson (Eds.), *Sociological theories in progress: New formulations* (pp. 73–99). Newbury Park, CA: Sage.

Foschi, M. (1986). Actors, observers, and performance expectations: A Bayesian model and an experimental study. *Advances in Group Processes: A Research Annual*, *3*, 181–208.

Foschi, M. (1989). Status characteristics, standards, and attributions. In J. Berger, M. Zelditch, Jr., & B. Anderson (Eds.), *Sociological theories in progress: New formulations* (pp. 58–72). Newbury Park, CA: Sage.

Foschi, M. (1990). *Double standards in the evaluation of men and women*. Paper presented at the Annual Meeting of the Canadian Sociology and Anthropology Association, Vancouver, B.C.

Foschi, M., & Foddy, M. (1988). Standards, performances, and the formation of self-other expectations. In M. Webster, Jr. & M. Foschi (Eds.), *Status generalization: New theory and research* (pp. 248–260, 501–503). Stanford, CA: Stanford University Press.

Foschi, M., & Foschi, R. (1976). Evaluations and expectations: A Bayesian model. *Journal of Mathematical Sociology*, *4*, 279–293.

Foschi, M., & Foschi, R. (1979). A Bayesian model for performance expectations: Extension and simulation. *Social Psychology Quarterly*, *42*, 232–241.

Foschi, M., & Freeman, S. (1991). Inferior performance, standards, and influence in same-sex dyads. *Canadian Journal of Behavioural Science*, *23*, 99–113.

Foschi, M., Lai, L., & Sigerson, K. (1991). *Double standards in the assessment of male and female job applicants.* Paper presented at the West Coast Conference on Small Group Research, San Jose, CA.

Foschi, M., & Plecash, J. (1983). *Sex differences in the attribution of success and failure: An expectation-states explanation.* Paper presented at the Annual Meeting of the Canadian Sociology and Anthropology Association, Vancouver, B.C.

Foschi, M., Warriner, G.K., & Hart, S.D. (1985). Standards, expectations, and interpersonal influence. *Social Psychology Quarterly*, *48*, 108–117.

Giele, J.Z. (1988). Gender and sex roles. In N.J. Smelser (Ed.), *Handbook of sociology* (pp. 291–323). Newbury Park, CA: Sage.

Goldberg, P. (1968). Are women prejudiced against women? *Transaction, 5*, 28–30.

Hansen, R.D., & O'Leary, V.E. (1985). Sex-determined attributions. In V.E. O'Leary, R.K. Unger, & B.S. Wallston (Eds.), *Women, gender, and social psychology* (pp. 67–99). Hillsdale, NJ: Erlbaum.

Harvey, J.H., & Weary, G. (1984). Current issues in attribution theory and research. *Annual Review of Psychology*, *35*, 427–459.

Harvey, O.J. (1953). An experimental approach to the study of status relations in informal groups. *American Sociological Review*, *18*, 357–367.

Heider, F. (1944). Social perception and phenomenal causality. *Psychological Review*, *51*, 358–374.

Hewstone, M., & Jaspars, J. (1982). Intergroup relations and attribution processes. In H. Tajfel (Ed.), *Social identity and intergroup relations* (pp. 99–133). Cambridge: Cambridge University Press.

Higgins, E.T., Strauman, T. & Klein, R. (1986). Standards and the process of self-evaluation: Multiple affects from multiple stages. In R.M. Sorrentino & E.T. Higgins (Eds.), *Handbook of motivation and cognition: Foundations of social behavior* (pp. 23–63). New York: Guilford Press.

Howard, J.A. (1990). A sociological framework for cognition. *Advances in Group Processes: A Research Annual*, *7*, 75–103.

Humphrey, R. (1985). How work roles influence perception: Structural-cognitive processes and organizational behavior. *American Sociological Review*, *50*, 242–252.

James, W. (1981). [Originally published in 1890]. *The principles of psychology*, Vol. 1. Cambridge, MA: Harvard University Press.

Kanter, R.M. (1977a). *Men and women of the corporation.* New York: Basic Books.

Kanter, R.M. (1977b). Some effects of proportions on group life: Skewed sex ratios and responses to token women. *American Journal of Sociology*, *82*, 965–990.

Kelley, H.H., & Michela, J.L. (1980). Attribution theory and research. *Annual Review of Psychology*, *31*, 457–501.

Latham, G.P., & Yukl, G.A. (1975). A review of research on the application of goal setting in organizations. *Academy of Management Journal, 18*, 824–845.

Lee, T.W., Locke, E.A, & Latham, G.P. (1989). Goal setting theory and job performance. In L.A. Pervin (Ed.), *Goal concepts in personality and social psychology* (pp. 291–326). Hillsdale, NJ: Erlbaum.

Lewin, K., Dembo, T., Festinger, L., & Sears, P.S. (1944). Level of aspiration. In J.M. Hunt (Ed.), *Personality and the behavior disorders* (Vol. 1, pp. 333–378). New York: Ronald Press.

Lips, H.M. (1988). *Sex and gender: An introduction.* Mountain View, CA: Mayfield.

Locke, E.A., Shaw, K.N., Saari, L.M., & Latham, G.P. (1981). Goal setting and task performance: 1969–1980. *Psychological Bulletin, 90*, 125–152.

Lockheed, M.E. (1985). Sex and social influence: A meta-analysis guided by theory. In J. Berger and M. Zelditch, Jr. (Eds.), *Status, rewards, and influence: How expectations organize behavior* (pp. 406–429). San Francisco: Jossey-Bass.

Lockheed, M.E., & Hall, K.P. (1976). Conceptualizing sex as a status characteristic: Applications to leadership training strategies. *Journal of Social Issues, 32*, 111–124.

Lott, B. (1985). The devaluation of women's competence. *Journal of Social Issues, 41*, 43–60.

Maslin, A., & Davis, J.L. (1975). Sex role stereotyping as a factor in mental health standards among counselors-in-training. *Journal of Counseling Psychology, 22*, 87–91.

McArthur, L.Z. (1985). Social judgment biases in comparable worth analysis. In H.I. Hartmann (Ed.), *Comparable worth: New directions for research* (pp. 53–70). Washington, DC: National Academy Press.

McDill, E.L., Natriello, G., & Pallas, A.M. (1986). A population at risk: Potential consequences of tougher school standards for student dropouts. *American Journal of Education, 94*, 135–181.

Meeker, B.F., & Weitzel-O'Neill, P.A. (1977). Sex roles and interpersonal behavior in task-oriented groups. *American Sociological Review, 42*, 91–105.

Moore, J.C., Jr. (1968). Status and influence in small group interactions. *Sociometry, 31*, 47–63.

Moore, J.C., Jr. (1969). Social status and social influence: Process considerations. *Sociometry, 32*, 145–158.

Natriello, G., & Dornbusch, S.M. (1984). *Teacher evaluative standards and student effort.* New York: Longman.

Natriello, G., & McDill, E.L. (1986). Performance standards, student effort on homework, and academic achievement. *Sociology of Education, 59*, 18–31.

Nielsen, J.M. (1990). *Sex and gender in society: Perspectives on stratification* (2nd ed.). Prospect Heights, IL: Waveland Press.

Nieva, V.F., & Gutek, B.A. (1980). Sex effects on evaluation. *Academy of Management Review, 5*, 267–276.

Olson, J.M., & Ross, M. (1985). Attribution research: Past contributions, current trends, and future prospects. In J.H. Harvey & G. Weary (Eds.), *Attribution: Basic issues and applications* (pp. 281–311). Orlando, FL: Academic Press.

Paludi, M.A., & Strayer, L.A. (1985). What's in an author's name? Differential evaluations of performance as a function of author's name. *Sex Roles, 12*, 353–361.

Pugh, M.D., & Wahrman, R. (1983). Neutralizing sexism in mixed-sex groups: Do women have to be better than men? *American Journal of Sociology, 88,* 746–762.

Ridgeway, C.L. (1982). Status in groups: The importance of motivation. *American Sociological Review, 47,* 76–88.

Ridgeway, C.L. (1988). Gender differences in task groups: A status and legitimacy account. In M. Webster, Jr. & M. Foschi (Eds.), *Status generalization: New theory and research* (pp. 188–206, 495–497). Stanford, CA: Stanford University Press.

Ross, M., & Fletcher, G.J.O. (1985). Attribution and social perception. In G. Lindzey & E. Aronson (Eds.), *Handbook of social psychology* (3rd ed., Vol. 2, pp. 73–122) New York: Random House.

Sears, D.O., Freedman, J.L., & Peplau, L.A. (1985). *Social psychology* (5th ed.). Englewood Cliffs, NJ: Prentice-Hall.

Sherif, M., White, B.J. & Harvey, O.J. (1955). Status in experimentally produced groups. *American Journal of Sociology, 60,* 370–379.

Sohn, D. (1982). Sex differences in achievement self-attributions: An effect-size analysis. *Sex Roles, 8,* 345–357.

Sontag, S. (1972, September 23). The double standard of aging. *Saturday Review,* 29–38.

Stewart, P. (1988). Women and men in groups: A status characteristics approach to interaction. In M. Webster, Jr. & M. Foschi (Eds.), *Status generalization: New theory and research* (pp. 69–85, 484–486). Stanford, CA: Stanford University Press.

Tudor, W., Tudor, J., & Gove, W.R. (1979). The effect of sex role differences on the social reaction to mental retardation. *Social Forces, 57,* 871–886.

Wagner, D.G. (1988). Gender inequalities in groups: A situational approach. In M. Webster, Jr. & M. Foschi (Eds.), *Status generalization: New theory and research* (pp. 55–68, 480–484). Stanford, CA: Stanford University Press.

Wagner, D.G., Ford, R.S., & Ford, T.W. (1986). Can gender inequalities be reduced? *American Sociological Review, 51,* 47–61.

Wallston, B.S., & O'Leary, V.E. (1981). Sex makes a difference: Differential perceptions of women and men. In L. Wheeler (Ed.), *Review of personality and social psychology* (pp. 9–41). Beverly Hills, CA: Sage.

Webster, M., Jr., & Driskell, J.E., Jr. (1978). Status generalization: A review and some new data. *American Sociological Review, 43,* 220–236.

Webster, M., Jr., & Entwisle, D.R. (1976). Expectation effects on performance evaluations. *Social Forces, 55,* 493–502.

Webster, M., Jr., & Foschi, M. (1988). Overview of status generalization. In M. Webster, Jr. & M. Foschi (Eds.), *Status generalization: New theory and research* (pp. 1–20, 477–478). Stanford, CA: Stanford University Press.

Whitley, B.E., Jr., McHugh, M.C., & Frieze, I.H. (1986). Assessing the theoretical models for sex differences in causal attributions of success and failure. In J.S. Hyde & M.C. Linn (Eds.), *The psychology of gender: Advances through meta-analysis* (pp. 102–135). Baltimore: Johns Hopkins University Press.

Wiley, M.G. (1986). How expectation states organize theory construction. *Contemporary Sociology, 15,* 338–341.

Zander, A., & Cohen, A.R. (1955). Attributed social power and group acceptance: A classroom experimental demonstration. *Journal of Abnormal and Social Psychology, 51*, 490–492.

Zelditch, M., Jr. (1969). Can you really study an army in the laboratory? In A. Etzioni (Ed.), *A sociological reader on complex organizations* (2nd ed., pp. 528–539). New York: Holt, Rinehart, and Winston.

9
Gender, Interaction, and Inequality in Organizations

PATRICIA YANCEY MARTIN

People today live much of their lives in and through formal organizations. Worshipping, learning to add and subtract, having babies, fighting wars, and making laws are organizational activities. The thesis of this chapter is that formal organizations are highly gendered, in addition to being ubiquitous, and are excellent sites for studying gender interaction and inequality (cf. Acker, 1990; Burrell & Hearn, 1989).

Organizations mirror society. They reflect gender inequality in addition to race/ethnic stratification, class stratification, and age stratification (Martin & Chernesky, 1989; Miller, 1986). The gendering practices of families and other existential groups—e.g., neighbors, play groups, prayer groups, friendship cliques—are paralleled in the formally organized arenas of paid work. But organizations do more than mirror; they also *create*. They create ideologies, norms, and practices that produce and reproduce *gendered activities and social relations* within their walls.

Most economic activity is performed in formal organizations. Gender is such a constitutive part of formal organizations that efforts to match *worker and activity* are often efforts to match *gender and activity*: finding men to do men's work, finding women to do women's work (Acker, 1990; Cockburn, 1988). Labor markets, jobs, occupations, organizational hierarchies, work groups, work activities, technology uses, supervisory practices, and procedures for promotion, hiring, and advancement, and so on, are gendered (Bibb & Form, 1977; Cockburn, 1988; Reskin & Roos, 1990). The gendered arrangements and practices of markets and economic organizations are consequential for all women and men, even those who do not work for pay, because they influence arrangements and practices in other institutional spheres (Lorber, 1991).

This chapter concerns *how* organizations create and sustain gender inequality. Many theories characterize bureaucratic organizations as gender blind and jobs as "empty positions" waiting to be filled by the best applicants, regardless of gender. I suggest alternatively that organizations *gender their members proactively* through a range of mechanisms that are mediated by *interactional encounters* (Bergmann, 1986; Cohn, 1985;

Cockburn, 1988; Hearn & Parkin, 1987; 1988; Martin, 1985). Interactional encounters are, in turn, mediated by the cultural and social context of the organization which is itself mediated by the cultural and social features—ideologies, arrangements, practices—of the broader society. A focus on interaction relative to the creation and re-creation of gender inequality *in and by* formal organizations calls for a rethinking of organizational theory (Acker, 1990; Blum, 1987, 1991).

This chapter has three purposes: (a) It locates organizations in a gendered sociocultural context—where labor market, work-family relations, and societal beliefs and practices engender paid work arrangements a priori. For example, when an organization requires *men/husbands/fathers* to work 60 hours a week, this effectively relegates responsibility for home/child care to *women/wives/mothers* (see Finch, 1981, and Margolis, 1979). (b) It identifies micro, interactional mechanisms through which organizations actively *gender* their members, work practices, and arrangements. (c) It calls for more research on groups. Understanding of the processes, conditions, and temporal determinants of gender inequality in formal organizations can increase if more attention is paid to the interactions among women, among men, and between women and men that occur in groups at work (McGrath, 1986; West & Zimmerman, 1987).

Background

Research documents the gendered character of the hierarchies, divisions, departments, internal labor markets, units, interpersonal relations, rhetoric and ideology, arrangements, and activities of work organizations. A minority of women and men work in truly mixed (gender) units (Bielby & Baron, 1986; Reskin, 1988; Wharton & Baron, 1987) or, if they do, they have different job titles and statuses. Men and women seldom hold similar amounts or forms of authority (Reskin & Ross, 1991). If gender is *irrelevant* to the organization of paid work, as gender-neutral theories of organizations claim (Acker, 1990), how is it possible that gender is so pervasively confounded with jobs, hierarchies, labor markets, and the entire organization of work, paid and unpaid?

Until recently, a conception of formal organizations as rational-technical tools for maximizing efficiency and productivity was widely accepted (Katz & Kahn, 1966; Thompson, 1967). Bias, discrimination, exploitation, politics, and "irrational" practices were claimed to be absent from formal organizations. Differential hierarchy, rewards, status, and privilege were said to be *necessary* for coordinated, efficient organization (Barnard, 1938). Such a view continues to be espoused by many management texts, training programs, and university courses.

But rational-technical theory is under attack. More recent theories depict organizations as sexist, racist, class-based and -driven, conflict-ridden, politicized, and ideological (e.g., Dressel et al., 1988; Hearn & Parkin, 1983, 1987; Kanter, 1977). Exploitation, self-interest, and politics are often as important to organizational elites as efficiency, rationality, and productivity are (e.g., Connell, 1987; Edwards, 1979; Jackall, 1988; Martin, 1990; Meyer & Rowan, 1977). New theories reject claims that jobs are gender-neutral, "empty positions" waiting to be filled by objectively best-qualified candidates (Acker, 1990; Cockburn, 1988; Cohn, 1985). They claim that biological sex, sexuality, and gender are fundamental aspects of organizational practice and structure (Burrell & Hearn, 1989). Politics and the pursuit of self-interest foster the recruitment and promotion of men over women, and whites over minorities (Martin & Chernesky, 1989; Reskin, 1988). Privileged persons devise rules for advancement and hiring that protect their positions (Lieberson, 1985) and they rarely sacrifice their status, rewards, or power for the sake of organizational efficiency or goals (Jackall, 1988).

A body of research documents the gendering *of* and *in* work organizations. According to this evidence, most jobs are gendered—before they are filled, when they are filled or refilled, and as they are socially constructed, enacted, evaluated, or altered (Cockburn, 1988; Cohn, 1985; Reskin & Roos, 1990; Williams, 1989). To illustrate this claim, the next section reviews some of the ways organizations are gendered, partly as a result of their embeddedness in a culture and society that devalue and subordinate women and women's normative activities. This review provides an introduction to the mechanisms that organizations employ to *actively gender* their internal arrangements and practices and their members' options, activities, and work and extra-work lives (cf. Finch, 1981; Hochschild, 1983; 1989; Lewis, 1989).

Gendered Markets, Jobs, Hierarchies, and Groups

The Gendered Labor Market

Dual, segmented, or split labor markets theory claims that women and men constitute different, and differently advantaged, labor markets (Baron & Bielby, 1984; Baron & Norris, 1976; Bibb & Form, 1977; Miller, 1986; Tienda, Smith, & Ortiz, 1987). This theory views majority (white) men who are neither young nor old as the primary or core market and women along with minority men and young or old white men as the secondary or peripheral market (Dressel, 1987; Dressel et al., 1988). Miller (1986) reports that majority men, majority women, minority men, and minority women form *four different labor markets* both outside and inside work organizations and, in line with the theory, finds that majority men are advantaged in both spheres.

Dual labor markets theory claims that women and men have different opportunities and experiences in organizations because they enter the job search arena through different starting gates. Among the reasons for women's disadvantaged start are girls' socialization by family, school, peers, the media, the church, and so on, to pursue traditional women's fields (including full-time marriage and motherhood) and to avoid math, science, and authority, which normatively belong to boys and men. Women's expectations, experiences, and qualifications, along with assumptions and preferences about men's versus women's commitment and relation to paid employment combine to situate men and women differently when they join the labor force. Women and men do not arrive at the organization's door as equals.

The Gendered Organization

Organizations are pervasively gendered, largely to women's detriment (Acker, 1990; Martin, 1991). This was the case, furthermore, from the earliest days of centralized production (i.e., the factory system). Early English capitalists had trouble luring men into factories where work was supervised and monitored but were more successful in recruiting women, the men's daughters and wives (Clegg & Dunkerley, 1979; Marglin, 1976). Men were recruited, eventually, to supervise these women. From the factory's early days, most jobs, positions, and activities were the purview primarily of women or primarily of men. Though the particulars of gender arrangements change with time—as in a shift from men to women for clerical work (Cohn, 1985)—the treatment of particular jobs, activities, and positions as men's or as women's continues (Bielby & Baron, 1986; Reskin & Roos, 1990).

Gendered Occupations

Occupations are broad groupings of work activities such as sales, accounting, and medicine and *occupational sex segregation* refers to the clustering of men and women in different occupations (Reskin & Hartmann, 1986; Reskin & Roos, 1987). Women predominate in secretarial, clerical, and nursing work; men predominate in engineering, heavy construction, and mining work. Research by Cohn (1985) showed that *employers sought out* women or men employees, depending on the labor needs or capital intensity of their organization. Studies over time show that occupations "tip" from men's to women's work when men abandon them because of declining rewards, status, or opportunities (Baran, 1985; Reskin, 1988). Occupational changes are generally *from* men's work *to* women's work, not to a stable mixed condition (Reskin & Roos, 1990).

The dynamics of occupational sex segregation are only starting to be understood. Computing work, a new occupation, would seem to provide opportunity for a true gender mix and more options for women. But computer work is stratified internally into men's work and women's work.

Men perform head work—computer scientist and programmer—and women do the routine work—data entry and computer equipment operator (Glenn & Tolbert, 1987). The *interactional mechanisms* that separate workers by gender need to be documented, as this chapter underscores. (See Bergmann, 1986, Bielby & Baron, 1987, and Reskin, 1988, for examples of such mechanisms.)

Gendered Jobs

Jobs are more gendered than occupations are (Acker, 1990; Baron & Bielby, 1985, 1986; Bielby & Baron, 1984). Jobs are positions with associated activities that comprise the official division of labor of an organization. Bielby and Baron (1986) found that the large majority of jobs in 393 establishments were, over a 20-year period, completely sex-segregated (the percentage of jobs that contained *only* women or *only* men was 93.4%). Even when aggregate data suggested otherwise, detailed analysis showed that most women and men were segregated into different jobs, units, departments, divisions, or physical locations. Job segregation occurs in two ways.

1. *Men's work, women's work.* Many jobs are viewed from their inception as women's work or men's work (Acker, 1990). Work viewed as men's work in one organization or historical era may be viewed as women's work in another. Employers make decisions—based on the nature of work activities, labor supply and costs, and men's willingness to perform certain jobs—and invoke gender-based arguments to justify them. Ideological invocations of gender stereotypes (Cohn, 1985) may reflect material and status differences between the genders in the organization. For example, claims that women are *better* at assembling computer chip boards because their fingers are smaller or that they *prefer* detailed work may be used to obscure the fact that men refuse to do such work because it is repetitive, boring, a strain on the eyes, and/or place-bound (cf. Cockburn, 1988; Cohn, 1985). Women lack the power and status in society to refuse such work.
2. *Identical work, different titles.* Jobs involving identical work activities are called by different names so that men and women *do not appear to do equal work* (Baron & Bielby, 1985, 1986; Bielby & Baron, 1986). A woman's job may be labeled Techician I and a man's Assembler I, although an observer would be unable to discern a difference in work activity (Acker, 1989). Titling men's and women's jobs differently when they involve identical tasks is usually attributed to management's goal of separating men from women in order to justify men's higher rate of pay. Separation and differential compensation almost always favor men (Baron & Newman, 1990; Blum, 1991; Reskin, 1988).

Gendered Bureaucratic Hierarchy

Most economic organizations are structured as bureaucratic hierarchies of administrative positions that confer differential power, perks, resources, options, and rewards. Men predominate at the upper echelons, numerically and positionally, and most women, even those in management, occupy low pay, minimal power, and limited opportunity positions (Hardesty & Jacobs, 1986; Kanter, 1977; Morrison & Von Glinow, 1990; Reskin & Ross, 1991). Women are crowded into lower echelons, regardless of the type of organization or industrial sector involved (Brown, 1988; Hearn & Parkin, 1988). Many men supervise women; few women supervise men (Boyd, Mulvihill, & Myles, 1990). Even in mixed groups, men and women rarely work together as equals. Typically, men and women are differentiated simultaneously by bureaucratic hierarchy *and* by gender hierarchy, so that official rank and gender status are confounded (cf. Blau, 1977; Martin, 1985). The consequences of this confounding are discussed below.

Gendered Job Ladders

Related to bureacratic hierarchy, but also different, are job ladders or internal labor markets. (Job ladders can exist independently of bureaucractic hierarchies, e.g., in civil service or union seniority systems where education or tenure lead to incremental raises in pay grades, wages, etc.) Internal labor markets are job hierarchies along which workers can advance in pay, seniority, job security, and, in some instances, supervisory status. Research shows that internal labor markets are highly gendered (Baron, Davis-Blake, & Bielby, 1986; Bielby & Baron, 1986, 1987). Many more women than men hold *jobs that are not in job ladders* (Baron et al., 1986), with material and social psychological consequences for men as well as women (cf. Edwards, 1979). Kanter (1977) found that the perception of opportunity *preceded* the creation of ambition in women; that is, women who did not *perceive advancement opportunities* did not aspire to advance. Thus, arrangements and practices that steer women (and minority men) into jobs that lie outside of job ladders dissuade them from aspiring to move up or seek jobs that are situated in job ladders.

Gendered Unions

Unions have influenced gender relations since they began (Marglin, 1976). They have often failed to recruit women as members or, when they have, to support them for leadership positions (Izraeli, 1984). Historically, unions have pursued bargaining agreements that ignored women's circumstances and material needs and excluded women from jobs and economic activities that would allow women to compete with men for jobs, lower men's wages, and so on (Cornfield, 1989; Feldberg, 1980; Marglin, 1976; Martin, Seymour, Godbey, Courage, & Tate, 1988; Milkman, 1980, 1982).

With the recent growth in professional and white collar unions (e.g., Associated Federal, State, and Municipal Employees), unions have begun recruiting women and, in some instances, have made women's issues a union priority. Public employee unions and the American nurses' union have bargained for pay equity policies for women in public sector jobs (Acker, 1989; Godbey, 1987; Steinberg, 1987). Research by Martin et al. (1988) found that women union leaders were more supportive than men union leaders of organizational benefits and policies to help employees with their family responsibilities. Male leaders differed little from their management counterparts, male and female, in their lukewarm support for such policies; thus, conflicts about gender in unions will likely continue.

Gendered Groups

Men and women work together in groups, e.g., a surgical team of male physicians and female nurses, but few interact with opposite gender *peers* (Baron & Bielby, 1986; Bielby and Baron, 1986). Nevertheless, most interactional encounters at work occur in group contexts (cf. Alderfer & Smith, 1982; Izraeli, 1983; McGrath, 1986; Schwartzman, 1986) and the effects of group dynamics on gender inequality need to be explored. The next section reviews some mechanisms through which organizational arrangements and activities *gender* members' activities and social relations, and the following section focuses on selected group dynamics that contribute to gender inequality in the organization.

Gender Mechanisms in the Organization

Where does gender importation from other institutional spheres leave off and *original gendering* by organizations begin? A male boss may rhetorically (cf. Miller, 1991) represent a job as women's work because the activity is consistent with women's family roles, e.g., child care, nursing, tending the elderly or retarded. He may invoke expectations, assumptions, and norms associated with women's so-called natural caretaking or nurturing responsibilities. This is a case of *gender importation*: gender is imported from the broader context to justify internal arrangements. But what if the work activity *contradicts* normative expectations for women—as in shipbuilding, welding, or longshoring jobs in World War II? What does the boss say then?

Other rhetorical claims are invoked to justify work as acceptable for women or men. An employer may acknowledge that work is appropriately men's but claim that extraordinary circumstances, such as war or a short labor supply, require women to perform it. Women may be asked to show their patriotism or help the community by doing *men's* work. In noncrisis times, employers may claim that women have special attributes such as good hand-eye coordination, small fingers, a preference for repetitive, detailed, or place-bound work, or other qualities that make certain jobs uniquely theirs. Employers use arguments like this to justify women's predominance in computer-chip work and wiring-board work (cf. Pringle, 1989). Such arguments have no parallel in other institutional spheres and are examples of *gender origination or creation* by the organization.

Many mechanisms contribute to gendering and women's subordination in organizations and many of them involve interaction—among men, among women, and between men and women. A review of some mechanisms follows.

Organizations Gender Their Tasks and Activities

All societies allocate tasks, activities, and behaviors by gender. In our society, formal organizations participate in this allocational process—affecting children as well as adults. (See Scott, 1986, on how schools gender students; and Cockburn, 1988, Kanter, 1977, and Pringle, 1989, on adults). Organizations *gender* members through their conception, assignment, and evaluation of tasks, activities, and behaviors (Baron & Newman, 1990). As noted above, some tasks are gendered outside of work—e.g., in the family such as caring for children, nurturing, and caretaking, making decisions, controlling people and money—and affirmed and re-created through organizational arrangements, practices, and ideology. In other cases, gendering at work contradicts assumptions on the outside, e.g., as when women were recruited in World War II to perform traditional men's work or when men are required to be secretaries and clerks in the military.

Organizations do not consistently view activities or jobs as female-appropriate or male-appropriate. Cockburn's (1988) research shows that the demands of technology relative to gender are minimal. Claims about technological imperatives are invoked, however, to *justify* assigning tasks and jobs to women or to men. As an example, clerical work was men's work for most of the 19th century but after the typewriter was invented, clerical work became routinized. It no longer provided entry into the organization's internal labor market, women could be hired to perform it for less pay, and men were able to obtain work that paid more and led to more opportunities. Thus, employers regendered clerical work as women's work rather than men's (Cohn, 1985).

Employers Seek Women as Cheap Labor

From the start of the industrial revolution, capitalist owners sought cheap labor (Marglin, 1976). Women's labor was and is cheapened by a variety of gender-related mechanisms. Fears that women's entry will lower men's wages prompted early union men to oppose women in jobs that men valued. This and other forces forced women to crowd into jobs that pay less. Too many applicants for these jobs cheapened women's labor even more. The crowding of women into few positions heightened women's competition with each other, lessening the odds of collective organization and protest. Women's need for work (e.g., to feed their children) influenced them to work for less (Bianchi & Spain, 1986). Beliefs and stereotypes that discredit women's qualifications for managerial jobs—particularly when they involve authority over men (Boyd et al., 1990)—also cause women to be excluded from upper echelon positions. As a result, some jobs are earmarked for women because women will work for less (Baran, 1985; Baron & Newman, 1990; Cohn, 1985).

Cohn (1985) reports that employers sought women to perform low-paying, labor-intensive clerical work in the British post office in the late 19th century because their labor was cheap. The decision to use women clerks was not a decision to help women or harm men but to find cheap labor. Baran (1985) reports similar reasons for the relocation of American insurance companies to the suburbs and the downgrading of claims adjustor work in the 1980s. They moved to find well-educated, middle-class housewives who would work part-time, for low pay and few benefits (pp. 165–166). With the advent of computers, and home-based work, employers were able to reduce plant, land, and overhead costs and to de-skill jobs that were previously considered professional and that had been held by men. Women were recruited for work that was being automated and was losing the skills, discretion, high pay, and professional status it formerly had. Insurance jobs slated for complete automation were held by minority women, indicating that race/ethnicity in addition to gender are implicated in organizational decisions (Baran, 1985; also Miller, 1986). For many reasons, a search for cheap labor is a gendered search—a search for women (and minority) workers (Dressel et al., 1988). This search affects majority men also because the jobs they hold may be eliminated, or downgraded, when cheaper workers are hired.

Male Managers Act to Preserve Male Privilege and Jobs

Another gender mechanism involves male manager's efforts to reserve privilege and jobs for men. In any bureaucracy, the better-paying, more rewarding, and more powerful positions are scarce and coveted (Cohn, 1985; Reskin, 1988). Men's overwhelming predominance in these positions allows them to exercise control and, importantly, to choose their successors. They (correctly) see that most other men and all women are their competitors. According to Kanter (1977), male managers practice "homosocial reproduction" in an attempt to recruit men who like and admire them, share their goals and values, and will protect them by maintaining the status quo. Very different replacements—such as majority women or minority women or men—may have different goals and values and may favor change that disadvantages incumbents.

When jobs are scarce, male managers may protect ordinary jobs from women (Cohn, 1985). For example, male managers in the British railway industry delayed converting clerical work from men's to women's work long after other industries had made the switch (Cohn, 1985). Because only a few types of jobs existed in this capital-intensive industry, protecting the clerical jobs from women was a way of preserving these jobs for men. Such tactics are grounded in cultural assumptions that men deserve to have paid work more than women do.

Male Peers Exclude Women from Their Jobs and Groups

Male peers may prevent the admission of women to their jobs, units, or organizations if they believe women's entry will lower their material and symbolic statuses (Bergmann, 1986; Cockburn, 1988; Cohn, 1985; Zimmer, 1987). Given women's lower status and rates of pay, women's entry into all-male jobs or units—such as prison guard, fire department, mining crew, law firm, or academic department—may indeed lower pay and status (Toren & Kraus, 1987). Zimmer (1987) found that women prison guards were viewed by men guards as violating the job's masculinity assumptions and requirements (also Reskin & Padavic, 1988). The job's *masculine* qualities—being tough, in control, or macho—were called into question by women's entry. To protect their material and symbolic advantages, therefore, some men excluded, threatened, and undermined women applicants and peers (Bergmann, 1986; Cohn, 1985).

Small-group researchers should explore this perceptual and interactional dynamic. Male peers who exclude women to preserve their privileges may be especially resistant to affirmative action remedies and goals (Toren & Kraus, 1987). Men's use of the ideology and rhetoric of objectivity and achievement to justify women's exclusion at work is discussed by Martin and associates (DiNitto, Martin, & Harrison, 1982; Martin, 1980; 1982; Martin, Harrison, & DiNitto, 1983). They contend that women's so-called qualification and performance deficits at work are often *post hoc rationalizations* rather than *a priori causes*. Whereas the devaluation of women qua women is viewed as illegitimate, or sexist, the use of so-called objective criteria to devalue women is legitimate. Assessments of *objective* qualifications and performance are *subjectively* made, however, and since male-normative assumptions undergird conceptions of work qualifications and performance (Martin, 1985), the odds are substantial that men will make self-interested, male-favoring judgments when assessing women at work (cf. Acker, 1989; Blum, 1991).

Male Workers Refuse to Accept Dead-End, Repetitive, Place-Bound, Low-Pay Jobs

Women are allocated the least rewarding and most deadening jobs in organizations partly because men have more power to have themselves otherwise assigned. Cockburn (1988) found that male supervisors and employees colluded to preserve for men the jobs that were least repetitive, boring, place-bound, and physically abusive. Women were given the undesirable jobs. Due to their disadvantaged labor market status, and to dynamics and conditions that devalue them in the organization, women often have no choice but to take demanding, unrewarding jobs (cf. Edwards, 1979).

Men's Masculinity Displays and Competitiveness Handicap Women

The gender dynamics of relations *among* men and *among* women, as well as between them, are consequential for women at work. The enactment of gender-normative behaviors is called *gender displays* by West and Zimmerman (1987). Men's *masculinity displays* can exclude, diminish, and offend women even when they are not intended to. For example, a Wall Street bond trading firm refers to top achievers as "Big Swinging Dicks" and has a practice of broadcasting pornography over the loud-speaker system in the mornings (Lewis, 1989). Such appellations and practices are not directed at women but women who work there are unlikely to feel included or affirmed by them.

An example from a law firm illustrates how men compete with each other to maintain valued identities. When the firm's president resigned, the top candidate for the job was a competent, well-liked, senior partner—a man. Other senior men agreed he was the best candidate but blocked his election because "it would make him [the candidate] too powerful." The resigning president had jeopardized the firm's financial status and the man in question was acknowledged as the best person to turn things around. Ultimately, the senior men made the candidate vice president and gave him operational authority over the firm but they never made him president. The partner who reported the story, a woman, saw her male colleagues as more concerned with their own status than the firm's welfare. In her view, the candidate's interpersonal skills and intelligence, plus the power of the presidency, threatened the other men; they were reluctant to make their peer president, although he was right for the job, because it would elevate him over themselves (cf. Aires, 1976; Martin & Shanahan, 1983).

This interpretation confirms Cockburn's (1988) finding that men at work perceive other men as competitors and have little trust of each other. The men in her sample were far more threatened by other men than by women. Men are sometimes threatened by women, however. Generally, men assume they can always beat a woman—that a woman will never be "real competition" for them. If by chance a woman reaches a competitive position or demonstrates enough skill to become true competition, men are *more* threatened by her than by a man. This is due to the status loss associated with losing to a woman.

Managers Segregate Women and Men to Facilitate Pay Differentials and Minimize Inter-Gender Comparisons and Contacts

The strategy of segregating women and men at work benefits male managers and workers and generally penalizes women. Segregation takes several forms including the recruitment and assignment of women and men to jobs with different titles and their placement in separate job ladders, hierarchical positions, and physical locations. Male managers— and the organizational balance sheet—benefit from segregation because they can pay women less for work that is comparable (or equal) to men's, partly because of women's lesser value in the labor market and partly because of women's crowding into a few jobs (cf. Bielby & Baron, 1987). Male workers benefit from higher pay for work that is no more difficult, and is often more interesting, varied, and easier, than the work women do. Segregation reduces the opportunities for invidious comparisons by women who see that their work is similar in difficulty and skill to men's (Bielby & Baron, 1987). If women cannot observe men at work, they cannot determine if men's work is more difficult, skilled, or demanding than their own.

Managers segregate women and men also to minimize social contacts and discourage heterosexual intimacy and liaisons (Burrell & Hearn, 1989). Many employers claim that allowing women and men to work together causes problems (Quinn, 1980). Research on intimacy shows that men who become romantically involved with women at work are rarely penalized whereas women who become involved are usually transferred, fired, or otherwise sanctioned. Gutek (1985, 1989) finds that gender segregation reduces women's exposure to sexual harassment at work, by reducing the opportunties for cross-gender contact. Lower odds of being sexually harassed at work are, thus, a benefit of segregation for women. In other respects, sex segregation is a liability for women (Reskin and Roos, 1990).

Male Managers and Workers Invoke Gender Ideology, Including Sexuality Assumptions, to Prevent Women's Unfettered Participation

Gendered beliefs about women—their abilities, skills, preferences, constraints, circumstances—are invoked to devalue women's worth to the organization (Bergmann, 1986; Chase, 1988; West, 1982). Assertions that women cannot travel on the job, are physically weaker, are absent more than men due to sickness or childcare demands, are more emotional (meaning soft-hearted), or cannot bond with men (cf. Williams, 1989) imply that women, as a class of worker, are less able, qualified, or appropriate. The ideal worker (manager, employee) is normatively *masculine*: a full-time employee who can devote most of his [sic] energies and time to the job and whose family responsibilities, other than providing a paycheck, are assumed by a full-time homemaker wife and mother, that is, a woman (Acker, 1990; Hearn & Parkin, 1988).

Claims that bodies, sexuality, and sexual relations are irrelevant to organizations are pervasive, yet recent research is challenging them (see Acker, 1990). Many managers have commented to me on the destructiveness of sexuality, a synonym for women (cf. Burrell & Hearn, 1989), to organizational processes and outcomes. Women are said to cause problems for men workers on construction sites, ships, military units, coal mines—a claim that is used to justify women's exclusion from many jobs and groups. The owner of a painting firm explained how he would *never* hire women painters because his painters worked out of town and he had to provide housing accommodations. Women painters would cause problems, he said. "I have enough headaches with drugs and alcohol; I'd be crazy to put women in there too." Sexuality problems are blamed on the devalued class, that is, women.

Groups and the Gendering Process in Organizations

Most mechanisms through which organizations gender their members and activities involve interaction. Understanding gendering as produced through interaction requires attention to group dynamics. Yet group dynamics in organizations are not well understood. This section discusses the limitations of the classic groups literature on gender interaction and inequality in organizations. It also discusses selected dynamics that create or sustain gender inequality in organizations. These include the interaction of gender status with formal rank, and gender displays in relation to leadership displays and identity—including the way gender displays interpenetrate organizational behavior and even subvert organizational rationality and meritocratic considerations—gender interaction as discourse, and identity group processes.

Two examples show how interpersonal interaction contributes to gender inequality at work. Bergmann (1986) describes how women are *steered* toward typical women's jobs, and away from men's, in employment interviews. A personnel officer can steer a woman applicant away from the better jobs by saying, "I wonder if you wouldn't be happier in this job" or "Your qualifications make you a better candidate for this job than that one." If the officer steers her to low status, low pay, low opportunity, women-crowded jobs, s/he contributes to the perpetuation of sex segregation. Encouraging her to stay away from jobs that are high status, lucrative, and so on, harms the woman individually and all women collectively. Repeated micro-exchanges like this help to create a sex-segregated work context.

Another example involves a man's request for coffee. A male superior asks a female subordinate to bring him a cup of coffee. She does so and gender inequality is created. The exchange may seem natural to both parties—although probably more to him than to her—but it is consequential. If it happened only once or if they took turns bringing coffee to each other, it would not create inequality. But if the same scenario happens many times—each day, week, and year in many offices across the nation—it *creates* inequality. Through his request, and receipt of service, the man enacts dominance; through her accommodation to the request, the woman enacts subservience. His status as boss probably accounts for his request and her status as subordinate no doubt explains her compliance. But, her female gender and his male gender *make the exchange a gender exchange* in addition to a boss-subordinate exchange. Gender inequality is the interactional result.

Limitations of Classic Groups Literature

Overall, organizational sociologists have paid little attention to groups at work and the research that has been done has problems. For example, one study of gender composition skirts the question of what a group is by allowing respondents to self-define their *work group* (South, Bonjean, Markham, & Corder, 1982, 1983), another treats an entire law school class as a group (Spangler, Gordon, & Pipkin, 1978), and a third treats an entire organization—a university—as a group (Szafran, 1983).

Many types of *in vivo groups* influence the creation and maintenance of gender inequality in organizations. These groups range from functional work units (e.g., operating room staff, miners) and secretarial pools to committees, task forces, quality circles, management teams, entire departments, social and friendship groups, and identity groups (Alderfer & Smith, 1982; McGrath, 1986). As shown earlier, organizational members and contexts are gendered in many ways. In vivo groups can be studied to find out how a priori gendering is played out in interpersonal exchanges—e.g., the male official who asks a woman subordinate to bring him coffee.

The ways in which in vivo groups *originate* gendering practices and arrangements should also be explored.

Among the questions that scholars might pursue are the following. Which groups should students of gender inequality study and why and how? Are members affected most by groups in which they carry out their work? Are the gendering dynamics of some groups more consequential than others? How does group size affect gendering dynamics? Are 50 seamstresses with a male supervisor less likely to be sexually harassed than the secretary in a male manager's office? Should people who interact to discharge their work be considered a group, irrespective of office, rank, or job (e.g., a judge, bailiff, court reporter, prosecutor and defense attorney)? Are groups that are informal or formal, permanent or temporary, or heterogeneous or homogeneous more consequential in producing gender inequality? How so and why?

The Convergence of Gender Rank and Official Rank

Most research on gender in groups holds constant other status differences. This is unfortunate because official rank and gender rank are generally *confounded* in organizations. Many men have authority over women at work whereas few women have authority over men (Boyd et al., 1990; Reskin & Ross, 1991). A man who bosses women is their superior on two counts: official rank and gender rank. A man who bosses only men or a woman who bosses only women is superior only on official rank. A woman who bosses men is superior on official rank but inferior on gender; a woman who bosses men may have trouble gaining their compliance or support (Kanter, 1977). A woman boss of men has little leeway for mistakes; if she falters or errs, her male subordinates may oppose her with a vengeance (Pringle, 1989). Organizational authority is not gender-neutral. Rather, it is confounded with gender in ways that profoundly affect interactional encounters among women, among men, and between women and men (cf. Acker, 1990). These ways are only starting to be studied and understood (cf. Fenstermaker, West, & Zimmerman, 1991; Pringle, 1989).

Some predictions are suggested by these observations. "Two pluses for him, two minuses for her" is a highly asymmetrical relationship. In this circumstance, official rank is likely to *compound* the effects of gender inequality. As research confirms, sexual harassment by men bosses of women subordinates is common whereas sexual harassment by women bosses of men subordinates is rare (Gutek, 1985, 1989). When official rank is the *only* status difference, supervisors should abuse authority less than when official and gender rank converge (Martin, 1985; Skvoretz, 1981). When official and gender rank contradict each other, one proffering privilege and the other retracting it, a woman boss may have trouble gaining her male subordinates' compliance (Pringle, 1989). (This should be true for minority supervisors of majority supervisees also.) Regardless of a woman's actual talents or skills, she is likely to have problems with male subordinates because of her inconsistent gender and official statuses (Chase, 1988; West, 1982). Indeed, Eagly, Makhijani, and Klonsky (in press) find that women in leadership positions are evaluated less favorably, especially by men, when they engage in directive behaviors (see Johnson, Chapter 2 in this volume, for a discussion).

An account by filmmaker Gale Anne Hurd (Rosen, 1989) who supervised an all-male camera crew on location in England illustrates the point. Despite her authority over the male camera crew, as director and co-producer, Hurd was resented and treated rudely by the men.

The only time I really encountered sexism was in England when we were making *Aliens*. I couldn't believe it, England, where the prime minister is a woman. I'm not sure what people said behind my back, but to my face they called me "ruthless" and said, "Women shouldn't be like you, they should be compassionate and kind." And I said, "I am compassionate and kind but I have a budget and a schedule, and if someone tells me, that I shouldn't fire him because he's got house payments, I can only point out that I'm not in a charitable position. I have to get my movie done." (Rosen, 1989, p. 70)

Sigourney Weaver, an actress in the film, confirmed Hurd's report, saying that, ". . . the British crew made constant fun of Gale . . . These guys hated having a woman as a producer" (Rosen, 1989, p. 70). As if affirming Hurd's femininity, Weaver praised Hurd for her *womanly* gender displays—of dignity, kindness, and fairness—toward the antagonistic men.

The Divergence of Leadership Displays and Gender Displays (at Least for Women)

Recent analyses of gendering as process have directed attention to gendering *activities* in addition to gender statuses (Fenstermaker et al., 1991; West & Zimmerman, 1987). Men and women (boys and girls) are normatively expected to demonstrate gender-appropriate behaviors—words, mannerisms, facial expressions, tones of voice, attributional accounts, emotions—at all times and in all institutional spheres, including the workplace. Groups at work provide a useful site for studying the effects of gender displays on gender inequality.

Women may have problems at work when norms associated with valued organizational statuses, e.g., leadership or the exercise of authority, contradict norms associated with their status as females (cf. Ridgeway, 1982, 1988). Leadership displays involve taking control, making decisions, exercising authority. Leading is male-normative behavior; following is female-normative behavior. Leadership displays are highly compatible with, indeed almost one and the same as, male-normative displays. But leadership displays contradict female-associated norms. Women leaders are required to display behaviors that are normative for leaders but when they do, they violate norms associated with their status as women (Chase, 1988; Martin, 1985; West, 1982). In short, women leaders are caught in a bind.

I return to the Gale Hurd example. In behaving like a director/ producer, Hurd displayed leader-normative behaviors. She directed, gave orders, made decisions, exercised control. In acting this way, she *behaved like a man*. In behaving like a man, she violated female-associated norms. The crew perceived her as ruthless. She failed to display compassion and kindness, *like a woman*. In behaving like a leader/man, she violated the expectation for women that she *serve, not control, men*. A woman who behaves like a man—e.g., Claudette Claudill, sculptress and companion of Rodin who was described as "sculpting like a man"—is denigrated ("She's a witch").

A woman who occupies a leadership position will be judged foremost as a woman, second as a leader. It is impossible for her to make leadership displays that are *identical* to a man's. Her status as woman will color her actions in the eyes of those who observe, react to, and evaluate her, particularly if they are men (Taps & Martin, 1990). Gendering is thus a constituent part of organizational dynamics that affects the assessment of qualifications, performance, and appropriateness. In respect to valued statuses, jobs, and rewards at work, women are and will remain, unless organizations change, *the other* (de Beauvoir, 1974; Smith, 1987).

Gender Interaction as Discourse

Some research on gender dynamics in organizations focuses on the analysis of talk *between* men and women or *about* men and women (Chase & Bell, 1990). This analysis has as its goal the understanding of how talk, or discourse, is constructed and used to shape and control gender relations and outcomes at work (see Gronn, 1983; also Bartlett, 1990; Ferguson, 1984). The use of talk to establish and maintain the conversational agenda or to sustain particular interpretations of situations or events is a potent interpersonal tool (cf. West & Zimmerman, 1987). Viewpoints expressed through speech, written or spoken, can either reinforce or challenge practices that privilege men and disadvantage women at work (Chase & Bell, 1990; Scott, 1986). The results of two discourse studies of gender inequality in organizations illustrate these points.

Pringle (1989), in a study of secretaries and their bosses, analyzed talk as a clue to status. She found that male secretaries talked much more freely and opinionatedly about their female bosses than they did about their male bosses. They also talked more freely than female secretaries did about their bosses of either sex. Consistent with points made earlier, Pringle concluded that male secretaries with women bosses view their *gender* subordination as questionably legitimate (cf. Ridgeway, 1988; Zimmer, 1988) and feel they have a right to express their opinions and judgments, even if they contradict their bosses. Their rebellious talk reflected both an awareness of and a resistance to the perceived illegitimacy of their inconsistent statuses: subordinate job and superior gender.

Chase and Bell (1990) interviewed gatekeepers (men and women school board members) in school districts with women school superintendents about why women had been hired and how they were doing in their jobs. In explaining their views, gatekeepers invoked two discourses that reinforced rather than challenged the dominance of men in school superintendent positions (women hold less than 3% of all superintendency jobs nationally). According to Chase and Bell, these discourses—of individual achievement and gender neutrality—*dissimulate* the reality of gender inequality and the social dynamics and arrangements that sustain it. Although the gatekeepers were intending to express support for women superintendents, their talk unwittingly affirmed the underlying assumptions upon which gender inequality and women's exclusion are built. Chase and Bell conclude that well-meaning people may support inequitable, unjust arrangements through participating in talk that reflects the underlying assumptions upon which dominance systems are built. Talk is in this sense a political tool that shapes the meanings, interpretations, and practices of gender dominance and subordination.

These studies suggest that talk about women and men both reflects and shapes interaction at work in subtle but consequential ways. The role of various discourses in creating and sustaining gender inequality in organizations needs to be investigated. Miller's (1991) study of rhetoric as an occupational (and political) tool and recent work on attributional accounts as shapers of gender interaction in task groups can serve as guides to this type of analysis (see, for example, Taps & Martin, 1990).

Identity Groups

Identity groups are aggregates of persons in organizations who share a common status marked by one or more easily identifiable sociodemographic characteristic(s)—such as gender, race or ethnicity, nationality, social class, or age (Alderfer & Smith, 1982). For example, all women, all African-Americans, all Hispanic men, all Chicanos, all Italian-Americans, and all majority men are identity groups. Identity groups are not interactional groups, like work units or organizational departments, nor do their members necessarily hold meetings. Identity group members are attentive to what happens to persons like themselves in the organizations, however.

Little is known about identity group dynamics in organizations. How, if at all, do they influence organizational processes? Do identity groups become interest groups and, if so, under what conditions? Do minority members meet face to face to discuss experiences and strategies in organizations? Do women? Research by Mueller (1984) found that women legislators in some states organized into caucuses and met to plan strategies and agendas pertinent to women's issues and concerns. Women in other states were so divided along party and/or ideological (e.g., abortion) lines, however, that they never met or cooperated on legislative agendas.

Some research indicates that majority men perceive their common interests and cooperate to preserve their control over privileged positions and opportunities (Bergmann, 1986; Cohn, 1985; Kanter, 1977; Reskin, 1988). Yet, if this is so, little is known about how it works. Is gender inequality re-created and sustained through the identity group politics of majority men? Do majority men make and enforce succession, hiring, and advancement rules in full knowledge that they are protecting and benefiting themselves? Research by Jackall (1988) suggests they do and Michael Lewis's (1989) account of Salomon Brothers in the mid-1980s agrees.

Numerous scholars conclude that organizations will not improve their treatment of women unless women organize among themselves and press for change (Acker, 1989; Hardesty and Jacobs, 1986; Martin, 1991; Martin and Chernesky, 1989). In this view, majority men who benefit from current arrangements will not change voluntarily and lasting change will not occur unless women become a *group for themselves*. (This is no small task given the many divisions among women—due to race, ethnic, educational, and social class differences.) Research on identity groups and networks, including how they are activated into interest groups and how they operate once activated, can increase understanding of the effects of interaction on gender inequality in organizations.

References

Acker, J. (1989). *Doing comparable worth: Gender, class, and pay equity.* Philadelphia: Temple University Press.

Acker, J. (1990). Jobs, hierarchies, and sexuality: Some further thoughts on gender and organizations. *Gender & Society, 4,* 139–158.

Aires, E. (1976). Interaction patterns and themes of male, female, and mixed groups. *Small Group Behavior, 7,* 7–18.

Alderfer, C.P., & Smith, K.K. (1982). Studying intergroup relations embedded in organizations. *Administrative Science Quarterly, 27,* 35–65.

Baran, B. (1985). Office automation and women's work: The technological transformation of the insurance industry. In M. Castells (Ed.), *High technology, space, and society* (pp. 143–171). Beverly Hills: Sage.

Barnard, C.I. (1938). *The functions of the executive.* Cambridge, MA: Harvard University Press.

Baron, J.N., & Bielby, W. (1984). The organization of work in a segmented economy. *American Sociological Review, 49,* 454–473.

Baron, J.N., & Bielby, W. (1985). Organizational barriers to gender equality: Sex segregation of jobs and opportunities. In A. Rossi (Ed.), *Gender and the new life course* (pp. 233–251). New York: Aldine.

Baron, J.N., & Bielby, W. (1986). The proliferation of job titles in organizations. *Administrative Science Quarterly*, *31*, 561–586.

Baron, J.N., Davis-Blake, A., & Bielby, W.T. (1986). The structure of opportunity: How promotion ladders vary within and among organizations. *Administrative Science Quarterly*, *31*, 248–273.

Baron, J.N., & Newman, A.E. (1990). For what it's worth: Organizations, occupations and the value of work done by women and nonwhites. *American Sociological Review*, *55*, 155–175.

Baron, R.D., & Norris, G.H. (1976). Sexual divisions and the dual labor market. In D. Leonard & S. Allen (Eds.), *Dependence and exploitation in work and marriage* (pp. 47–69). London: Longman.

Bartlett, K.T. (1990). Feminist legal methods. *Harvard Law Review*, *103*, 829–888.

de Beauvoir, S. (1949/1974). *The second sex*. New York: Vintage Books.

Bergmann, B. (1986). *The economic emergence of women*. New York: Basic Books.

Bianchi, S.M., & Spain, D. (1986). *American women in transition*. New York: Russell Sage.

Bibb, R., & Form W.H. (1977). The effects of industrial, occupational, and sex stratificaton on wages in blue collar markets. *Social Forces*, *55*, 974–996.

Bielby, W.T., & Baron J.N. (1984). A woman's place is with other women: Sex segregation within organizations. In B. Reskin (Ed.), *Sex segregation in the workplace: Trends, explanations, remedies*. Washington, DC: National Academy Press.

Bielby, W.T., & Baron, J.N. (1986). Men and women at work: Sex segregation and statistical discrimination. *American Journal of Sociology*, *91*, 759–799.

Bielby, W.T., & Baron, J.N. (1987). Undoing discrimination: Job integration and comparable worth. In C. Bose & G. Spitze (Eds.), *Ingredients for women's employment policy* (pp. 211–229). Albany: SUNY Press.

Blau, P.M. (1977). *Inequality and heterogeneity*. New York: Free Press.

Blum, L. (1987). Priorities and limits of the comparable worth movement. *Gender & Society*, *1*, 380–399.

Blum, L. (1991). *Between feminism and labor: The significance of the comparable worth movement*. Berkeley: University of California Press.

Boyd, M., Mulvihill, M.A., & Myles, J. (1990). *Patriarchy and postindustrialism: Women and power in the service economy*. Departmental Working Paper 90–1. Carleton University: Department of Sociology and Anthropology, Ottawa, Canada.

Brown, L.K. (1988). Female managers in the United States and in Europe: Corporate boards, MBA credentials, and the image/illusion of progress. In N.J. Adler & D. Izraeli, (Eds.), *Women in management worldwide*. London: M. E. Sharpe.

Burrell, G., & Hearn, J. (1989). The sexuality of organization. In J. Hearn et al. (Eds.), *The sexuality of organization* (pp. 1–28). London: Sage.

Chase, S.E. (1988). Making sense of "the woman who becomes a man." In A.D. Todd & S. Fisher (Eds.), *Gender and discourse: The power of talk*. Norwood, NJ: Ablex Publishing Co.

Chase, S.E., & Bell C.S. (1990). Ideology, discourse, and gender: How gatekeepers talk about women in a male-dominated occupation. *Social Problems, 37*, 163–177.

Clegg, S., & Dunkerley, D. (1979). *Organization, class, and control.* London: Routledge and Kegan Paul.

Cockburn, C. (1988). *Machinery of dominance: Women, men, and technical know-how.* Boston: Northeastern University Press.

Cohn, S. (1985). *The feminization of clerical labor in Great Britain.* Philadelphia: Temple University Press.

Connell, R.W. (1987). *Gender and power: Society, the person, and sexual politics.* Sydney: Allen and Unwin.

Cornfield, D.B. (1989). *Becoming a mighty voice: Conflict and leadership in the United Furniture Workers of America.* New York: Russell Sage Foundation.

DiNitto, D., Martin, P.Y. & Harrison, D. (1982). Sexual discrimination in higher education: A multi-level model for cross-national analysis of women's problems and prospects. *Higher Education Review, 14*, 33–54.

Dressel, P. (1987). Patriarchy and social welfare work. *Social Problems, 34*, 294–309.

Dressel, P., et al. (1988). Welfare workers as surplus population: A useful model. *Journal of Sociology and Social Welfare, 15*, 87–103.

Eagly, A., Makhijani, M.G., & Klonsky, B.G. (in press). Gender and the evaluation of leaders: A meta-analysis. *Psychological Bulletin.*

Edwards, R. (1979). *Contested terrain: The transformation of the workplace in the twentieth century.* New York: Harper Colophon.

Feldberg, R. (1980). "Union fever": Organizing among clerical workers, 1900–1930. *Radical America, 3*, 53–67.

Fenstermaker, S., West, C., & Zimmerman, D.H. (1991). Stalking gender inequality: New conceptual terrain. In R. Lesser Blumberg (Ed.), *Gender, family and economy: The triple overlap.* Beverly Hills: Sage.

Ferguson, K. (1984). *The feminist case against bureaucracy.* Philadelphia: Temple University Press.

Finch, J. (1981). *Married to the job: Women's incorporation in men's work.* London: Allen and Unwin.

Glenn, E., & Tolbert, C. (1987). Technology and emerging patterns of stratification for women of color: Race and gender in computer work. In B. Wright (Ed.), *Women, work and technology,* (pp. 318–331). Ann Arbor: University of Michigan Press.

Godbey, K.L. (1987). *Explaining State Comparable Worth Initiatives in the United States.* Unpublished dissertation, Florida State University.

Gronn, P.C. (1983). Talk as the work: The accomplishment of school administration. *Administrative Science Quarterly, 28*, 1–21.

Gutek, B.A. (1985). *Sex and the workplace: Impact of sexual behavior and harassment on women, men, and organization.* San Francisco: Jossey-Bass.

Gutek, B.A. (1989). Sexuality in the workplace: Key issues in social research and organizational practice. In J. Hearn, D.L. Sheppard, P. Tancred-sheriff, & G. Burrell (Eds.), *The sexuality of organization* (pp. 56–70). London: Sage.

Hardesty, S., & Jacobs, N. (1986). *Success and betrayal: The crisis of women in corporate America.* New York: Franklin Watts.

Hearn, J., & Parkin, P.W. (1983). Gender and organizations: A selective review and critique of a neglected area. *Organization Studies, 4*, 219–242.

Hearn, J., & Parkin, P.W. (1987). *Sex at work: The power and paradox of organization sexuality*. New York: St. Martin's.

Hearn, J., & Parkin, P.W. (1988). Women, men and leadership: A critical review of assumptions, practices, and change in the industrialized nations. In N.J. Adler & D. Izraeli (Eds.), *Women in management worldwide* (pp. 17–40). New York: M. E. Sharpe.

Hochschild, A. (1983). *The managed heart: Commercialization of human feeling*. Berkeley: University of California Press.

Hochschild, A. (1989). *The second shift: Working parents and the revolution at home*. New York: Viking/Penguin.

Izraeli, D. (1983). Sex effects or structural effects? An empirical test of Kanter's theory of proportions. *Social Forces, 61*, 153–165.

Izraeli, D. (1984). The attitudinal effects of gender mix in union committees. *Industrial and Labor Relations Review, 37*, 212–221.

Jackall, R. (1988). *Moral mazes: The world of corporate managers*. New York & London: Oxford University Press.

Kanter, R.M. (1977). *Men and women of the corporation*. New York: Basic.

Katz, D., & Kahn, R.L. (1986). *The social psychology of organizations*. New York: Wiley.

Lewis, M. (1989). *Liar's poker: Rising through the wreckage of Wall Street*. New York: W. W. Norton.

Lieberson, S. (1985). *Making it count*. Berkeley: University of California Press.

Lorber, J. (1991). *Gender as a social institution*. New Haven: Yale University Press.

Marglin, S.A. (1976). What do bosses do? The origins and functions of hierarchy in capitalist production. In A. Gorz (Ed.), *The division of labour: The labour process and class struggle in capitalism* (pp. 13–54). Sussex: Harvester Press.

Margolis, D.R. (1979). *The managers: Corporate life in America*. Boulder, CO: Westview Press.

Martin, P.Y. (1980). Women, labor markets, and work organizations: A critical analysis. In D. Dunkerley & G. Salaman (Eds.), *The international yearbook of organization studies 1980* (pp. 128–150). London: Routledge and Kegan Paul.

Martin, P.Y. (1982). "Fair Science": Test or assertion? Reply to Cole's *Women in Science. Sociological Review, 30*, 478–508.

Martin, P.Y. (1985). Group sex composition in work organizations: A structural-normative model. In S. Bacharach & R. Mitchell (Eds.), *Research in the sociology of organizations* (Vol. 4, pp. 311–349). Greenwich, CT: JAI Press.

Martin, P.Y. (1990). The moral politics of organizations: Reflections of an unlikely feminist. *Journal of Applied Behavioral Science, 25*, 451–470.

Martin, P.Y. (1991). Feminism and management. In E. Fagenson (Ed.), *Women in management: Trends, perspectives, and challenges*, Newbury Park, CT: Sage Publications.

Martin, P.Y., & Cherneskey R.H. (1989). Women's prospects for leadership in social welfare: A political economy perspective. *Administration in Social Work, 13*, 117–143.

Martin, P.Y., Harrison, D. & DiNitto, D. (1983). Advancement for women in hierarchical organizations: A multi-level analysis of problems and prospects. *Journal of Applied Behavioral Science, 19*, 19–33.

Martin, P.Y., Seymour, S., Godbey, K., Courage, M., & Tate, R. (1988). Corporate, union, feminist, and pro-family leaders' views on work-family relations. *Gender & Society, 2*, 385–400.

Martin, P.Y., & Shanahan, K. (1983). Transcending the effects of sex composition in small groups. *Social Work with Groups, 6*, 19–32.

McGrath, J.E. (1986). Studying groups at work: Ten critical needs for theory and practice. In P.S. Goodman (Ed.), *Designing effective work groups* (pp. 362–391). San Francisco: Jossey-Bass.

Meyer, J., & Rowan, B. (1977). Institutionalized organizations: Formal structure as myth and ceremony. *American Journal of Sociology, 83*, 44–63.

Milkman, R. (1980). Organizing the sexual division of labor: Historical perspectives on women's work and the American labor movement. *Socialist Review, 10*, 95–150.

Milkman, R. (1982). Redefining women's work: The sexual division of labor in the auto industry during World War II. *Feminist Studies, 8*, 337–372.

Miller, G. (1991). Human service work as rhetoric. In *Enforcing the work ethic* (pp. 1–33). Albany, NY: SUNY Press.

Miller, J. (1986). *Pathways in the workplace*. Cambridge and New York: Cambridge University Press.

Morrison, A.M., & Von Glinow, M.A. (1990). Women and minorities in management. *American Psychologist, 45*, 200–208.

Mueller, C.McC. (1984). Women's organizational strategies in state legislatures. In J.A. Flammang (Ed.), *Political women: Current roles in state and local government* (pp. 156–176). Beverly Hills: Sage.

Pringle, R. (1989). *Secretaries talk: Sexuality, power, and work*. New York: Verso.

Quinn, R.E. (1980). Coping with cupid: The formation, impact, and management of romantic relationships in organizations. In D.A. Neugarten & J.M. Shafritz (Eds.), *Sexuality in organizations* (pp. 38–52). Oak Park, IL: Moore Publishing Company.

Reskin, B. (1988). Bringing men back in: Sex differentiation and the devaluation of women's work. *Gender & Society, 2*, 58–81.

Reskin, B., & Hartmann, H. (1986). *Women's work, men's work: Sex segregation on the job*. Washington, DC: National Academy Press.

Reskin, B., & Padavic, I. (1988). Supervisors as gatekeepers: Male supervisors' response to women's integration in plant jobs. *Social Problems, 35*, 536–550.

Reskin, B., & Roos, P. (1987). Sex segregation and status hierarchies. In C. Bose & G. Spitze (Eds.), *Ingredients for women's employment policy*. Albany: SUNY Press.

Reskin, B., & Roos, P. (1990). *Gender Queues, job queues: Explaining women's inroads into male occupations*. Philadelphia: Temple University Press.

Reskin, B., & Ross, C. (1991). *Job segregation, authority and earnings among women and men managers*. Univeristy of Illinois: Department of Sociology.

Ridgeway, C. (1982). Status in groups: The importance of motivation. *American Sociological Review, 47*, 76–88.

Ridgeway, C. (1988). Gender differences in task groups: A status and legitimacy account. In M. Webster & M. Foschi (Eds.), *Status generalization: New theory and research* (pp. 188–206). Palo Alto: Stanford University Press.

Rosen, M. (1989, September). The Hurd instinct. *MS Magazine*, 66–71.

Schwartzman, H.B. (1986). Research on work group effectiveness: An anthropological critique. In P.S. Goodman (Ed.), *Designing effective work groups* (pp. 237–276). San Francisco: Jossey-Bass.

Scott, K.P. (1986). Effects of sex-fair materials on pupils attitudes, comprehension, and interest. *Amercian Educational Research Journal, 23*, 105–116.

Skvoretz, J. (1981). Extending expectation states theory: Comparative status models of participation in N person groups. *Social Forces, 59*, 752–770.

Smith, D. (1987). *The everyday world as problematic: A feminist sociology.* Boston: Northeastern University Press.

South, S.J., Bonjean, C.M., Markham, W.T., & Corder, J. (1982). Social structure and intergroup interaction. *American Sociological Review, 47*, 587–599.

South, S.J., Bonjean, C.M., Markham, W.T., & Corder, J. (1983). Female labor force participation and the organizational experiences of male workers. *The Sociological Quarterly, 24*, 367–380.

Spangler, E., Gordon, M.A., & Pipkin, R.M. (1978). An empirical test of Kanter's hypothesis. *American Journal of Sociology, 84*, 160–170.

Steinberg, R. (1987). Radical challenges in a liberal world: The mixed success of comparable worth. *Gender & Society, 1*, 466–475.

Szafran, R. (1983). A note on recruitment and reward equity of organizations: U.S. universities before affirmative action. *Social Forces, 61*, 1109–1118.

Taps, J., & Martin, P.Y. (1990). Gender compsition, attributional accounts, and women's influence and likability in task groups. *Small Group Research, 21*, 471–491.

Thompson, J.D. (1967). *Organizations in action.* New York: McGraw-Hill.

Tienda, M., Smith, S.S., & Ortiz, V. (1987). Industrial restructuring, gender segregation, and sex differences in earnings. *American Sociological Review, 52*, 195–210.

Toren, N., & Kraus, V. (1987). The effects of minority size on women's position in academia. *Social Forces, 65*, 1090–1100.

West, C. (1982). Why can't a woman be more like a man? *Work and Occupations, 9*, 5–29.

West, C., & Zimmerman, D. (1987). Doing gender. *Gender & Society, 1*, 125–151.

Wharton, A., & Baron, J.N. (1987). So happy together? The impact of gender segregation on men at work. *American Sociological Review, 52*, 574–587.

Williams, C. (1989). *Gender differences at work: Women and men in nontraditional occupations.* Berkeley: University of California Press.

Zimmer, L. (1987). How women reshape the prison guard role. *Gender & Society, 1*, 415–431.

Zimmer, L. (1988). Tokenism and women in the workplace: The limits of gender-neutral theory. *Social Problems, 35*, 64–77.

Author Index

Subject Index